# THE NEW JERSEY WEATHER BOOK

*The Great Falls of the Passaic in winter dress.*
*(Courtesy of Paterson Museum Archives)*

# THE NEW JERSEY WEATHER BOOK

DAVID M. LUDLUM

RUTGERS UNIVERSITY PRESS
New Brunswick, New Jersey

To the weather observers of New Jersey, the thousands of men and women who have recorded atmospheric activities over the Garden State since its first settlement, and to those who have transmitted, analyzed, and preserved the data. Without their dedicated service over the years, the preparation of this work would not have been possible.

Library of Congress Cataloging in Publication Data

Ludlum, David McWilliams, 1910–
The New Jersey weather book.

Bibliography: p.
Includes index.
1. New Jersey—Climate. I. Title.
QC984.N5L83 551.69749 81–5193
ISBN 0–8135–0915–7 AACR2
ISBN 0–8135–0940–8 (pbk.)


Manufactured in the United States of America

Design by Anistatia Vassilopoulos

# CONTENTS

## CHAPTER 1



## CHAPTER 2



## CHAPTER 3



## CHAPTER 4

## CHAPTER 5

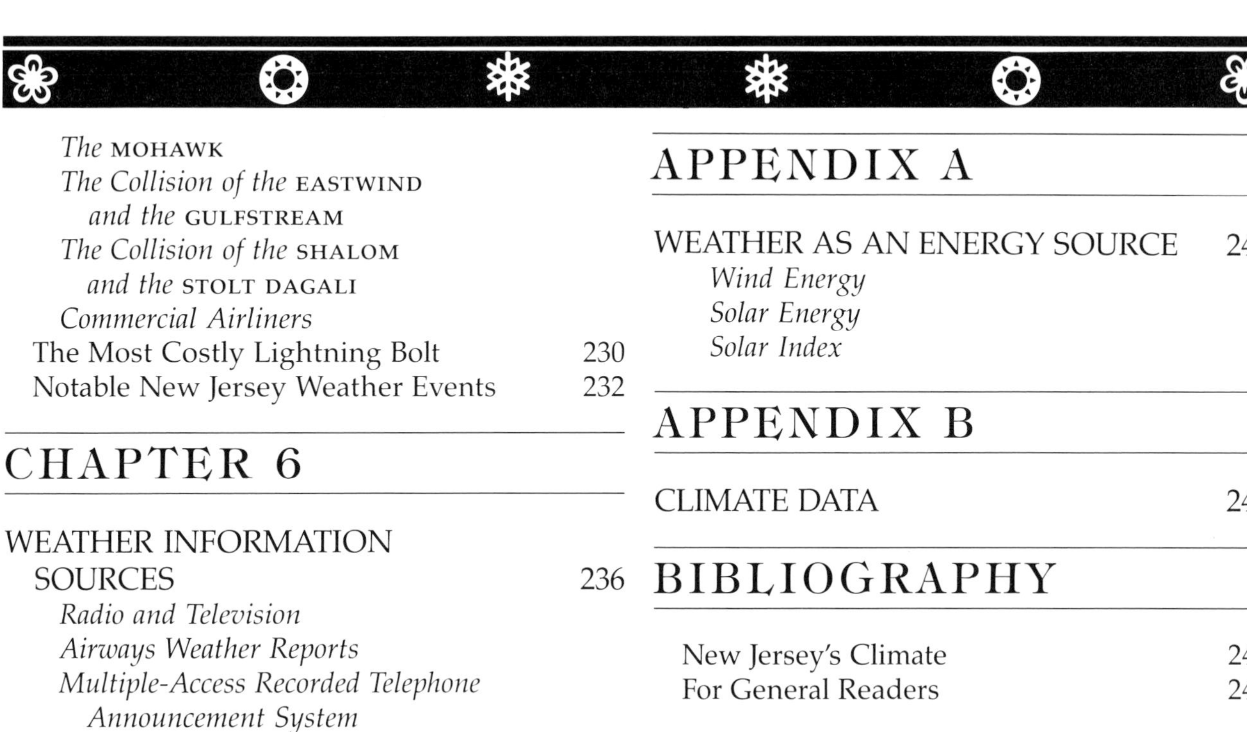



## CHAPTER 6



## APPENDIX A



## APPENDIX B



## BIBLIOGRAPHY

*This lithograph by N. Currier depicts the wreck of the ship* JOHN MINTURN *off the coast of New Jersey in a gale, February 15, 1846. Thirty-eight people were drowned or frozen to death.*
*(The Harry T. Peters Collection, Museum of the City of New York)*

# THE NEW JERSEY WEATHER BOOK

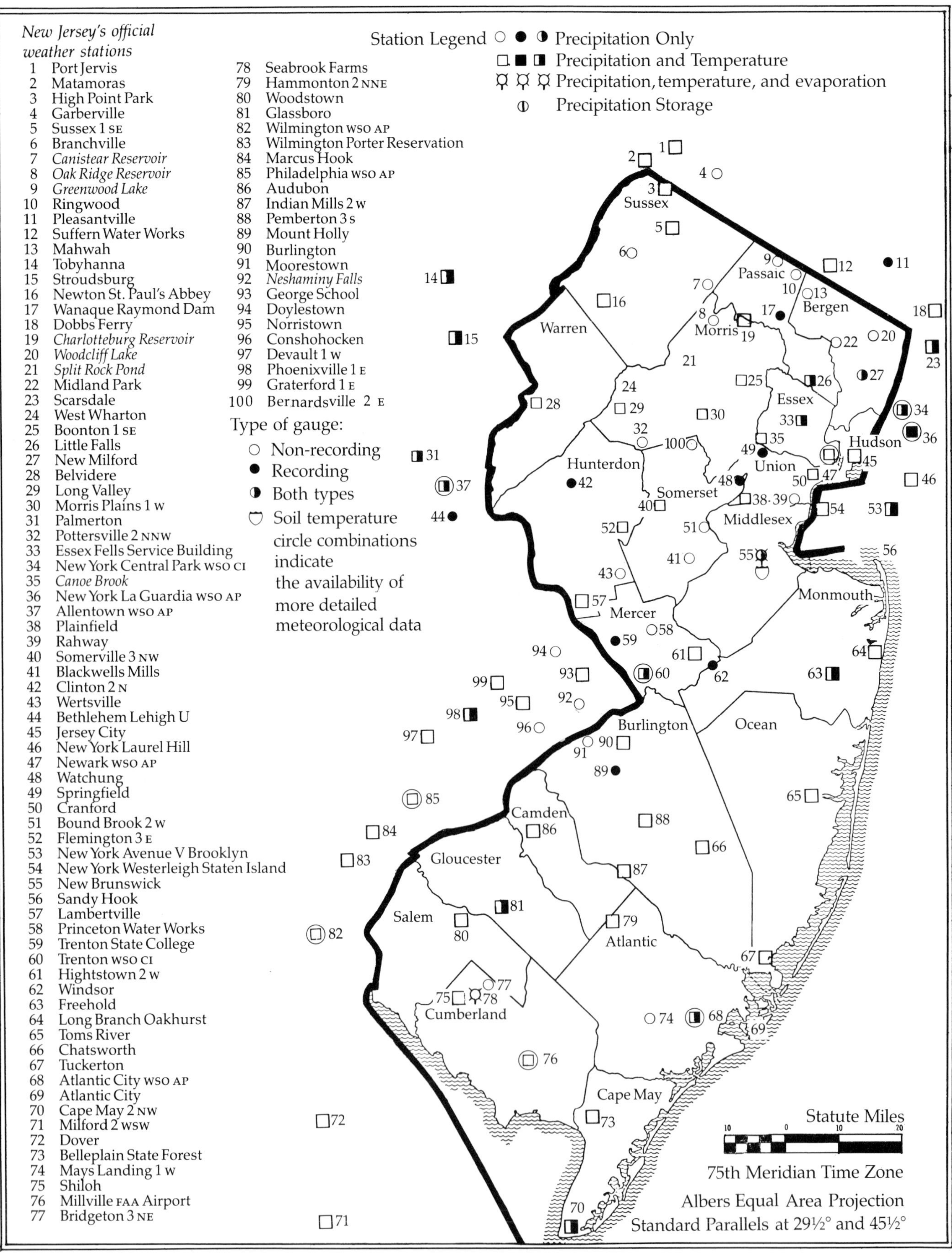
New Jersey's official weather stations
1 Port Jervis
2 Matamoras
3 High Point Park
4 Garberville
5 Sussex 1 SE
6 Branchville
7 Canistear Reservoir
8 Oak Ridge Reservoir
9 Greenwood Lake
10 Ringwood
11 Pleasantville
12 Suffern Water Works
13 Mahwah
14 Tobyhanna
15 Stroudsburg
16 Newton St. Paul's Abbey
17 Wanaque Raymond Dam
18 Dobbs Ferry
19 Charlotteburg Reservoir
20 Woodcliff Lake
21 Split Rock Pond
22 Midland Park
23 Scarsdale
24 West Wharton
25 Boonton 1 SE
26 Little Falls
27 New Milford
28 Belvidere
29 Long Valley
30 Morris Plains 1 W
31 Palmerton
32 Pottersville 2 NNW
33 Essex Fells Service Building
34 New York Central Park WSO CI
35 Canoe Brook
36 New York La Guardia WSO AP
37 Allentown WSO AP
38 Plainfield
39 Rahway
40 Somerville 3 NW
41 Blackwells Mills
42 Clinton 2 N
43 Wertsville
44 Bethlehem Lehigh U
45 Jersey City
46 New York Laurel Hill
47 Newark WSO AP
48 Watchung
49 Springfield
50 Cranford
51 Bound Brook 2 W
52 Flemington 3 E
53 New York Avenue V Brooklyn
54 New York Westerleigh Staten Island
55 New Brunswick
56 Sandy Hook
57 Lambertville
58 Princeton Water Works
59 Trenton State College
60 Trenton WSO CI
61 Hightstown 2 W
62 Windsor
63 Freehold
64 Long Branch Oakhurst
65 Toms River
66 Chatsworth
67 Tuckerton
68 Atlantic City WSO AP
69 Atlantic City
70 Cape May 2 NW
71 Milford 2 WSW
72 Dover
73 Belleplain State Forest
74 Mays Landing 1 W
75 Shiloh
76 Millville FAA Airport
77 Bridgeton 3 NE
78 Seabrook Farms
79 Hammonton 2 NNE
80 Woodstown
81 Glassboro
82 Wilmington WSO AP
83 Wilmington Porter Reservation
84 Marcus Hook
85 Philadelphia WSO AP
86 Audubon
87 Indian Mills 2 W
88 Pemberton 3 S
89 Mount Holly
90 Burlington
91 Moorestown
92 Neshaminy Falls
93 George School
94 Doylestown
95 Norristown
96 Conshohocken
97 Devault 1 W
98 Phoenixville 1 E
99 Graterford 1 E
100 Bernardsville 2 E
Station Legend
Precipitation Only
Precipitation and Temperature
Precipitation, temperature, and evaporation
Precipitation Storage
Type of gauge:
Non-recording
Recording
Both types
Soil temperature
circle combinations indicate the availability of more detailed meteorological data
Sussex
Passaic
Bergen
Warren
Morris
Essex
Hudson
Hunterdon
Somerset
Union
Middlesex
Mercer
Monmouth
Burlington
Ocean
Camden
Gloucester
Salem
Atlantic
Cumberland
Cape May
Statute Miles
10 0 10 20
75th Meridian Time Zone
Albers Equal Area Projection
Standard Parallels at 29½° and 45½°

CHAPTER 1

# New Jersey's Place under the Sun

The sun shines over New Jersey every day of the year as it probably has for billions of years, ever since the big bang started things and our planetary system evolved. However, sometimes various combinations of physical matter in the earth's atmosphere intercept much of the solar radiation before it reaches the surface of the earth. Then all kinds of natural phenomena result, and that is what this book is all about—the vagaries of New Jersey's weather.

The sun, as the ultimate source of energy on earth over the ages, has provided New Jersey with very different climates over geologic time—climates ranging from lush tropical forests to barren arctic wastes—that belie its present name as the Garden State. Even at the present period the annual increasing and decreasing angles of the incoming solar rays cause the change of seasons, from the cold of winter to the heat of summer.

New Jersey occupies a favored grid position on the face of the globe. A little less than halfway between the equator and the North Pole, on the eastern periphery of the North American land mass, its geographic location makes for an energetic environment for human activity, with stimulating temperature conditions and an adequate moisture supply.

The intersection of the 40° north parallel and the 75° west meridian lies in Burlington County close to the Delaware River, on the grounds of the Riverton Golf Club in Cinnaminson. Following that line of latitude east, one would reach Portugal and central Spain; going west, St. Louis, Kansas City, Denver, and northern California lie close to New Jersey's latitude. To the immediate east lie 3,000 miles of ocean—a source of moisture; to the west lie 3,000 miles of land—a source of dryness. Following the 75° west meridian north, one would pass close to the eastern shore of Hudson Bay and meet the Arctic Circle on Baffin Island, 1,750 miles from New Jersey. Dropping southward, the 75° west meridian passes over the Atlantic Ocean off Cape Hatteras and meets the Tropic of Cancer in the central Bahama Islands, about 1,150 miles from New Jersey. To the north lies the subboreal mass of eastern Canada—a source of cold; to the south are the semitropical waters of the Atlantic Ocean—a source of warmth.

Rhythmic successions of wet and dry, hot and cold airstreams converge over New Jersey and make up the daily weather whose most notable characteristic is its changeableness. The almost infinite variety of New Jersey's weather year-round was succinctly and imaginatively described by the Reverend Jedidiah Morse, America's foremost geographer during the early days of the Republic:

> The changes of weather are great, and frequently sudden. On the whole, it appears that the climate is a compound of most of the climates of the world. It has the moisture of Ireland in spring; the heat of Africa in Summer; the temperature of Italy in June; the sky of Egypt in autumn; the snow and cold of Norway in winter; the tempests (in a certain degree) of the West Indies, in every season; and the variable winds and weather of Great Britain in every month of the year.
>
> *Geography Made Easy,* 1800

THE START.

*Scenes of the toboggan slide at Orange, 1886. (Courtesy of* Harper's Magazine*)*

# New Jersey Weather Compared to Worldwide Extremes

New Jersey's small geographical area receives only a minuscule portion of the sun's total incoming radiation. A consideration of this energy's effect on the range of the state's weather extremes, in comparison with the rest of the United States, North America, and the world, places our climate in its proper perspective. Tables 1.1–1.4 present the generally accepted extremes of temperature, precipitation, and atmospheric pressure experienced since weather measurement by scientific instruments under standard exposure conditions came into practice.

### Temperature

| Extremes | °F | °C | Place and date |
|---|---|---|---|
| Maximum | 110 | 43 | Runyon, Middlesex County, New Jersey, July 10, 1936 |
| | 134 | 57 | Death Valley, California, July 10, 1913 |
| | 136 | 58 | El Azizia, Libya, September 13, 1922 |
| Minimum | − 34 | −37 | River Edge, Bergen County, New Jersey, January 5, 1904 |
| | − 69 | −56 | Rogers Pass, Montana, January 20, 1954 |
| | − 79.8 | −62.1 | Prospect Creek, Alaska, January 23, 1971 |
| | − 81 | −63 | Snag, Yukon Territory, Canada, February 3, 1947 |
| | −126.9 | −88.3 | Vostok, Antarctica, August 24, 1960 |

### Precipitation

| Totals | Inches | Millimeters | Place and date |
|---|---|---|---|
| Greatest in 24 hours | 14.81 | 376 | Tuckerton, Ocean County, New Jersey, August 19, 1939 (official gauge) |
| | 22.40 | 569 | Ewan, Gloucester County, New Jersey, September 1, 1940 (type gauge unknown) |
| | 43.00 | 1,092 | Alvin, Texas (between Houston and Galveston), July 24–25, 1979 |
| | 73.62 | 1,870 | Cilaos La Reunion, Indian Ocean, March 15–16, 1952 |
| Greatest in one month | 25.98 | 660 | Paterson, Passaic County, New Jersey, September 1882 |
| | 71.54 | 1,817 | Helen Mine, California, January 1909 |
| | 107.00 | 2,718 | Kukui, Maui, Hawaii, March 1942 |
| | 366.00 | 9,296 | Cherrapungi, Maghalaya, India, July 1861 |

## Precipitation (*continued*)

| Totals | Inches | Millimeters | Place and date |
|---|---|---|---|
| Greatest in one year | 85.99 | 2,184 | Paterson, Passaic County, New Jersey, 1882 |
| | 184.56 | 4,688 | Wynochee Oxbow, Washington, 1931 |
| | 332.29 | 8,440 | MacLeod Harbor, Alaska, 1976 |
| | 578.00 | 14,681 | Kukui, Maui, Hawaii, 1950 |
| | 905.00 | 22,987 | Cherrapunji, Maghalaya, India, calendar 1861 |
| | 1,042.00 | 26,467 | Cherrapunji, Maghalaya, India, season August 1860–July 1861 |
| Least in one year | 19.85 | 504 | Canton, Salem County, New Jersey, 1965 |
| | 0.00 | 00 | Death Valley, California, 1929 |
| | .00 | 00 | Bagdad, California, October 3, 1912–November 8, 1914 |
| | .00 | 00 | Arica, Chile, October 1903–December 1917 |

## Snowfall

| Totals | Inches | Centimeters | Place and date |
|---|---|---|---|
| Greatest in 24 hours | 29.7 | 75 | Long Branch, Monmouth County, New Jersey, December 26–27, 1947 |
| | 75.8 | 193 | Silver Lake, Colorado, April 14–15, 1921 |
| Single storm | 34.0 | 86 | Cape May, Cape May County, New Jersey, February 11–14, 1899 |
| | 189.0 | 480 | Mt. Shasta Ski Bowl, California, February 13–19, 1959 |
| Calendar month | 50.1 | 127 | Freehold, Monmouth County, New Jersey, December 1880 |
| | 390.0 | 991 | Tamarack, California, January 1911 |
| Season | 108.1 | 275 | Culvers Lake, Sussex County, New Jersey, 1915–1916 |
| | 1,122.0 | 2,850 | Paradise Ranger Station, Mount Rainier, Washington, 1971–1972 |

## Atmospheric Pressure

| Extremes | Inches | Kilopascals | Place and date |
|---|---|---|---|
| Highest | 31.09 | 105.3 | Newark Airport, Essex County, New Jersey, February 13, 1981 |
| | 31.40 | 106.3 | Helena, Montana, January 9, 1962 |
| | 31.43 | 106.4 | Barrow, Alaska, January 3, 1970 |
| | 31.53 | 106.8 | Mayo, Yukon Territory, Canada, January 1, 1974 |

Atmospheric Pressure (*continued*)

| Extremes | Inches | Kilo-pascals | Place and date |
|---|---|---|---|
| | 32.005 | 108.4 | Agata, Evenk N.O. district, Central Siberian Republic, 66°55′N, 93°30′E (approximately on Arctic Circle) |
| Lowest | 28.36 | 96.0 | Long Branch, Monmouth County, New Jersey, March 6, 1932 (mercurial barometer) |
| | 26.35 | 89.2 | Long Key, Florida, September 2, 1935 (tested aneroid) |
| | 25.87 | 87.6 | Typhoon June, Pacific Ocean, November 19, 1975 (aerial sounding) |
| | 25.69 | 87.0 | Typhoon Tip, Pacific Ocean, October 12, 1979 (aerial sounding) |

# Climates of the Recent Past

Not very long ago, in terms of historical geology, New Jersey had a terrain and a climate very different from what it now enjoys. For perhaps a thousand centuries during the most recent glacial period, when ice covered much of the northern part of the state, the region resembled the fringes of an arctic island. South of the glacier's terminal moraine across the neck of central New Jersey lay a desolate land similar to the outwash plains adjacent to present live glaciers, with melt water cutting channels to an ocean shoreline that was then about 100 to 150 miles (161 to 241 km) east of its present location.

Perhaps twenty-five thousand years ago all this began to change. Temperatures began to rise for reasons that paleoclimatologists have not yet agreed upon. Though there were fluctuations between retreat and advance of the glacier, the dissolution and ultimate disappearance of the ice sheet were inexorable. It appears that the last vestiges of the ice were gone from New Jersey soil about ten thousand years ago. The major terrain features that emerged largely resembled those of today except for the lack of flora and fauna; these gradually appeared over the next several centuries as a more beneficent climate encouraged their development and growth.

By this time the ocean level had risen about 250 feet (61 m) higher than it was during the glacial period, when so much atmospheric moisture was entrapped in the ice sheet. The continental shelf, extending about a hundred miles from the mainland, became submerged, as did the estuaries of the major river valleys—the Hudson, the Raritan, and the Delaware. The land mass, now free of the tremendous burden of the thick ice sheet, also rose slightly. In the northern sections some of the melt water from the glacier became trapped in the hollows and valleys scooped out by the ice; these formed the beds of the lovely lakes and ponds that make New Jersey's northern counties so attractive.

During the ten thousand years since the ice departed, New Jersey, along with the rest of the middle latitudes of North America, has undergone several swings of the climatic pendulum, though these have been minor compared with the catastrophic changes accompanying the glacial epochs.

Following the melting of the ice and the runoff of most of the glacial water into the seas, the climate gradually became less humid while continuing to warm. A so-called Climatic Optimum prevailed, with temperate, semihumid conditions persisting until about 3000 B.C. Temperatures were perhaps as much as 3.6°F (2°C) warmer than now, and rainfall was more plentiful. Rich forests of temperate zone species took over the land. This was followed by a slightly cooler and drier period with more frequent cyclonic activity; subboreal conditions returned and northern forest types flourished.

In the past two thousand years, two significant swings in the climatic pendulum of the Northern Hemisphere stand out. The first major period, from about 800 to 1200 A.D., brought another relatively warm, less stormy period, called the Little Climatic Optimum. This was the time when the Vikings ventured over the ice-free northern seas to settle Iceland, Greenland, and northern Newfoundland. A period of greater storminess and increasing cold followed from 1250 to 1350 A.D., causing the disappearance of the settlements in Greenland and Newfoundland and greatly reducing crop yields in Iceland, the British Isles, and Scandinavia. The second major climatic deviation of the recent past began about 1550 and continued for about three centuries. It is called the Little Ice Age, a period when mountain glaciers in Europe (and probably in Alaska and the western mountains of the continental United States) advanced down into the valleys and the cyclonic storm belt shifted southward, permitting the cold and snow of the subpolar region to advance deeper into the temperate zone than in the centuries preceding or following. Temperatures in the northeastern United States probably averaged about 3°F (1.5°C) below current levels. New Jersey had a shorter crop season, with earlier frosts in autumn and later frosts in spring; summers were cooler and rivers and harbors froze more solidly and for longer periods than now. The Little Ice Age lasted through the colonial period and extended into the early nineteenth century.

Sometime after the middle of the nineteenth century it was noticed that many glaciers in Europe had stopped advancing; they were soon in full retreat. Though a study of temperature at New Haven, Connecticut, revealed that there had been little temperature change from 1780 to 1870, it soon became apparent in the United States, too, that a warming trend had set in by the middle 1870s; temperatures were on the rise. Severe winters received much publicity in the last three decades of the nineteenth century, but they were interspersed with notably mild winters to balance the thermal scales.

A University of Maryland study* of Philadelphia records supplemented by other North American stations shows that since 1738 there has been little essential change in the long-term annual temperature means, though there have been some short-term trends in both directions and some marked fluctuations between individual years and series of years. The year 1881 was taken as a divide between two sections of the study. This is convenient for New Jersey data, since the first formal collection of records for the state dates from that time.

The study concluded that the years prior to 1881 were 0.36°F (0.2°C) colder than the almost one hundred years following—a rather small difference for such long periods. The coldest year was 1777, with an annual mean of 51.1°F (10.6°C); the warmest mean was 56.5°F (13.6°C), in several years, the latest being 1949—a difference of 5.4°F (3.0°C). Prior to 1881, the coldest years were 1784–1786 and 1810–1820, with a less extreme period in 1836–1838. A feature of the early nineteenth century was an outstanding warm period in 1824–1828.

In the last hundred years of the composite Philadelphia record, several trends were noted. The middle and late 1880s were cold, the 1890s generally milder. Individual cold years occurred in 1904, 1907, and 1917, but the general trend was toward higher temperatures.

The 1920s and 1930s were consistently warmer than normal, the years 1930–1933 outstandingly so. The year 1940 was cold, but then the decade became moderate and ended very warm in 1949. Mild conditions prevailed in the early 1950s through 1955. Then a colder trend set in and continued for fifteen years, through the end of the 1960s. The early 1970s were generally above normal, with the exception of 1972. It turned colder in 1976 and remained so through 1982.

A Rutgers University study of temperature trends during the first seven decades of the twentieth century tends to confirm the results of the Philadelphia analysis. The period from 1900 to 1969 was characterized by two major temperature trends in New Jersey. A pro-

*Landsberg, H. E., C. S. Yu, and Louise Huang. *Preliminary Reconstruction of a Long Time Series of Climatic Data for the Eastern United States*. Report II. Technical Note BN-571, September 1968. Baltimore: The Institute for Fluid Dynamics and Applied Mathematics, University of Maryland.

nounced warming started shortly after the turn of the century, with maximum temperatures being reached in the 1940s and early 1950s. A sharp cooling trend set in during the mid-1950s and persisted through 1969.

The principal feature of the 1970s was a marked warming in 1973, 1974, and 1975, followed by an equally marked reversal. The twelve months of 1973 averaged out as the warmest in two decades. The winters of these years were especially mild, with little snow. The second half of the decade reversed the warm trend. Both 1976 and 1978 were below normal, and 1977 ran just about normal. The winters of 1976–1977 and 1977–1978 ranked sixth and eighth respectively among cold winters over the past ninety years, and February 1979 proved a standout as the second coldest February of any in that long span. Despite the coldness of February and a cool summer period, the annual temperature for 1979 averaged above normal by about 1°F.

# Observers of New Jersey Weather

The earliest observers of the New Jersey weather scene were the aboriginal inhabitants whose outdoor lives made their very existence dependent on their ability to cope with the vagaries of daily weather and general climatic conditions. Unfortunately for us, they possessed no means of transmitting their experience to future generations, so we have no firsthand knowledge of their weather wisdom or the actual climate conditions of pre-Columbian North America.

## Pioneer Observers

The first European to leave a daily record of New Jersey weather was Robert Juet of Limehouse, England, who served as first mate on Henry Hudson's *Half Moon*. On August 28, 1609, the ship sailed through the entrance to Delaware Bay and soon encountered shoals and small islands along the north shore. Hudson decided that the bay could be explored only with a small boat, and he put to sea again. He sailed off the sand-barrier islands from Cape May northward until he sighted the highlands at the southern entrance to New York Bay. Excerpts from Juet's log describe the weather on these days:

> The nine and twentieth [of August 1609], faire weather, with some thunder and showers, the winde shifting betweene the south south-west and the north north-west.

*The* HALF MOON *sailed around New Jersey's coast in 1609. First mate Robert Juet was the first European to leave a record of New Jersey's weather. (The Bettmann Archive)*

. . . And at foure of the clocke . . . it was calme. . . . Then the winde came to the north north-west. . . . [Inside Delaware Bay near north shore]

The thirtieth, in the morning . . . the winde at north north-west. . . . In the after-noone, the winde came to north by west . . . and it was little winde untill twelve of the clocke at mid-night; then wee had a gale a little while. [Outside entrance to Delaware Bay]

The one and thirtieth, faire weather and little wind. At sixe of the clocke in the morning we cast about to northward, the wind being at the north-east, little wind. At noone it fell calme. . . . From noone till foure of the clocke in the after-noone it was calme. At sixe of the clocke we had a little gale southerly, and it continued all night, sometimes calme and sometimes a gale. . . . [Off Delaware coast]

The first of September, faire weather, the wind variable betweene east and south; we steered away north north-west. [Off South Jersey]

> The second, in the morning, close weather, the winde at south in the morning. . . . At five of the clocke we anchored, being little winde, and rode in eight fathoms of water; the night was faire. . . . This is very good land to fall with, and a pleasant land to see. [Near the site of what is now Ambrose Light]

> The third, the morning mystie, untill ten of the clocke; then it cleered, and the wind came to the south southeast, so wee weighed and stood to the northward. [Entering New York Bay]

Another early account of the daily weather along the periphery of New Jersey comes from the Swedish settlement at Fort Christiana on Delaware Bay near what is now Wilmington. The young Reverend John Campanius came out to the colony in 1642 and soon set to work to compare the natural history of the New World with that at home. This led him to keep a journal of the weather "every day and night of every month" for 1644 and 1645. Campanius's observations have been preserved only in condensed form by his grandson, Thomas Campanius Holm of Stockholm, who used them in a study he published on America in 1702. Professor James V. Havens, when he was a student at Florida State University, analyzed and reduced the data to summaries of three ten-day periods in each month. Modern weather map symbols have been employed in Chart 1 to illustrate the type of weather reported in the Campanius record. Incidentally, the National Weather Service currently honors outstanding weather observers each year with the John Campanius Holm Award.

Though weather conditions were recorded with instruments in Europe from the 1660s on, we hear of no thermometer or barometer being safely transported to America until the early eighteenth century. The first series of instrumental weather records of substantial duration were begun at Charleston, South Carolina, in 1737 by Dr. John Lining and at Cambridge, Massachusetts, in 1742 by John Winthrop. Only a summary abstract of the Charleston record survives, but Winthrop's complete day-by-day record in the original manuscript through 1779 now rests in the Archives of Harvard University. Though Benjamin Franklin and his associates possessed thermometers at least as early as 1749, no continuous record for Philadelphia is extant until 1758, when individuals associated with the American Philosophical Society began observations. From 1771 to 1778, daily records are available in manuscript form. Though there was a thermometer at Kings College about 1765, no regular record of the daily weather for New York City has survived until Henry Laight of the

New York Insurance Company started his forty-eight-year series in 1788.

There is no mention in historical literature of the presence of a thermometer or barometer in New Jersey until the War of Independence. A thermometer reading at Princeton is mentioned in a contemporary newspaper account of 1778, and a barometer reading at Trenton in 1780. New Jersey appears to have been devoid of any meteorological record for years thereafter. Several diarists who paid attention to the current weather are helpful in filling in some of the story. These include Joseph Lewis of Morristown, 1783–1795, Sylvanus Seely of Chatham, 1768–1800, and Gerard Rutgers of Belleville, 1803–1829.

New Jersey made no move through the early nineteenth century to establish state-sponsored weather stations, though there was some activity in Pennsylvania, especially in Philadelphia, where the Franklin Institute and the American Philosophical Society maintained a Joint Committee on Meteorology during the 1830s and 1840s.

In 1848, the Board of the Smithsonian Institution appropriated one thousand dollars toward establishing a nation-wide weather-observing system. Circulars requesting the cooperation of people with scientific inclinations were distributed by congressmen throughout their districts. Among the 412 responses received in 1849 were several from New Jersey residents. The first reports that reached Washington for March 1849 included those from observers at Bloomfield, Burlington, Morristown, and Newark.

Usually a thermometer and rain gauge were supplied by the Smithsonian to the observers; as the scope of the network increased some received barometers and psychrometers. Three and later four observations a day were made, and the recording sheets were transmitted monthly to Washington by franked mail. During the next twenty-five years, twenty-nine New Jersey localities were listed as participants, with reports made by sixty-one different persons over the years.*

With the establishment of a storm-warning system by the Signal Service of the United States Army in 1870, the value of maintaining two separate weather organizations by government agencies came into question. Though the Smithsonian system remained strictly a climatological network reporting once a month and the Signal Service aimed at being a weather-warning system with thrice-daily telegraphic collectives, it was thought the two might function better under one head and supplement each other. Secretary Joseph Henry of the Smithsonian stated in his annual report for 1870 that he would be willing to transfer his observers to the military if some funds were

*Most of the records are currently available for study on microfilm at the National Climatic Center at Asheville, North Carolina, with duplicate prints at the National Archives in Washington.

provided. These were slow in forthcoming, so it was not until January 1874 that the transfer was made. Some of the Smithsonian observers ceased their public weather activities forthwith, while others submitted their reports through military channels.

## State Weather Service

The first periodical publication of a collective of New Jersey weather stations appeared in the annual reports of the New Jersey Board of Health from 1877 to 1887. The report for 1884 contained summaries of ten stations' records from 1878 to 1883. Beginning in 1882, a *New Jersey Weather Review* was produced by a group of volunteer observers with headquarters on Washington Street in Newark. The August 1884 issue contained summaries for ten New Jersey stations.

In September 1886 Professor George H. Cook announced a New Jersey State Weather Service along the lines being pursued in other states. It was described in an official publication as "an organization of voluntary observers, cooperating with the United States Weather Service, the State Agricultural Society, and the State Experimental Station; the National Service detailing an experienced observer who acts as Director and supervises the work carried on in a commodious office furnished by the State Experimental Station." The United States Signal Service cooperated by assigning a coordinator from a post at New Brunswick. The service formally began on November 1, 1886. The *New Jersey Weather Chronicle* was instituted in December 1886 and it contained the November weather data. It was published through June 1890.

By act of the New Jersey legislature on June 19, 1890, one thousand dollars were appropriated for the support of the weather service and the publication of a *Monthly Meteorological Bulletin*. The State Board of Agriculture appropriated a hundred dollars per year for the issue of a *Weekly Weather-Crop Bulletin* during the growing season. Both bulletins were reissued in an *Annual Report* in small bound volumes; the same text also appeared each year in the *State Legislative Documents*. These continued through 1905. On July 1, 1895, there were fifty-seven stations in the observing network.

Starting in January 1897, the United States Department of Agriculture published the first issue of *Climate and Crops, New Jersey Section*, which contained much of the data appearing in the state issue. This publication has been continued in various forms to the present day by the Environmental Data Service of the National Oceanic and Atmospheric Administration. Its title is *Climatological Data: New Jersey* and contains data for forty-four stations.

*The lighthouse at Sandy Hook warns those at sea of storms. (Special Collections, Rutgers University)*

# Army Signal Service

Several proposals were brought forward in the 1850s and again after the Civil War to establish a nation-wide meteorological service under the aegis of the federal government. A resolution passed both houses of Congress in early February 1870 authorizing the president to establish a weather-warning service. President Grant awarded the task of inaugurating the venture to the Army Signal Service. Several stations began taking observations for transmittal to Washington before the end of 1870; among these were New York and Philadelphia. The system's prime function as a storm-warning service was emphasized by the establishment of stations along the New Jersey sea coast: Atlantic City in 1871, and Cape May, Barnegat, Long Branch, and Sandy Hook in 1873.

# United States Weather Bureau

The Signal Service continued its meteorological activities for two decades. During its latter years it came under almost annual attack from members of Congress, who charged the military officers with inefficiency, favoritism, and outright fraud. In 1891, all weather functions were transferred to the United States Department of Agriculture, which reorganized the office and established the Weather Bureau.

Under the direction of the Department of Agriculture, the only station in New Jersey with first-class status was Atlantic City, which had both observing and forecasting duties. Another station of equal rank within the state was not established until 1913, when the chief of the Weather Bureau instituted services at Trenton, which then became the principal station for climatological activities. New Jersey weather data were published in *Climate and Crops: New Jersey Section*, 1896–1909; *Monthly Weather Review*, 1909–1913; and *Climatological Data, New Jersey Section*, 1914–present.

## National Weather Service

The increased importance of aviation led to the establishment of a station at Newark Airport in March 1929. And in 1940 the entire Weather Bureau was transferred to the Department of Commerce, which supervised other aspects of aviation throughout the country. Since then, the weather service has undergone several bureaucratic adjustments. In 1965 it came under the aegis of the Environmental

*William A. Whitehead, a nineteenth-century historian, was a pioneer New Jersey weather observer. (Collection of the New Jersey Historical Society)*

Science Services Administration (ESSA) and in 1970 under the National Oceanic and Atmospheric Administration (NOAA). The main forecasting functions are now carried out by the National Weather Service (NWS) and the climatological functions by the Environmental Data and Information Service (EDIS) of NOAA.

In 1980 the Environmental Data and Information Service of NOAA operated a network of weather stations for the collection of current climatological data (see map facing the opening of this chapter). Most of the stations take daily observations of temperature and precipitation; these are published monthly in *Climatological Data: New Jersey*.

Another federally funded activity in New Jersey is the Advisory Agricultural Weather Service Office on the New Brunswick campus of Cook College of Rutgers University. The objective of this office is to provide agriculture with specialized weather services, including observations, forecasts, warnings, and advisories to help increase farm production, improve agricultural efficiency, conserve energy, and protect the environment.

# Of Special Note

## Newark

William Adee Whitehead of Newark could well be called the dean of New Jersey's nineteenth-century weather observers. He kept an unbroken daily record of the weather from 1843 until his death in 1884. During this time he published monthly and annual summaries in the *Newark Daily Advertiser* without missing a single column. These are a pleasure to read not only for their scientific content but for their literary quality. When the Smithsonian Institution requested the submission of local weather observations, Whitehead dutifully sent his to Washington each month.

Whitehead's columns often described significant weather events that had occurred elsewhere in the state and nation, making them an informative source of meteorological news over many years when there was no national weather reporting agency.

Whitehead's successor as Newark's weatherman was his friend and associate Frederick W. Ricord. Ricord took over the weather observations immediately after Whitehead's death, so there was no break in the lengthy record until 1897, when Ricord died.

A second set of records had been started in 1892 by George C. Sonn who taught natural science at the old Newark High School on Washington Street. These were transferred to the new Barringer High School in 1899. Upon Sonn's death, William Wiener took over the supervision of the "weather boys" and moved this activity to Central High School on High Street, where he served as principal. When he retired in 1924, Wiener transferred his equipment to the roof of the Kresge Department Store on Broad Street opposite Military Park and served as unofficial city meteorologist. Since the exposure did not meet Weather Bureau specifications, the records were no longer published by that agency. They appeared daily, however, in the columns of the *Newark Evening News*.

## New Brunswick

Two sets of records were maintained at New Brunswick during the latter half of the nineteenth century. P. Vanderbilt Spader, an 1849 Rutgers graduate who lived at the northwest corner of George and Church streets, began his observations in 1847. An obituary noted: "Possessing ample means he never chose a profession, nor engaged in any business, but was enabled to cultivate his scholarly instincts and indulge his scientific and literary tastes." Spader started with only temperature and sky condition and expanded the scope of his observations by adding barometric pressure and precipitation recordings. His work was published in a thick volume, *Weather Record for New Brunswick, N.J., 1847–1890*. After January 1857, there are daily observations with very little missing data.

George H. Cook, who was instrumental in establishing the New Jersey Weather Service, came to the Rutgers College campus in 1853. He soon began a series of weather records at the College Farm and submitted them monthly to the Smithsonian Institution; they are now available on microfilm from June 1859 through May 1870.

The observational work he inaugurated was carried on for many years by the staff of the Agricultural Experiment Station and is now under the supervision of the Department of Meteorology and Physical Oceanography at Cook College of Rutgers University.

## Trenton

The first series of weather observations in the state's capital was the work of Dr. Francis Armstrong Ewing. He was a practicing physician and accomplished organist, singer, and historian. His meteorological observations began in 1840 and appeared in the *State Gazette* sporadically during the 1840s and 1850s. They consisted of temperature, wind, and sky condition taken three times daily.

A second Trenton record began on June 24, 1865. The thermometer was located at Cook's Jewelry Store in the heart of downtown Trenton. The observer was Captain E. Rezeau Cook. The series runs through 1909, though there is a break from March 1881 through September 1887. The records from 1865 to 1881 were forwarded monthly to the Smithsonian Institution and the Signal Service Office in Washington and have been preserved on microfilm. The reason for the 1881–1887 hiatus in the records is unknown. Starting in 1887 the reports appeared daily in the *State Gazette,* and a complete series of these have been preserved in a scrapbook in the Trenton office. When Cook died in 1910, Paul H. Wendel carried on the observation work from March 10, 1910, through January 31, 1912. For about a year, 1912–1913, the observer was James L. Bennett.

A first-class station of the United States Weather Bureau was established in the Broad Street Bank Building on April 1, 1913. The decision to place a station at Trenton had political overtones and a hint of scandal. To curry favor with future presidential candidate Woodrow Wilson, then governor of New Jersey, Weather Bureau Chief Willis L. Moore spent considerable bureau time and money to establish a weather station at Trenton. Moore also engaged in active promotion of Wilson's candidacy within the ranks of the bureau. News of this leaked out; members of Congress demanded an investigation. In March 1913 Moore resigned his position, effective July 31. The seriousness of the charges against Moore grew when the correspondence of his representative at Trenton during the election campaign was found and released to the press. President Wilson decided not to await the resignation date and removed Moore from his position on April 16, 1913. The affair was officially summarized as "Acceptance of resignation withdrawn, removed for irregularities and misuse of orders on conduct of business of the Bureau."

The Trenton weather station stayed at the Broad Street Bank Building until January 1, 1933; it was then moved to the Federal Building at State and Carroll streets. It was closed in 1982. Airway observations at the Mercer County Airport were begun in June 1930 and have continued since.

CHAPTER 2

# What Makes New Jersey's Weather

## Atmospheric Circulation

### Westerly Airstream

The dominant feature of the atmospheric circulation over North America—and New Jersey—is a great circumpolar movement of air whirling in a broad undulating flow from west to east over the middle latitudes of the continent. This flow has traditionally been known as the *prevailing westerlies*, but meteorologists now prefer the designation of *westerly airstream*. Migrating north and south with the seasons and waxing and waning periodically in strength, it controls most of the atmospheric traffic during the year from near the Arctic Circle to the tropical seas bordering the southern United States.

The westerly airstream is made up of contributions from many different regions. As the waves in its flow fluctuate across ocean and continent, they entrain reservoirs of resident air along its borders both to the north and the south. For a while these injections of homogeneous air dominate that section of the flow; after mixing with airstreams from other sources, the original characteristics of temperature and moisture content are modified.

New Jersey often lies close to or under the core of the vast westerly flow and is therefore subject to its varying condition. Thus, the daily weather over the state may be a composite of air that was originally conditioned in a variety of source regions: the arctic tundra of Canada and Alaska; the cool waters of the North Pacific; the hot desert lands of the American southwest and Mexico; the warm waters of the Gulf of Mexico, the Caribbean Sea, and the adjacent tropical North Atlantic; or the chill maritime environment of the North Atlantic east of Canada.

These reservoirs of air around the globe are known as *airmasses*. While they rest undisturbed in the source region for many days, their lower layers, through contact and convection, acquire the general properties of heat and moisture of the land or water surface beneath and possess related temperature and humidity characteristics throughout. This conditioning process continues until the dynamics of atmospheric circulation cause the airmass to be set in motion and become an airstream in the general westerly flow.

During its journey, the characteristics of an airstream may undergo modification either from the type of terrain over which it is passing—land or water, snow covered or bare, hilly or flat—or from contact and mixing with other airstreams from different source regions. If the trajectory from its source to New Jersey is relatively short and the terrain fairly uniform, the airstream will arrive with most of its native properties remaining; if it comes from a long distance and travels over diverse country, it will be modified considerably. The origin of an airstream and the history and length of its journey are important factors in determining the type of weather New Jersey experiences while under its influence.

The flow of westerly airstreams across the continent is not a simple straight-line procedure. Rather, they exhibit an undulating motion, partly as the result of the dynamics of air flow, and partly because of the varied topography of the North American continent. The most prominent feature is the great Western Cordillera, with its dual mountain ranges, the Cascades–Sierra Nevada chain and the Rocky Mountains, along with the intervening plateau, which forms a barrier either to block or to distort the strong westerly air flow from the Pacific Ocean. In the heart of the continent lie the vast Mississippi valley and the Great Lakes region, some fifteen hundred miles (2,400 km) in breadth, open on the north to arctic and polar influences and on the south to tropical influences. Here is the great meteorological mixing bowl of the continent, where airstreams of very different origins and characteristics meet, and here are generated many of the storm systems that will affect New Jersey in a matter of hours.

The Appalachian chain, whose crest runs from northeast to southwest and forms the watershed between the Mississippi valley and the Atlantic seaboard, presents a low barrier to migrating storm systems and air flow. It serves not so much as a blocking force but as a guiding influence. Storms generating in the western Gulf of Mexico and Texas tend to move northeast along the western flank of the mountains; eastern Gulf storms travel along the eastern slopes or the Atlantic seaboard toward Long Island and New England. At their northern end the Appalachians are not high enough to prevent polar airstreams from the Hudson Bay area of Canada from reaching New Jersey with much of their cold undiminished.

# Jet Stream

The most spectacular aspect of the westerly airstream centers in narrow currents of fast wind flow aptly called *jet streams*. These may be likened to swift currents in the middle of a relatively placid river. The principal jet stream circles the greater part of the Northern Hemisphere in a mean position between 30°N and 40°N. It sometimes strays a considerable distance north and south of its normal position and may often be broken into unconnected segments. Its greatest development lies above 25,000 feet (7,620 m), where speeds are normally in the 80- to 100-mile-per-hour (129- to 161-km/h) range but can reach as high as 200 miles per hour (322 km/h) and more.

The jet stream is a thermal product deriving its great dynamic energy from the temperature difference between warm air flowing northward out of the tropics and cold air coming southward from the polar regions. The importance of the jet stream lies in its activity in generating cyclonic storm systems and guiding their movement across the weather map. These usually generate just to the north of the core of the jet and are then steered by its undulating flow.

Across North America in winter there are two branches of the westerly jet. The main stream crosses the North Pacific in a mean position near 40°N and enters the continent over Oregon and Washington. It then trends southeast to the Kentucky and Tennessee area, where it meets with a subtropical jet that originates over the Pacific Ocean west of Mexico. Together they curve northeast and pass close to or over New Jersey and out into the Atlantic Ocean. In the warmer months of the year the subtropical jet is often absent from the weather maps for many weeks, and the main westerly jet migrates northward and crosses the continent along the Canadian border.

# Air-Flow Patterns

The weather at the earth's surface is largely controlled by the configuration of the upper-air circulation, which consists of a series of atmospheric waves with crests and troughs constantly undergoing transformations in length, amplitude, and location. Ordinarily, one full wave has a length of about 3,000 miles (4,828 km) from one crest to the next, or one trough to the next—an expanse covering the breadth of the continent across the United States. Normally the wavelength is such that there is only one crest and one trough over the actual land mass, but at other times the wavelength may contract, allowing for two full waves over the continent. The westerly flow is often complex, but four basic types of wave patterns are discernible.

A knowledge of these types is a big help in understanding the controls exerted on New Jersey's daily weather by the patterns of upper-air flow.

1. When there are no major ridges and troughs in the upper-air flow, a *straight west flow* prevails across the continent, with winds blowing roughly parallel to the lines of latitude, varying at times from west-southwest to west-northwest. The jet stream speeds across southern Canada, and cyclonic weather disturbances are carried rapidly eastward on a northerly track through southern or central Canada, normally requiring about three days for the transcontinental passage in winter. The conditioning area of the airstreams is the North Pacific, which imparts its coolness and wetness to the air. Most of the moisture is lost in ascending the coast ranges and crossing the elevated plateau of the Intermountain region; the air is warmed in its descent from the Rocky Mountains and emerges as a mild, dry airstream on the Great Plains. In the great central valley of the mid-continent the westerly flow may mix briefly with polar or tropical streams and the original air may become modified, but the flow from these regions is quickly shut off by a renewal of the westerly flow's strength. The modified air may travel as far as the Atlantic coast of New Jersey, bringing a mild, rather dry regime.

2. Under the *western trough-eastern ridge* wave pattern, storm systems move into the Pacific Northwest from the Gulf of Alaska and produce heavy precipitation at both coastal and mountain stations from northern California to the Alaskan panhandle. In their passage over the Intermountain region the centers and fronts often become disorganized in structure and appear on weather maps only as low-pressure troughs. There is a marked tendency for redevelopment to the lee of the eastern slopes of the Rocky Mountains from Alberta south to Colorado. The rejuvenated disturbances move northeast in the broad southwest flow on the eastern side of the upper-air trough, producing heavy rain or snow in the northern Plains, upper Mississippi valley, and Great Lakes once the moisture source of the Gulf of Mexico is tapped and carried northward in the southerly flow. East of the Appalachians, storminess is generally confined to the northern portion, though trailing cold fronts may bring periods of shower-type precipitation to the Middle Atlantic states. The strong southwesterly flow preceding the trough of low pressure carries mild air to New Jersey, and conditions are warm for the season until the cold front of the storm system arrives.

3. The *western ridge-eastern trough* type places a strong ridge of high pressure over the Intermountain and Rocky Mountain regions with a low-pressure axis in the form of a north-south trough over the Appalachians or along the Atlantic coast. Storms from the North Pacific are steered north around the high pressure, forming the core of the ridge over Idaho and Utah. Once the cyclonic disturbances circumvent the ridge and enter the northwest flow on its eastern flank, they are carried rapidly southeast and are followed by fast polar flow from Canada. Little precipitation results, since no substantial source of moisture has been tapped by the airstreams preceding or following the disturbance. To the east of the Rocky Mountains, the entire Mississippi valley is subject to cold outbreaks of polar or arctic air which may penetrate in the winter season all the way to the Gulf Coast and Florida.

   As cold fronts enter the southern end of the trough over the Gulf states or along the South Atlantic coast, a secondary center may develop and soon acquire considerable energy. The storm moves northeast with driving snow in winter and cool rains the rest of the year, becoming one of the famous coastal storms or northeasters of the Atlantic coastal plain. With storm tracks lying along the coast or just offshore, cold air is drawn from central Canada, and then the Middle Atlantic states and New England experience their severest cold waves, especially if the low-pressure center is blocked in its northeast progress and stalls off New England or Nova Scotia.

4. The *western ridge-central trough-eastern ridge* type represents a modification of the two preceding alignments. Its main feature is a well-marked low-pressure trough running south and southwest from the Hudson Bay area through the Mississippi valley to the Gulf of Mexico or Texas. There are strong ridges of high pressure to the west over the Pacific states and to the east over the Atlantic states, and temperature contrasts across the country are sharp, since there is great north and south transport of air taking place over the mid-continent.

   Storm centers move from the North Pacific around the northern periphery of the western ridge, cross the northern Plains, and move eastward near or over the Great Lakes. They usually then trend northeastward down the St. Lawrence valley. A notable feature of this kind of storm track is the tendency for vigorous secondary disturbances to form in the southern end of the trough, either in southeast Colorado, Texas, or the western Gulf of Mexico when the primary storm is passing over the northern Plains or

Great Lakes. The secondaries move rapidly northeast toward the Ohio valley and soon become the main storm center bringing widespread storminess to all the Midwest. Heavy rainfall, thunderstorms, and tornadoes may occur east of the storm track, while snow, sleet, and possibly blizzard conditions prevail to the west and north. If the secondary forms in the eastern Gulf of Mexico, the course northeast is along the Atlantic seaboard and New Jersey experiences a coastal storm.

## Cyclones and Anticyclones

The most striking feature of the daily surface weather map is the succession of high-pressure and low-pressure zones moving alternately in a steady procession across the continent. These are designated *cyclones* and *anticyclones* by meteorologists; they are popularly called lows and highs, in reference to the relative height of the barometer at their centers. Though they vary greatly in surface configuration, these systems usually have centers enclosed by contours representing lines of equal barometric pressure, called *isobars*.

Anticyclones and cyclones extend upward to considerable heights. On charts of upper-air flow they appear as ridges of high pressure or troughs of low pressure. Sometimes they have distinct centers aloft surrounded by closed isobars and their own circulation; more often their isobars are open-ended, being appendages of more permanent pressure systems to the north for low-pressure troughs and to the south for high-pressure ridges. Winds in an anticyclone tend to circulate in a clockwise direction; in a cyclone they circulate in a counterclockwise direction. Direction is reversed in the southern hemisphere.

These circulatory systems are essentially eddies of various sizes embedded in the general circumpolar whirl moving from west to east around the globe. Migrating anticyclones may be as much as 1,500 miles (2,414 km) across and extend vertically to 4 or 5 miles (6 to 8 km). Cyclones, on the other hand, tend to be somewhat smaller in lateral breadth, 500 to 800 miles (805 to 1,288 km) being an average, but a well-developed cyclonic circulation may extend to the tropopause at the base of the stratosphere at altitudes of 6 to 8 miles (10 to 13 km).

Cyclones and anticyclones differ in the dynamics of their internal circulations. The winds moving around a cyclonic center generally converge toward the central core, circling in a counterclockwise direction, always moving inward and crowding air particles together. The only outlet is upward. The rising air cools as it ascends and eventually reaches its dew point, causing condensation of its moisture into solid droplets in the form of cloud and precipitation. Wet weather usually follows. Anticyclones, on the other hand, exhibit a clockwise circulation, with air particles descending and spreading out in a diverging pattern. In its downward motion the air column is warmed dynamically and its relative humidity lowered. This enables the air to hold additional moisture in the invisible, gaseous state, inhibiting cloud formation and preventing precipitation. Dry weather usually results.

## Storm Tracks

There are three regions of North America where contrasting airmasses regularly meet and storm generation is frequent. The Gulf of Alaska is the home of the semipermanent Aleutian low-pressure area, where cold airstreams from Siberia, Alaska, and Canada mingle with warm air flowing northward from the vast Pacific high-pressure area. The Gulf of Alaska, where cyclonic activity is most frequent and vigorous, has been called the greatest storm factory of the world.

Storm-Track Weather

| Area of origin | Season | Speed | Path in relation to New Jersey | Attendant weather in New Jersey |
|---|---|---|---|---|
| Alberta | Frequent all year | Fast, strong westerlies aloft | St. Lawrence valley and north | Preceded by high clouds; narrow band of low clouds; light rain or snow at frontal passage; quick clearing |
| North Pacific | Only cold months | Moderate at steady pace | Great Lakes to St. Lawrence valley | Usually occluded front, with showers at frontal passage |
| South Pacific | Similar to Texas type throughout | | | |
| North Rockies | Similar to North Pacific type throughout | | | |
| Colorado | Mainly cold months | Slow movers at first; then faster on northeast track; southwesterly flow aloft | Over upper Great Lakes, Ontario, St. Lawrence valley; secondaries from Ohio may pass near New Jersey | Extensive cloud cover; moderate to heavy rain; warm spell precedes, cold follows |
| Texas and West Gulf | Only cold months | Fast movers on northeast track; southerly flow aloft | West of Appalachians; secondaries may form over Carolinas | Moderate to heavy snow, sleet, or rain; often extended storm period |

Storm-Track Weather (*continued*)

| Area of origin | Season | Speed | Path in relation to New Jersey | Attendant weather in New Jersey |
|---|---|---|---|---|
| East Gulf and South Atlantic | Mainly cold months | Fast movers along coast, but occasionally slowed by blocking | Along Atlantic seaboard or offshore waters | Northeasters, often with heavy rain or snow, strong winds |
| Tropical | June through November | Speed varies, usually 30–40 miles per hour off New Jersey | Tracks erratic, usually offshore | Occasionally violent, with hurricane-force winds and storm tide; heavy rain producers with flood potential |

The second region, an extension of the Aleutian low-pressure area, runs eastward through British Columbia and southeast along the crest of the Rocky Mountains into the United States. It marks the meeting place of cold, dry polar air from central Canada and mild, moist air from the Pacific Ocean. New storm circulations may form at any place along this extensive frontal zone, or old disturbances moving eastward over the Intermountain region may regenerate into active storm systems. Eastern Colorado, to the lee of the Rocky Mountains, is the site of most frequent cyclogenesis in the colder months of the year.

A third storm-generating region extends in a sweeping arc from northwest Texas southeast across the Gulf of Mexico to north Florida and northeast to the waters of the Atlantic Ocean off Georgia and the Carolinas. Tropical air originating in the Gulf of Mexico, the Caribbean Sea, or the tropical North Atlantic lies poised here to challenge southward-moving outbreaks of polar air; in the process cyclonic storms are born along the front.

The presence of the jet stream over these cyclogenetic areas often contributes to the genesis and development of cyclonic storm systems. Weather observers keep a close check on the jet's whereabouts and behavior in order to anticipate storm development.

# Airmasses

An *airmass* is a large expanse of the atmosphere possessing generally similar qualities of heat, moisture, and stability. At equal elevations above the surface of the earth, one would find nearly identical temperatures, humidities, and cloud conditions throughout the airmass. In certain regions of our hemisphere, such as the tundras of northern Canada, the vast stretches of the Atlantic and Pacific oceans, and the tropical waters of the Gulf of Mexico and the Caribbean Sea, the air often stagnates for days at a time. Like giant air conditioners, these surfaces impart their native characteristics of temperature and moisture to the air above. These source regions can usually be identified on a weather map by the persistence of high pressure there for several days in a row. At birth and during their early days, stable airmasses are usually associated with anticyclonic conditions. Later, when airmasses have become moving airstreams, they are modified in their structure by passing over varied terrain surfaces and by mixing with air in a cyclonic storm situation. They are transformed into unstable, weather-active airstreams.

### Airmass Weather

| Type | Source region | Properties in source region | Season in New Jersey | Properties in New Jersey | Attendant weather in New Jersey |
|---|---|---|---|---|---|
| Arctic | Northern Canada | Very cold and dry | Infrequent; only in winter outbreaks | Frigid, dry | Clear skies day and night; produces arctic "sea smoke" when it passes over unfrozen bodies of water |
| Polar Continental | Northern or central Canada | Cold, dry | Frequent all seasons | Cold for season, usually dry, but may be unstable | Nights clear and cold; daytime cumulus clouds; sometimes snow or rain showers over northern hills |
| Polar Maritime Pacific | North Pacific south of Alaska | Cool, moist | Infrequent; mainly spring or fall | Modified, usually mild for season, and dry | Mostly fair skies; cool at night, moderate daytime temperatures |
| Polar Maritime Atlantic | Atlantic Ocean east of Canada and Maine | Cool, moist | Infrequent; any season, but most often in spring | Cool, moist all seasons | Morning fog, low clouds, drizzle on coast; when overrun by maritime tropical in northeasters, steady rain or snow follows |

Airmass Weather (*continued*)

| Type | Source region | Properties in source region | Season in New Jersey | Properties in New Jersey | Attendant weather in New Jersey |
|---|---|---|---|---|---|
| Tropical Maritime | Gulf of Mexico, Caribbean Sea, tropical Atlantic | Warm, humid | Frequent all seasons; most often warm months | Warm and humid all seasons; copious moisture | Low clouds on coast with fog and drizzle; broken clouds inland, fog at night, especially with snow cover; often convective or frontal showers in warm season |
| Tropical Continental | Southwestern United States and northern Mexico | Very hot, very dry | Infrequent; only in heat waves | Hot, dry | Fair hazy skies; attends extreme heat waves |

# Cold Fronts

A cold front is the leading edge of a cool or cold airmass that is actively on the move. What furnishes the front's dynamic energy is the dense cold air of a high-pressure system, usually consisting of fresh polar air from central Canada or, less frequently, North Pacific air greatly modified by a transcontinental journey.

Since cold fronts generate the most spectacular action in cyclonic storms, they are the features of the weather map that must be kept under constant watch by the forecaster. The arrival of a cold front in an area not only brings turbulent conditions but also introduces a complete change of airmass with different temperature and humidity conditions. The cold front's passage signals the concluding phase of cyclonic controls and the introduction of anticyclonic controls over the local weather.

No two cold fronts have the same structure or behave in the same manner. Some are activists, others create little change. Some are fast moving, others sluggish or even stationary. Some slope steeply to considerable heights, others are shallow with gradual slopes. The characteristics of an individual cold front may vary from day to day, even from hour to hour.

Cold-Front Weather

| Time | Temperature | Humidity | Barometer | Wind | Ceiling and visibility | Attendant weather in New Jersey |
|---|---|---|---|---|---|---|
| Prefrontal | Gradual rise | Steady increase | Steady fall | Increasing, veering from southeast-south to southwest | Lowering and decreasing | Increasing upper and middle clouds |
| At passage | Marked drop | Increase; then gradual fall | Sharp drop, then abrupt rise | Gusty, with shift to west or northwest | Decreasing, sometimes to zero-zero briefly | Low clouds, showers, thunder-storms in summer; brief rain or snow showers in winter |
| Postfrontal | Gradual decrease | Steady decrease | Rising, then steady | Strong, then decreas-ing, steady west or northwest | Quick improvement | Clearing, unless air very unstable, then continued showers |

NOTE: When the cold air behind a cold front has caught up with the warm air preceding a warm front, an occluded front is formed, and the weather behavior usually resembles that of a cold-front passage, though often in more subdued form.

# Warm Fronts

A warm front is the leading edge of an advancing mass of warm air that is displacing a cooler or colder airmass. Since warm air is lighter than cold air, it tends to glide up over the wedge of cold air hugging the surface. While the upper strata speed ahead two or three hundred miles, the main body of the warm air continues to advance along the surface at a slower pace.

The approach of a warm front is a subtle performance, with weather changes coming more gradually than with the bustling cold front. A warm front heralds the end of settled, anticyclonic conditions and the beginning of an unsettled period of cyclonic activity with cloudiness and precipitation prevailing. Forecasters take heed when a warm front is charted to the south or southwest of their areas.

The first sign of an approaching warm front appears on the southwest to northwest horizon in the form of cirrus cloud streamers at elevations of six miles or more. These climb to the zenith and in a couple of hours may cover almost the entire sky. The frozen ice crystals composing the cirrus clouds indicate that moist air is arriving overhead. Sometimes they may cause solar or lunar haloes. The cloud sheet gradually thickens and lowers, and clouds appear at middle elevations in a few hours, followed by low clouds. Warm fronts are the principal rain producers for New Jersey in the cooler months of the year. Since their behavior does not always follow the textbook description, the timing of the onset and the amount of precipitation is most difficult to forecast.

Warm-Front Weather

| Time | Temperature | Humidity | Barometer | Wind | Ceiling and visibility | Attendant weather in New Jersey |
|---|---|---|---|---|---|---|
| Prefrontal | Gradual rise | Increase | Falling slowly | Light, but increasing, veering from northeast-southeast to southeast-south | Lowering and decreasing steadily | Increasing clouds, first upper, then middle; steady rain sets in with low clouds and fog forming |
| At passage | Quick rise | Marked increase | Unsteady | Sometimes gusty, gradual shift to south-southwest | Low, often near zero-zero | Rain ending, often foggy |
| Postfrontal | Gradual rise, or no change | Gradual increase | Steady or falling slowly | Steady from south-southwest | Improvement, though sometimes restricted | Clouds break, sometimes complete clearing; warm and humid for the season |

# Climatic Sections

Though New Jersey is compact, it experiences a great variety of weather conditions over its land area of 7,836 square miles (covering a little over two degrees of latitude and one degree of longitude). Within the state there are five main climatic sections. Each has a homogeneity of its own in relation to basic geologic structure and geographic placement of land and sea areas. The relative proximity of each to the prevailing airstream and storm track of the day varies in slight but significant degree. These factors combine to produce distinctive local weather types in each of the five sections.

About one-third of New Jersey makes up the northern climatic zone. Its elevated highlands and valleys are part of the Appalachian uplands. The central zone of lowlands extends across the state like a waistband; it is marked by many water courses. The southwest is made up of a low plain with tidewater streams along the lower reaches of the Delaware River. The southern interior is distinguished by the Pine Barrens, or Pinelands, which cover a large area inland from the ocean and the Delaware estuary. The coastal zone stretches from Sandy Hook south 123 miles (198 km) to Cape May in a strip that penetrates no more than 5 to 10 miles (8 to 16 km) inland.

Though all sections of New Jersey experience related types of weather on most days, each of the five areas has some characteristics peculiar to itself. The following section seeks to identify these and show how they affect the weather locally, but it is not intended as a full survey of all the climatological features of the region.

## North

The most prominent features on a relief map of northern New Jersey are the ranges of low mountains running in parallel ridges from southwest to northeast and the numerous lakes and ponds interspersed here and there among the lower hills and valleys. Geologic maps show that the ranges of highlands reflect the basic rock structure of the region, though the surface topography was greatly modified by the glacial ice sheets. Since the melting of the ice about ten thousand years ago, this highland-and-lake region has exhibited a rather homogeneous pattern in its development, the result in part of its basic geography and in part of its weather regime. It is distinct in both regards from the central and southern sections of the state.

The northern region is surrounded by land, unlike the other sections, which all have close-by oceanic influences. Wind flow from all directions except east through south comes from the interior of the North American land mass, making for a continental type of climate, since the predominating winds vary from southwest in summer to northwest in winter. Being the farthest north in the state and having elevations from 500 to 1800 feet (152 to 549 m) above sea level, it experiences a colder regime, especially in winter, when the difference between Sussex and Cape May counties amounts to a full ten degrees Fahrenheit in average temperature; the record extremes have ranged from −34°F (−37°C) in the north to −3°F (−19°C) in the south. The snowfall variance is also marked, amounting annually to about 40 inches (102 cm) in Sussex County and about 15 inches (38 cm) along the southeast coast in Atlantic and Cape May counties.

Northern New Jersey lies close enough to the main storm track

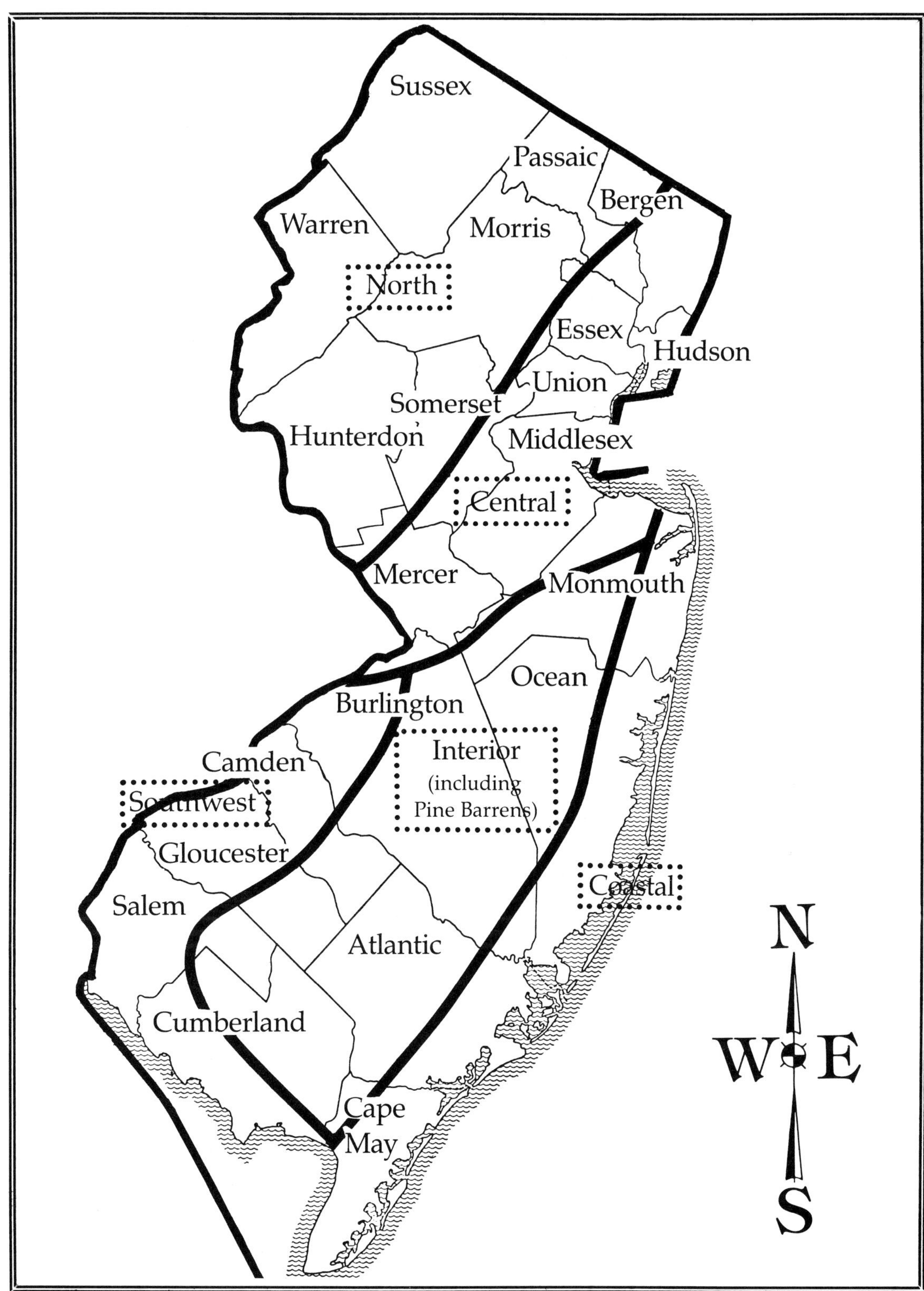


*New Jersey's climatic regions*

leading from the continent's interior to share in its cyclonic activity. This runs from the heart of the Mississippi valley over the Great Lakes and down the St. Lawrence valley. Trailing fronts from storm systems moving on this track cause heavier precipitation in the north than in the south. Furthermore, the precipitation shields of coastal storms moving offshore often reach far enough inland to cover the northern counties and augment the precipitation totals of the region.

The elevated terrain of the northern mountains and highlands creates some of its own weather. Upslope winds from the south or southeast result in orographic precipitation and occasionally intense downpours that sometimes result in flash floods when the narrow river courses cannot carry off the excessive precipitation. Further, wind flow over the rough terrain has a distinct effect on outbreaks of cold polar air following the passage of a cold front, since the ranges lie at right angles to a northwest flow. If the airstream is unstable, these serve as barriers and cause rising vertical currents in the wind flow, which in turn result in strato-cumulus cloudiness that may persist for hours while the smoother terrain to the south soon becomes cloudless. Mountain-type showers can occur with this type of instability, and in the colder months the precipitation may fall as snow showers.

Thunderstorms form a substantial portion of the warm season's rainfall budget, when cyclonic storms and frontal passages are less frequent. Many afternoon thundershowers develop in the mountains of Pennsylvania and New York State to the west and northwest and are carried by the prevailing upper-air wind flow across northern New Jersey, where they reach their maximum development in the evening. Sussex County has about twice as many thunderstorms per year as does Cape May County.

The colder regime in the north makes for a shorter growing season. The average date for the last killing frost in spring is about May 4 and that of the first in the fall is October 6, giving an average growing season of about 155 days. These dates, of course, can vary widely: there have been killing frosts at Layton in Sussex County as early as September 11 and as late as June 20. The shortness and variation of the length of the growing season excludes many products that can be commercially grown farther south.

Though the cold mornings keep the snow crisp and skiable for many weeks in a normal winter, the cold does of course add to heating bills—on the basis of total degree-days, the heating requirements run 35 percent more in Sussex County than at Atlantic City.

# Central

The central climatic region extends in a northeast-to-southwest zone from the waterway complex making up New York Harbor and the lower Hudson River to the great bend of the Delaware River in the vicinity of Trenton, Bordentown, and Burlington. The northern border runs from the highlands of northern Bergen County, along the Watchung Mountains and their Sourland Mountain extension, and through the hills of Mercer County north of Princeton and Trenton. The southern boundary extends from the hills of northern Monmouth County, passing near Freehold and through the rolling country of Burlington County north of Fort Dix. This zone includes the Hackensack, lower Passaic, lower Raritan, Millstone, and Assunpink drainage basins.

The central zone is strategically located to receive the residue of the pollutants emitted by the industrial plants lying to the west. When the prevailing wind is from a westerly quarter, all the atmospheric pollution of the middle and lower Delaware valley, stretching from the steel mills at Fairless Hills in Bucks County, Pennsylvania, to the petrochemical complexes of the Delaware estuary, is carried over New Jersey; the many New Jersey manufacturing and industrial plants add to the load of pollutants carried by the atmosphere. The web of highway traffic coverging toward the Hudson River crossings, plus heavy local traffic, pour additional fumes into the air. All human additives tend to change the chemical composition of the atmosphere; distinct weather conditions are sometimes created over the northeast portion of the state when a stable atmosphere becomes overburdened with its load of these additives.

Another distinctive feature of the central section lies in its predominantly urban environment. With large buildings and extensive paved areas serving as thermal reservoirs, the cities retain much of their daytime heat input, while the round-the-clock combustion of hydrocarbon fuels creates additional warmth, which modifies the atmosphere above. These conditions result in urban zones where nighttime temperatures remain higher than in the surrounding suburban and rural areas. Meteorologists call these zones *heat islands*; their significance lies in the presence of temperature inversions that trap impurities, warm the lower atmosphere, and cause smog conditions. The murky air overhanging some of New Jersey's—and the region's—large cities can often be seen as one approaches, and once within one can sense the locally created climate conditions by the thermometer reading, poor visibility, and physiological reactions. Morning commuters from the North Jersey suburbs often hear on the radio that the temperature in New York's Central Park is anywhere from 10° to 20°F

(6° to 11°C) warmer than at home and know they will soon be entering a different atmospheric environment.

A line of critical temperature change forms an additional climatic feature of the northern edge of this region; it runs from northern Bergen County along the ridges of the Watchung range and reaches the Delaware River between Lambertville and Trenton. In winter, this often marks the location of the 32°F (0°C) isotherm separating freezing from nonfreezing areas. During a storm period the fluctuation of the thermometer can determine whether precipitation will fall in frozen form as snow or ice pellets or as liquid rain drops. At times the heights of the Watchung range are sheathed in sparkling ice while the lowlands remain dripping wet with rain. In a summer heat wave, this narrow zone often marks the dividing line between comfortable and uncomfortable sleeping conditions. If the nighttime minimum fails to drop below a certain critical temperature, from about 72° to 76°F (22° to 24°C)—it varies according to the individual—sleeping may not be optimally restful. A temperature difference may be present on a summer afternoon, too: Newark averages twenty days per summer with a maximum temperature of 90°F (32°C) or more; there are only six such days at Charlotteburg high in Passaic County and ten at Long Valley in western Morris County.

## Pine Barrens

The most distinctive region of the state in topography and ground cover is the Pine Barrens. Also known as the Pinelands, they occupy the greater part of the interior south. The region includes all of Cape May County, half of Cumberland, all of Atlantic, bits of Gloucester, nearly half of Camden, nearly two-thirds of Burlington, almost all of Ocean, and a coastal belt of Monmouth County. The soil is made up mainly of white sands of the Lakewood series. Soil subtypes designated as Hammonton and Cape May phases of the Sassafras series are found in sizable areas of this zone, especially at the northern and southern extremes. The outstanding characteristic of these soils is their infertility; they sustain only scrub pine and oak forests, hence the historic reference to the region as the Pine Barrens.

The region's sandy soils play an important part in shaping its climate characteristics. The soil absorbs solar radiation in daytime but radiates the acquired heat to outer space at night. This creates temperatures that are warmer by day and colder by night than if the soil were less conducive to radiation. Some of the lowest night temperatures in the state are registered in the Pinelands, despite their relatively southerly latitude. Atlantic City Airport, surrounded by sandy soil, may run 15° to 20°F (8° to 11°C) less than the exposure at the

Marina on the bay, only about thirteen miles (21 km) away.

The very porous and permeable sands allow rapid infiltration of precipitation downward into the lower aquifer, leaving the surface quite dry. Most of the Pine Barrens are in reality rather arid most of the time. This greatly delays the biological breakdown of dead plant material, leaving the surface litter of dry leaves and branches as ideal tinder. Forest fires have swept the area periodically over the years, and now with more development in the region the potential for destruction is greatly increased.

## Southwest

The counties in the lower Delaware drainage basin form a distinct zone; their unity derives from sharing a low elevation with tidal creeks penetrating well inland, a soil very productive for agricultural purposes when evenly watered, and a southerly latitude (most of the area lies south of the Mason-Dixon line). All these factors contribute to making it a distinctive climatic zone. Most of the land lies below the hundred-foot elevation contour; Delaware Bay and its wide estuary provide a maritime influence over the land. This section includes the western third of Burlington County, about half of Camden, most of Gloucester, all of Salem, and about half of Cumberland County.

Temperatures here rise to the highest average levels of any place in the state. The southerly latitude accounts for high daytime maximums, and the presence of Delaware Bay, with its moist atmosphere and frequent fogs, tends to lessen nighttime radiation and maintain high minimum temperatures. These influences make for the most temperate climate in the Garden State.

The southwest also experiences less precipitation than the northern or central sections. There are no mountains or elevated plateaus to cause orographic precipitation, nor do thunderstorms form as readily over the flatlands as they do over the varied elevations of the north. The southwest is also more distant from the major storm track through the Great Lakes and the St. Lawrence valley and sometimes too far inland for the canopy of heavy rain of a coastal storm to reach. Conditions approaching drought appear almost every summer, and irrigation is necessary for commercial agricultural enterprises.

Prevailing winds blow from northwest through southwest, with the latter predominating except in winter. Usually wind movement is sufficient to provide adequate ventilation of the atmosphere, but in times of light air flow attending anticyclonic situations, pollution from the petrochemical and other industrial plants along the Delaware River causes smog and its usual resulting unsatisfactory air quality.

When wind flow is from northeast through south, it has an over-water trajectory, and the area is subject to maritime influences, with moderate temperatures and high humidities. The first autumn frosts often occur four weeks later and the last spring frosts four weeks earlier than in the north. Thus, the growing season is the longest in New Jersey.

## Coastal Zone

The coastal zone stretches 123 miles (198 km) from Sandy Hook to Cape May. It forms a distinct climate province wherein a battle between oceanic and continental influences is constantly in progress. There are many ebbs and flows in this contest as opposing airstreams advance and retreat. Sometimes one air flow may take control of the scene for several days, and at other times its domination may be limited to a few hours or a day before a resurgence of the opposing wind flow regains control and brings changes in the local weather.

Wind flow over the coastal zone coming from northeast through southeast to south, having an over-water trajectory, is conditioned by the temperature characteristics of the ocean surface. These vary according to season, water being a conservative body that changes gradually. In autumn and early winter the ocean gives up its heat slowly and remains warm relative to the land, keeping the coastal zone warmer than the interior. In spring and early summer the ocean continues cooler longer than the land, which reacts more speedily to the increasing altitude and duration of solar rays. The seasons change more gradually and to less of an extreme in the coastal zone than elsewhere in the state.

An oceanic influence of shorter duration occurs during the approach and passage of a cyclonic storm moving from the southwest or west. With a substantial anticyclone moving eastward offshore after a period of fair weather, the wind shifts to the southeast and immediately brings oceanic influences over the land; this means lowering clouds, fog, and, eventually, precipitation. The flow then veers more to the south and perhaps to southwest after the passage of the warm front, bringing air flow that has been conditioned off the South Atlantic coast or over the Gulf of Mexico. After a few hours of this flow, the passage of the cold front shifts the wind to west or northwest, and continental influences rout the oceanic influences and dominate both land and offshore waters. The new airmass and air flow usually continue until the ridge line or central axis of the next high-pressure area passes eastward of the meridian of New Jersey. Then the wind shifts around to southeast or south and a noticeable warming of the coastal zone takes place again under oceanic controls.

A brief influence, often limited to only several hours, may take place on an ordinary spring or summer day when the ocean is still relatively cool. Daytime heating of the land causes the development of a sea breeze system whereby the heated air over the land rises and is replaced by a flow of cool air from the ocean surface. This exchange of air between ocean and land may begin in the late morning or early afternoon and continue as long as the heating of the sun is able to cause convective currents over the land. Ordinarily, the sea breeze penetrates only a short distance inland, limited to about five to ten miles. But if the pressure gradient is favorable, the penetration may be as far as twenty-five to forty miles (40 to 64 km) and greatly temper the daytime heat well inland. At night there may be a less pronounced reversal of the system, with winds blowing from the cool land to the warmer ocean.

The outstanding weather specialty of this region is the coastal storm, which may arrive at any time of the year but is most frequent from October to April. The storm systems move northward over the coastal plain or a short distance offshore. They are accompanied by northeast winds on the New Jersey coast if the center passes to the east and by southeast winds if the center passes over land between the Appalachians and the coast. Winds may mount to gale and even hurricane force in a well-developed coastal storm, and barometric pressure may sink below 29.00 inches (98.2 kilopascals [kPa]). Hardly a season goes by without at least one storm of this type, and in some seasons there may be a series of three or four. When a coastal disturbance occurs at the time of astronomical high tide, the waves may drive over the beaches, through or around the protective dunes, and into built-up areas containing buildings and roads. The Great March Storm of 1962 provides an example of the extreme destruction such a storm can cause. Hurricanes, too, are a special concern of the coastal zone; they are discussed in detail on p. 89.

*Cape May's shoreline is constantly being eroded, as this stranded fire hydrant illustrates. (Courtesy of Princeton University Library)*

CHAPTER 3

# New Jersey Almanac

The BURLINGTON

ALMANACK,

FOR

The Year of our LORD, 1771;

Being the Third after LEAP-YEAR.

*Fitted to the Latitude of Forty Degrees, and a Meridian of near Five Hours Weſt from* London.

CONTAINING,

The Motions of the Sun and Moon; the true Places and Aſpects of the Planets; the Riſing and Setting of the Sun; the Riſing, Setting and Southing of the Moon; the Lunations, Conjunctions, Eclipſes, Riſing, Setting and Southing of the Planets; Length of Days; Judgment of the Weather; Feſtivals, and other remarkable Days; High Water at Philadelphia.—*Alſo,*

Some uſeful Hints, from a late approved Treatiſe on Health; Quakers General Meetings; a Table of Intereſt at Six and Seven per Cent, with other uſeful Tables; a Point of Law relative to Wills explained; Courts, Receipts, Fairs, Roads, *&c.* Together with a Variety of uſeful and entertaining Matter.

By *TIMOTHY TRUEMAN,* Philom.

TIME *turns his Glaſs, and round the Pole*
*Another Year begins to roll.*
*Touch'd by the Sun's returning fire,*
*Stern* WINTER *ſhall ere long retire;*
*Soon the all-animating* SPRING
*Shall make the Hills and Vallies ſing;*
*The* SUMMER *ſhall adorn the Plain*
*With purple Fruits and golden Grain;*
*And* AUTUMN *preſs the loaded Floor,*
*Till thankful Man ſhall aſk no more.*

*BURLINGTON:*

Printed and Sold by ISAAC COLLINS.

*A page from the 1771* Burlington Almanack. *(Special Collections, Rutgers University)*

# January Day-by-Day

January is the prime winter month in New Jersey. Snow and cold strive to dominate the scene. The sun has made its turnaround and climbs 5°36′ toward the zenith, but temperatures continue their downward trend until the last week when an upward trend begins. The days grow longer, with an additional fifty minutes of daylight by the month's end; the increased daylight shortens the duration of overnight radiational cooling and extends the period for the sun to warm the daytime air. Often cold, dry anticyclonic conditions produce those bright, blue January days when the landscape sparkles in the sunshine, giving the winter-weary a psychological boost after the dreariness of December.

The January thaw is a popular feature of the weather-lore calendar and has been since colonial times. The daily mean temperatures in many Januarys do show an upward trend sometime between January 18 and the twenty-seventh. A Rutgers University study found that a "seasonal trend curve" brings higher temperatures on January 22 and 23 and lower readings on January 29 than seasonally expected. The January thaw may thus be considered a floating feature on the meteorological calendar. It may be completely absent, however, in some years that feature steady cold. The January thaw results from adjustments in the atmospheric circulation over the continent from a high-winter to a late-winter pattern. The supply of cold air over central Canada is temporarily exhausted and high pressure in the Arctic diminishes. A low-pressure trough in the Midwest and a temporary northward movement of the Bermuda high set the stage for warm airstreams from the Gulf of Mexico to advance into the northeastern United States for several days in a row.

In January the Pacific high, that great controller of atmospheric traffic across the vast ocean, lies at its most southerly position, and its counterpart to the north, the Aleutian low, is well developed. The mean jet stream position continues its December behavior by tracking from an entry point on the continent in southern British Columbia southeast to the Ohio valley, where it is usually joined by the southerly jet coming northeast from northern Mexico. The combined fast flow moves over the New Jersey area and into the Atlantic Ocean.

The main storm track across the continent originates in Alberta, trends southeast to the Great Lakes, then moves down the St. Lawrence valley, with the trailing fronts of the cyclonic systems moving over New Jersey. The plains of the Southwest produce the Texas-type cyclone which normally travels a northeasterly course to the west of the Appalachians over Ohio and the lower Great Lakes. Rain-producing or snow-changing-to-rain storms in New Jersey, as well as some of the heaviest January rains, come from warm frontal actions of this type. There is also a cyclogenetic area off the coast of Georgia and the Carolinas at this season which produces midwinter storms of varying intensity. Their path northward is all-important in determining the type—frozen or liquid—and intensity of precipitation. These coastal storms or northeasters can cause severe beach erosion and heavy damage to shore installations.

Mean temperatures for January average about 3°F colder than for December. The highest mean is at Shiloh in Cumberland County, with 33.2°F (0.7°C); the lowest is at Newton in Sussex, with 25.2°F (−3.8°C), making a difference of 8°F (4.4°C) between representative stations in the north and south. Probably there is a 10°F (5.6°C) spread between the absolute coldest and warmest locations in January, but we do not have records to substantiate this. Over the years of record since 1885, thermometers in January have ranged from a maximum of 78°F (25.6°C) in 1890 to a minimum of −34°F (−36.7°C) in 1904. The coldest January occurred in 1918, with a statewide mean of 20.2°F (−6.5°C); the warmest was in 1932, with a mean of 42.4°F (5.8°C). During the recent cold, windy winter of 1976–1977, January was almost as cold as the record January 1918.

January is a relatively dry month because of the predominance of northwest winds that flow from the dry land mass of the interior of the continent, and the concomitant infrequency of moist wind flow from the ocean. January is drier than December and about equal in precipitation to February. The state-wide average is 3.05 inches (77 mm). The amounts are generally higher in the eastern portions; Atlantic City Airport reports an average of 3.56 inches (90 mm) compared to 2.82 inches (72 mm) at Moorestown in Burlington County. The January state-wide averages over the years of record have ranged from 9.09 inches (231 mm) in 1979 to 0.68 inch (17 mm) in 1955.

Snowfall in January averages about 9 inches (23 cm) in the northwestern counties and drops to about 5 inches (13 cm) along the southeast coast. The snow cover usually lasts longest in January because of the low temperatures, but February has more actual snowfall. Snows of 12 inches (30 cm) or more are rare, but lighter falls of the dry variety are often driven by northeast gales into deep drifts and can disrupt transportation for days afterward. The greatest January storm in recent years came on January 19–20, 1961 and dropped as much as 26 inches (66 cm) in the extreme northern part of the state. It is known in weather circles as the Kennedy Inaugural Storm.

1 / 1877 Snowiest New Year's Day: 15 inches at Newark.

1918 Coldest New Year's Day: −24°F at Culvers Lake in Sussex County.

1966 Warmest New Year's Day: 69°F at Belleplain in Cape May County.

2 / 1925 Big snowstorm: 18.5 inches at Newark, 27.5 inches at South Orange "by accurate measurement," according to *Climatological Data*.

3 / 1914 Second severe coastal storm of winter did immense damage at Long Branch: east gales continued for twenty-seven hours, peak gust 93 miles per hour; hotel toppled into sea; railroad tracks and station swept away.

4 / 1918 Climax of eight-day cold wave: date records still stand at New York City for seven of eight days.

5 / 1835 Nighttime radiation during cold week dropped thermometers to −32°F in Sussex County, −20°F at Belleville in Essex, −13°F at Newark.

1904 Record all-time lows: −34°F at River Vale in Bergen County; −30°F at Layton in Sussex; −28°F at Englewood in Bergen.

6 / 1910 Severe ice storm: rain fell at temperature range from 16°F to 25°F; ice ¾ inch thick at Jersey City; widespread wire and tree destruction.

7 / 1841 The Bridges Flood, greatest on Delaware River since 1810: six major bridges destroyed; also damage on Passaic River, where four of six bridges were lost.

8 / 1866 Cold Term of '66 from January 4 to 9: −14°F in New York City, −12.7°F at Newark, −12°F at Trenton, −14°F at Haddonfield in Camden County; barometer "highest ever known," according to a Philadelphia observer writing in the *Journal* of the Franklin Institute.

9 / 1793 First balloon flight in America, Philadelphia to Woodbury in Gloucester County, under clear skies and almost calm conditions.

10 / 1859 Coldest daylight on record, below-zero maximums in north: −5°F at Newton in Sussex County, −0.5°F at Newark.

11 / 1922 Severe coastal storm plus spring high tides caused beach erosion: barometer 28.74 inches at Sandy Hook; winds 60 miles per hour at Long Branch.

12 / 1720 Hudson River could be crossed on ice from Manhattan to Bergen Point.

1890 78°F at Cape May Court House: all-time state record high for January.

13 / 1915 Coastal storm on 12–13: barometer 28.78 inches at Long Branch, northeast wind at 65 miles per hour; 3.62 inches of rain at Newark in twenty-four hours.

1978 Ice storm in north with 3-inch snow and ice accumulation: traffic accidents; power outages affected over a hundred thousand people.

14 / 1932 Heat wave during warmest-ever January: 68°, 70°, 67°F on January 13–15.

15 / 1831 Great Snowstorm, January 14–16: 18 to 30 inches fell over south; Cape May had "nearly three feet" according to a local newspaper, depths not equaled until 1899.

1961 Air Force Texas Tower Number 4, a radar site located sixty-five miles east of Barnegat, collapsed during storm, killing twenty-eight.

16 / 1893 Cold wave in a severely cold month dropped thermometer to −7°F at Cape May Court House.

1924 *Shenandoah*'s Wild Ride in nighttime storm; southeast gale of 57 miles per hour ripped the airship from its new mooring mast at Lakehurst; it was buffeted over North Jersey before control was regained.

17 / 1977 Cold wave: −10°F at High Point in Sussex County, 2°F at Cape May City.

1982 "Cold Sunday." Temperature at Newark Airport dropped from 21°F at 10:00 P.M. to a morning reading of −4°F on January 17, later to −7°F, for coldest daylight period of modern record. Trenton reached minimum of −9°F, Atlantic City −6°F. Strong northwest gales all day caused excessive wind chill temperatures.

18 / 1857 Cold Storm of 1857: snow began with temperature at zero; 12 inches fell, with gales creating huge drifts; railroads blocked.

19 / 1810 Cold Friday: temperature dropped 40°F overnight, with northwest gales causing severe wind chill.

20 / 1961 Kennedy Inaugural Snowstorm: 16 to 26 inches fell across north; gales caused great drifting; in Sussex County temperature dropped from 20°F to −20°F on January 21.

21 / 1881 Damaging ice storm knocked out all communications in many cities in northern part of state.

1979 Hard coastal storm: barometer dropped to 28.85 inches; rainfall over 3 inches.

22 / 1961 Most prolonged cold wave in century: temperature remained below freezing from January 21 to February 4 in north; low of −29°F at Layton in Sussex County.

23 / 1857 Cold Friday II: cold northwest winds all day, record low readings on morning of January 24; −30°F at Cornley's Mill and −28°F at Frenchtown, both in Hunterdon County.

24 / 1925 Total solar eclipse over extreme north under clear skies and zero temperatures; most of Sussex, Passaic, and Bergen counties in path of totality.

25 / 1821 Record cold wave: Hudson River frozen over, people crossed on foot; "refreshment taverns" set up on ice; −14°F at New York.

26 / 1944 Extreme January thaw set in: Pleasantville near Atlantic City had 65°F on January 26, 69°F on twenty-seventh.

1978 Severe storm passed north over Ohio with low barometers widespread eastward, 28.75 inches at Philadelphia; quick January thaw.

27 / 1927 High pressure of great magnitude, with cold wave: barometer 31.03 inches at Verona in Essex County; −12°F at Culvers Lake in Sussex; 6°F at Cape May City.

28 / 1805 Big Snow of 1805 was the "worst since 1780": 24 inches estimated at Newark during sixty-hour snowfall; snowiest January ever.

1935 Second coldest January on record: −26°F at Runyon in Middlesex County.

29 / 1780 Coldest morning of the Hard Winter of 1780: thermometer in New York City reported at −16°F; heavy guns hauled over ice of Upper Bay from Manhattan to Staten Island.

30 / 1966 Blizzard conditions prevailed: 12 inches of snow fell over north; maximum 13°F on January 29 at Sussex, falling to 0°F on January 30; Atlantic City had winds of 60 miles per hour.

31 / 1920 Great anticyclone peaked at 30.98 inches at Trenton and Sandy Hook; temperature dropped 43°F at Sussex to −6°F.

# February Day-by-Day

"Half the wood and half the hay, you should have on Candlemas Day," says an old English proverb. The second of February has long been regarded as a pivotal day in the course of the winter. It comes forty-three days after the winter solstice and forty-seven days before the spring equinox. According to heating-degree data, half the heating requirements in most New Jersey locations have been met by January 25, so in most winters by the time February begins the worst is over. And there's always the prognostic tradition of the groundhog and his shadow on February 2—either winter is at an end or a second winter of six weeks' duration will follow Groundhog Day.

In February the main features of the winter weather maps attain their southernmost latitudes in both the Pacific and Atlantic oceans. The Azores-Bermuda high lies off the northwest African coast, with a long arm of high pressure extending westward to southern Florida. The Icelandic low occupies the southeast corner of Greenland and adjacent waters with a mean central pressure down to 29.38 inches (99.5 kPa). The jet streams cross the country a little south of their January tracks, meeting over Tennessee and departing the coast in the vicinity of Norfolk, Virginia. With the westerlies at relatively low latitudes and flowing stronger than in January, an area of maximum cyclogenesis develops in the Gulf of Mexico, and a storm track leads northeast along the Atlantic seaboard, usually passing about 150 to 250 miles (241 to 402 km) off the New Jersey coast. The state's severest northeasters occur from storms moving along this track. At the same time the storm tracks from the interior of the continent continue to converge toward the eastern Great Lakes and move down the St. Lawrence valley, with their trailing fronts causing frequent changes in New Jersey's weather.

The sun climbs about nine additional degrees toward the zenith in February, and there is an increase of about 4°F (2.2°C) in heat as a result. Mean temperatures range from 27.1°F (−2.7°C) at Sussex to 35.4°F. (1.9°C) at the Atlantic City Marina. The warmest February occurred in 1890, with a state-wide average of 39.9°F (4.4°C); the coldest was in 1934, with an average of 18.6°F (−7.4°C). The warmest February temperature on record is 80°F (26.7°C); occurring in 1930. The lowest was −26°F (−32.2°C) in 1934, closely followed by −25°F (−31.7°C) in 1943.

February days are slightly drier than those in January. The coastal region continues to be the wettest area, averaging 0.17 inch (4 mm) of precipitation more than the south and 0.24 inch (6 mm) more than the north. Individual stations show much greater discrepancies: Long Branch averages 3.52 inches (89 mm), Newton only 2.46 inches (62 mm). Four wet coastal stations average 0.77 inch (20 mm) more than four dry western stations. The wettest February came in 1896, with a state-wide average of 6.77 inches (172 mm); the driest was 1901, with only 0.94 inch (24 mm).

February is the snowiest month of the year despite its relative shortness; the February full moon is appropriately designated the Snow Moon in Indian lore. Monthly averages are above 10 inches (25 cm) at Charlotteburg in Passaic County, Flemington in Hunterdon, and Sussex, all in the north. In the south the average is about 5 inches (13 cm). The snow pattern is occasionally reversed, with the south receiving more than the north; this happened in February 1967, when Atlantic City Airport measured 35 inches (90 cm) of snow.

*This sleetstorm hit Trenton in February 1902. (Courtesy of Trenton Public Library)*

1 / 1920 Barometers remained high to set February records: 31.00 inches at New York City, 30.98 at Sandy Hook and Trenton; cold wave continued, with −16°F at Layton in Sussex County.

1935 Radiational cooling on sandy soil dropped mercury to −31°F at Runyon in Middlesex County; Freehold had −8°F, New Brunswick −7°F.

2 / 1915 Damaging coastal storm: winds of 54 miles per hour at Long Branch with 3 inches of rain on February 1, 1.65 inches on February 2.

3 / 1961 Third big snow of season on February 3–4: from 5 inches in southeast to 27 inches in north; Long Branch had east winds of 73 miles per hour; long below-freezing spell ended; 50 inches of snow accumulated at Layton.

4 / 1920 Great snow and sleet storm, February 4–7: 17 inches of mixed precipitation accumulated on ground with water content of over 4 inches, all frozen into solid mass; auto traffic impeded until end of month.

5 / 1947 Precipitous temperature drop from 56°F to 4°F in fifteen hours at Pleasantville near Atlantic City; 50°F to 8°F at Cape May.

6 / 1978 Severe coastal erosion in big northeast storm; heavy snow state-wide: 22 inches at Newton in Sussex County, 23 inches at Woodbridge in Middlesex; 20 inches at Toms River in Ocean; −10°F at Charlotteburg in Passaic County.

7 / 1861 Sharp cold front arrived: 45°F at Newark at 2:00 P.M., dropped to 3°F by 9:00 P.M., reached −7.5° on morning of February 8.

8 / 1895 Southeast gales caused floods, dam breaks, washouts as very deep storm center moved over Pennsylvania.

9 / 1870 President Grant signed a measure establishing a storm-warning service under control of U.S. Army Signal Service. Atlantic City was first station established in New Jersey.

1934 Coldest morning in coldest month in official records for New Jersey: minimum of −31°F at Culvers Lake in Sussex County; −26°F at Canoe Brook in Essex; −25°F at Indian Mills in Burlington.

10 / 1969 Biggest snowstorm since 1961: airports isolated, traffic blocked; 16 inches at Rahway, 13.8 inches at Newark, 13 inches at Flemington.

11 / 1899 Arctic week of intense cold well established; minimum dropped to 6°F or below every night from February 9 to 16; lowest −10°F on tenth.

12 / 1899 Greatest snowstorm in modern New Jersey history began: dropped 34 inches at Cape May to increase snow cover there to 41 inches; severe storm throughout state, with bitter wind chill.

13 / 1914 Third severe coastal storm of season caused more erosion; Sandy Hook peninsula broken through by tidal surge.

1923 Severe hailstorm during winter thunderstorm in Sussex County, where temperatures ranged from 19°F to 37°F.

14 / 1940 Valentine's Day storm: heavy mixture of snow and sleet equaling 2 inches of melted precipitation; wind of 54 miles per hour at Atlan-

tic City; barometer 28.89 inches at Trenton; highways impassable for several days.

15 / 1855 Thaw after hard winter brought earliest opening of Delaware-Raritan Canal (in use from 1834 to 1888).

1949 Mid-February heat wave: 77°F at Lakewood, 76°F at Newark and other stations; 77° second highest ever in February.

16 / 1943 Bitter cold wave: Charlotteburg in Passaic County dropped from 34°F on February 14, to −16°F on fifteenth and to −25°F on sixteenth; −24°F at Long Valley in Morris County.

17 / 1958 Great eastern snowstorm swept from Georgia to Nova Scotia: up to 21 inches fell in North Jersey; winds of 70 miles per hour at Atlantic City; massive drifting; transportation snarled.

18 / 1927 Icing during coastal storm caused wire and tree damage inland; 65-mile-per-hour wind at Atlantic City undermined structures and caused beach erosion.

1979 Climax of record long cold period that began on February 9: −18°F at Sussex.

19 / 1979 Very heavy snowstorm climaxed wintry period: snowfalls of up to 20 inches were whipped by strong gales, especially severe in south.

20 / 1934 Blizzard conditions prevailed during severe cold wave; 7.6 inches of snow fell in north; Charlotteburg dropped from 32°F to 4°F; drifting closed many highways.

21 / 1822 Heavy rains and snowmelt caused rapid rise of streams; seven county bridges carried away in Hunterdon County, as well as several on the Passaic River; many dams and mills destroyed.

22 / 1902 Widespread ice storm, "the most destructive we have record of," according to *Climate and Crops*: wires down; great tree damage, pine forests suffered severely.

23 / 1974 Northwest gales caused damage to utilities and blew in windows: building unroofed at Edison.

24 / 1977 Flash flooding in Passaic valley: Lodi in Bergen County on Saddle River suffered worst damage; 2 inches of rain fell on wet soil with frozen base.

25 / 1930 80°F at Pleasantville near Atlantic City, highest ever in state in February (had been −7°F on February 17); 79°F at Asbury Park.

26 / 1902 Great rainfall, February 25–28, resulted in very high floods, especially in Passaic River valley: 0.98 inch on February 25–26, 2.65 inches on February 28 at Charlotteburg.

27 / 1717 First of series of storms making up the legendary Great Snow: 36 to 48 inches in New England, depths in New Jersey unknown.

28 / 1934 Cold ending of coldest month in modern history: −23°F at Layton in Sussex County and at Canoe Brook in Essex; −8°F at Indian Mills in Burlington County; barometer peaked at high figure of 30.95 inches.

29 Leap Day: Newark's coldest was 5°F in 1884; its warmest was 63°F in 1880; Trenton's extremes were 5°F in 1884 and 67°F in 1880; Tuckerton reached 72°F in 1972.

# March Day-by-Day

March is the month of the vernal equinox, the beginning of both the astronomical and meteorological year. At noon on the day of the equinox, the direct rays of the sun fall on the equator and night and day are of almost equal length. Along the 75°W meridian the sun stands over a point in South America where the borders of Peru, Ecuador, and Colombia converge. The sun makes good progress northward during March, moving about 11°45′ and ending the month in the Northern Hemisphere at about 4°N. As a result, the duration of daylight increases about eighty-seven minutes from March 1 to March 31, and all living things respond to the added daylight and increased warmth. The cold dormancy of winter is over.

The storm tracks of winter still prevail in March, however. The area of cyclogenesis over the Gulf of Mexico migrates to the interior of East Texas, and the storm production area along the Georgia and Florida coasts is less active. The Atlantic coastal storm track is farther east than during the earlier winter months. The principal continental storm track over the Great Lakes and down the St. Lawrence valley continues to be a weather influence on New Jersey, with the fronts sweeping across the state periodically. Storms from the Texas area may move along either side of the Appalachians and can bring exceptional rainfalls, such as the one that occurred in March 1936, when the greatest snowmelt floods ever experienced in the Northeast sent New Jersey rivers on a rampage.

An important feature of the spring circulation comes to the fore in March—the blocking anticyclones that take up a position over the waters off Nova Scotia and Newfoundland and prevent the normal west-east movement of continental cyclones for several days in a row. The high-pressure area first appears over Hudson Bay and moves slowly southeast to assume its blocking stance over the offshore waters. A secondary anticyclonic track carries continental high-pressure areas across Ohio to New York and New England, where they join the ridge of high pressure over the cool waters of the North Atlantic.

The thermometer's response is marked, showing an increase of 11°F (6.1°C) during the month in state-wide mean temperatures. Local means range from 36.2°F (3.2°C) at Sussex to 42.4°F (5.8°C) at Shiloh in Cumberland County. The recorded extremes for the state during March are 92°F (33.3°C) in 1921 and −15°F (−26.1°C) in 1906.

March's average rainfall shows a sizable increase over February in all sections, being just over 1.00 inch (25 mm) in both the northern and southern zones and 0.80 inch (20 mm) along the coast. The wettest area is the northeast: Paterson and Elizabeth both report 4.42 inches (112 mm). The northwest is the driest: Newton reports 3.20 inches (81 mm); the southwest is next: Shiloh averages 3.48 inches (88 mm). The four wettest stations average 4.38 inches (111 mm) and the four driest 3.43 inches (87 mm). Over the years of record the wettest March came in 1912, with a state-wide average of 7.61 inches (193 mm). The driest March was in 1885, with an average of 1.10 inches (28 mm).

Snowfall continues heavy in the north throughout March: Charlotteburg averages 10.4 inches (26 cm), only a fraction down from the February figure. Both Flemington and Sussex expect 8.7 inches (22 cm), close to the February figure, but there is a sizable drop in the south, where Atlantic City Airport expects only 3.2 inches (8 cm) in March, about 60 percent of the February amount. The snowiest March came in 1914, with a state-wide average of 20.4 inches (52 cm). There have been three Marches with no measurable snow: 1903, 1921, and 1946. Thirty-six inches (91 cm) fell at Sussex in March 1967.

*Ice from the Delaware River jammed Trenton's Fair Street, March 1904. (Courtesy of Trenton Public Library)*

1 / 1914 Lionlike opening: heavy, wet, wind-driven snow crippled the state; "worst since '88"; 24 inches at Asbury Park; fourth severe storm of season; barometer at near-record low of 28.40 inches.

2 / 1846 Great coastal storm coming at time of perigean-spring tides raised water to highest level known for years.

1902 Snowmelt/rainstorm flood at crest in Passaic valley, highest since 1882; extensive damage around Pompton.

3 / 1940 Ice storm disrupted communications from Somerset to Bergen counties; Plainfield measured 2.27 inches with 34°F–32°F temperatures; 800 linemen used one million feet of wire for repairs.

4 / 1909 Backlash of storm deepening off coast provided President Taft's inauguration with a surprise snowstorm; 6 inches of snow, 35-mile-per-hour northeast winds at Atlantic City; communications with Washington severed.

5 / 1872 Severest March cold wave ever: 3°F at New York, 2.7°F at Newark, 5°F at Philadelphia.

6 / 1962 Great Atlantic coastal storm: from March 5 to March 7 five successive high tides topped by thirty-foot waves breached barrier beaches and caused great damage to shore installations.

7 / 1932 Record low barometer from deep coastal storm, March 5–7: Atlantic City 28.37 inches, Long Branch 28.36 inches; 62-mile-per-hour northeast winds at Atlantic City, but minimal damage.

8 / 1904 Ice-jam flood at Trenton raised Delaware River to record height: boilers in capitol building flooded; railroad traffic halted by blocks of ice.

9 / 1941 Big snow: depths ranged from 4 inches in south to 20 inches in north; Canoe Brook in Essex County had 2.69-inch water equivalent; storm left wet, heavy snowpack.

10 / 1954 Tornado moved from Woodbury in Gloucester County to Farmingdale in Monmouth: skip damage along sixty-mile path; funnel seen; ten injuries.

11 / 1936 First of two general rainstorms with heavy snowmelt raised rivers into preliminary flood stage; 3.52 inches at Charlotteburg in Passaic County and 3.26 inches at Dover in Morris County.

12 / 1888 Blizzard of '88 at height: Union reported 25 inches, Newark 19 inches; Trenton had 2.22 inches of rain on March 11, then 21 inches of snow on March 12–13.

13 / 1888 Entire state snowbound, with railroads blocked; bitter northwest gale with temperatures from 0°F to 10°F. Great shipping losses: thirteen vessels along the New Jersey coast and thirty-seven in Delaware Bay blown ashore, sunk, or damaged.

14 / 1846 Melting snow caused high freshet on Delaware and rivers of the northeast; rail traffic stopped near Bordentown in Burlington County.

15 / 1896 Third snowstorm of month: 12 inches fell in north, ending in rain.

16 / 1956 Snowy four days began: Newark had 5.6 inches on March 16–17 and 18.2 inches on March 18–19 from two coastal storms; wind gusts 40–48 miles per hour. Extensive damage to utilities; schools closed; traffic impeded.

17 / 1760 Woodbury in Gloucester County: "the snow on ye ground in Deer park in ye woods being then level was one yard deep—the deepest snow I ever remember." (From *Samuel Mickle's Diary*)

1892 Big St. Patrick's Day snowstorm in north: 14.6 inches fell in New York City.

1945 Hot St. Patrick's Day: Sussex in north and Hammonton in south both had 90°F.

18 / 1916 Record late-season cold: −9°F at Culvers Lake, 7°F at New York, 10°F at Philadelphia.

19 / 1936 Second big flood of March '36: Layton in Sussex County measured 4.07 inches of rain, Charlotteburg in Passaic 4.32 inches on March 17–22. Record high crests on Delaware; Trenton streets flooded.

20 / 1868 Great Equinoctial Storm: snows of 25 inches covered Cape May County; gales damaged shipping. Locally known as the McKane Storm for loss of two boys at the Bayside in Cumberland County.

1945 More early heat: Bridgeton in Cumberland County had 87°F, Sussex 86°F.

21 / 1885 Late-season cold wave dropped temperatures to 11°F, 10°F, and 12°F at New York City, and to 8°F, 6°F and 11°F at Philadelphia on March 20–22. Three consecutive date records still stand.

22 / 1920 Brilliant aurora reached to zenith circle with north and south arches; greatest at 10:00 P.M.; wire communications almost completely disrupted.

23 / 1894 Tornado at 1:30 A.M. at Bridgeton in Cumberland County destroyed barns, windmills, houses, and trees; trolley house wrecked; path was one hundred to two hundred feet wide.

24 / 1906 Lowest temperature so late in season: Layton had −6°F on March 23, −15°F on twenty-fourth, −14°F on twenty-fifth.

25 / 1765 Snow fell 30 inches deep, March 23–25, in South Jersey.

1876 Record March rainfall: 4.25 inches at New York City.

26 / 1954 Tornado at Neptune City in Monmouth County: funnel seen; two-story frame house demolished.

27 / 1921 Maximum 92°F at Woodbine in Cumberland County, but only 60°F at Cape May City, twenty-five miles away.

28 / 1921 Sudden change: temperature drop of 55°F in eighteen hours, and 20°F in twenty minutes; fairly well-developed tornado at Somerville.

29 / 1919 According to *Climatological Data: New Jersey Section*, "One of the longest continued and hardest blows this portion of the country has ever experienced" from March 27 to 30: Long Branch had winds up to 68 miles per hour; great damage to crops and small buildings.

30 / 1823 Easter Sunday storm: easterly gales uprooted trees, caused structural damage; 24 inches of snow fell in Sussex.

1970 Snowy Easter Sunday: 9 to 16 inches fell over north; temperature fell from 60°F on March 26 to 2°F on thirtieth.

31 / 1945 Lamblike ending: five-day heat wave with 91°F reading on March 29 concluded warmest March ever; growing season thirty days ahead of usual schedule.

# April Day-by-Day

April is a varied month, often opening in the cold lap of winter and ending in the warm embrace of spring. The first day of the baseball season often finds a chilly atmosphere unsuited for player or fan, yet by the end of April a shirtsleeved crowd may see a veteran pitcher enjoying enough summer balm to unlimber his arm for a full nine-inning stint on the mound.

April, of course, is associated with showers. Their presence indicates that local conditions are becoming important in the production of rain, while the general storm systems moving across the country contribute less to the total precipitation budget. The reason for the advent of the shower regime lies in the increased heat available at the earth's surface. Though the air remains cool aloft, the heating of the surface layer causes the air immediately above to expand, become less dense, and exhibit instability: a column of heated air rises, as a balloon does, and is propelled upward through the denser air aloft. During its ascent the air cools until reaching its dew point; then the moisture in the rising air column condenses to form a visible cloud. If conditions favor a continued ascent, the cloud top grows into a swelling cumulus, from which rain may fall. A shower is born. Further development of the cloud structure upward may result in the formation of a cumulo-nimbus or thunderhead cloud, with an array of meteorological elements coming into action.

During April the axis of the main westerly jet stream remains far south, crossing the Pacific coast at about 38°N, and the two areas of maximum storm generation lie in this latitude; one in the central Great Plains and the other off the Middle Atlantic coast. Accordingly, storm movement across New Jersey is frequent; some of the severest coastal storms have occurred during this month. The storm tracks of April across eastern North America closely resemble those of March. The Great Lakes–St. Lawrence stormway continues to carry the maximum traffic. The route from the southern Great Plains is less traveled as the spring season advances. A center of maximum anticyclonic frequency lies over South Dakota, from whence high-pressure areas dip southward into the Ohio valley and then curve northeast to pass over or close to New Jersey. The Hudson Bay–Quebec area also produces some strong anticyclones, which exhibit a tendency to track farther and farther eastward in the spring season.

Spring makes a great leap forward in April. With the sun climbing another 10°15′ toward the zenith, daylight lengthens by an hour and sixteen minutes. The final day of April is about fourteen hours long. The thermometer responds accordingly, rising 10°F (5.6°C) from the first to the thirtieth. The warmest stations are in the southwest: Shiloh, 52.9°F (11.6°C) and Burlington, 53.5°F (11.9°C). The coldest remain in the north: Charlotteburg, 47.8°F (8.8°C) and Newton, 48.3°F (9.1°C). April temperatures over the years have ranged from a statewide average of 56.3°F (13.5°C) in 1921 to 45.2°F (7.3°C) in 1907. The range of extremes is 98°F (36.7°C) in 1896 and 3°F (−16.1°C) in 1923.

The precipitation pattern changes markedly from March to April. In April the wettest part of the state is the northwest: Phillipsburg, 4.10 inches (104 mm) and Morris Plains, 4.09 inches (104 mm). This reflects the increasing importance of showers and the decline of coastal storms as precipitation contributors. The driest area is now the southwest: Shiloh, 3.04 inches (77 mm) and Burlington, 3.24 inches (82 mm). The wettest April occurred in 1973, with 6.77 inches (172 mm); the driest was in 1963, with 1.02 inches (26 mm).

Snow ceases to be a factor in April. There have been a number of Aprils without any snowfall, though often some falls in the northern highlands. Sussex, Newton, and Charlotteburg each average over one inch (2.5 cm) in April, other stations less. There have, however, been some heavy snows this month; witness the 21 inches (53 cm) that fell on April 3–4, 1915, across the central part of the state, and the remarkable two-foot snow cover that was reported at Sussex on April 28, 1874.

*This woodcut depicts the wreck of the* AYRSHIRE *off Squan Beach on the coast of New Jersey. Joseph Francis's innovative life car saved 201 people. (Moss Archives)*

1 / 1923 Coldest ever in April: 3°F at Layton in Sussex County, 16°F at Cape May City.

1924 April Fool's Day Snowstorm: 2 inches to 10 inches covered entire state; 54-mile-per-hour sustained wind at Atlantic City during northeaster.

2 / 1912 Tornado at Camden: two hundred buildings wrecked or seriously damaged in densely populated area; one killed; damage $100,000; funnel continued eastward through county.

1975 Stalled storm in Gulf of Maine caused destructive northwest gales for three days, April 2–5; Trenton had 47-mile-per-hour winds.

3 / 1915 Easter Saturday Snowstorm: Clayton in Gloucester County had 21.2 inches, Trenton 16.0 inches; barometer 29.44 inches at Atlantic City; Long Branch clocked 62-mile-per-hour northeast winds.

4 / 1933 U.S.S. *Akron* crashed in storm about twenty miles south-southeast of Barnegat Light at 12:30 A.M.; caught in fast-moving squall, cyclonic storm attended by severe thunderstorms; downdraft caused tail to hit water, leading to destruction of airship's frame.

5 / 1923 Locally violent storm in Hunterdon County, with high winds and hail.

1952 Tornado at Clark in Middlesex County, twenty-five homes and a school damaged.

6 / 1938 Heavy late snowstorm swept north with 9 inches at Sussex; skiing attempted by author in High Point State Park.

1944 Coldest for so late in season: 6°F at Layton in Sussex County, 9°F at Long Valley in Morris.

7 / 1972 Freezing rain in central and southern New Jersey caused hundreds of auto accidents.

8 / 1862 Snowstorm in south: sleighing at Atlantic City on April 8–9.

1895 Flood on Delaware: Trenton and Easton had highest stages since 1878, Lambertville since 1862, Bordentown since 1857; Flemington's Center Bridge floated away.

9 / 1980 Record heavy rains for April caused extensive flooding: high crests on Ramapo and Saddle rivers forced evacuation of homes.

10 / 1877 Coastal storm on April 8–10 did great damage to shore installations: *L'Amerique* ashore at Seabright but got off, towed to New York; steamer *Rusland*, ashore at Long Branch, broke up.

11 / 1894 Mixed snow, sleet, and rain at Freehold; 3 inches accumulated on ground.

12 / 1841 Great April snowstorm: snowed all day and all night, "about 18 inches on a level" at New York with temperature range 34°F to 30°F; 12 inches fell at Philadelphia, more in country.

13 / 1875 Snowstorm dropped 10 inches on New York City, 6.5 inches on Freehold.

1877 Second big coastal storm within a week extended shore damage and erosion.

1961 Wind, rain, snow: 6 inches in Sussex County; railroads flooded in Meadows, ferry service across Hudson River suspended.

14 / 1854 Great Easter weekend storm began: eighteen vessels wrecked between Cape May and Sandy Hook; big snow fell in interior with 24 inches at Newton and Flemington.

15 / 1914 Northeast storm of "hurricane force" caused wreck of three-masted schooner, with loss of eight lives at Long Branch; wind 68 miles per hour.

16 / 1854 Bark *Powhatan* with 311 German immigrants aboard wrecked on Long Beach Island; all aboard lost, for New Jersey's worst sea accident; schooner *Manhattan* also ashore, with loss of all nine crew members.

17 / 1854 Second coastal storm with heavy snow and much drifting: 18 inches fell at New Brunswick, melted down to 3 inches; Newark had 10 inches on ground at storm's end; much deeper in interior.

18 / 1896 Warmest ever in April; Paterson had 98°F.

1976 Second warmest in April: Plainfield at 97°F during heat wave April 17–20, with maximums of 95°F, 97°F, 95°F, 91°F.

19 / 1875 Late-season cold: 24°F at Cape May.

20 / 1941 Heat wave: Chatsworth in Burlington County hit 96°F, warmest April week since 1896.

1963 Pine Barrens fire, "the worst in 40 years": six firefighters killed.

21 / 1857 Late-season snowstorm: 6 inches at Belvidere in Warren County and 2–3 inches in Morris County.

22 / 1831 Heavy rains: flood took out six bridges on Rockaway River and damaged banks of Morris Canal.

23 / 1941 Pine Barrens fire: one hundred homes consumed by flames; no rain April 6–22; 0.50–0.75 inch fell to break spell on April 23.

24 / 1930 Late-season cold spell: temperature dropped to 21°F at Layton in Sussex County and to 34°F at Cape May City.

25 / 1874 Great end-of-April snow period began: 15 inches fell at Newton in Sussex County.

26 / 1842 Twin tornado funnels near Newton, one path five hundred yards wide and six miles long.

27 / 1890 Thunderstorm at Atlantic City: gales; 1.39 inches of rain fell in fifteen minutes.

28 / 1874 Additional snowfall of cold, snowy month raised total on ground to 24 inches at Newton; snow fell at New Brunswick on April 29; hard freeze in north on April 30.

29 / 1854 Floods from snowmelt damaged Erie and Morris & Essex railroads; Paterson factories suffered inundation; main street of Belleville in Essex County underwater; dams destroyed at Trenton.

1874 New York City measured half an inch of snow, the latest measurable snow in official records.

30 / 1857 Very late spring, "not a blossom unfolded at end of April." (*Sussex Register*)

# May Day-by-Day

"Faire, fresshe May" was Chaucer's greeting to what can be a delightful month. By the beginning of May the features that have directed the flow of airstreams over the winter undergo changes. Both the Pacific high to the west and the Azores-Bermuda high to the east start their annual northward migrations, with important consequences for the path of the westerly jet stream and storm tracks across the continent. The Bermuda portion of the Atlantic high-pressure zone is found along 35°N, and this effectively shuts off the Atlantic seaboard storm track as a major factor in New Jersey's weather. The westerly jet across the country has also shifted northward, moving over Ohio and Pennsylvania before crossing northern New Jersey. The Great Lakes–St. Lawrence valley storm path has moved northward well into Ontario and Quebec, so its influence on New Jersey's weather is of less consequence than in midwinter.

An area of increased anticyclonic frequency now lies in a ridge from Ontario southward to Tennessee. This sometimes develops into a blocking force to either prevent or slow the eastward movement of pressure systems, causing a persistence of the same type of weather for several days. The presence of a strong ridge of high pressure from New England and the Canadian Maritimes southward can also be important. This also acts as a blocking feature and introduces a northeast air flow along the Atlantic coast from Maine to the Carolinas; a chill maritime fog prevails on the immediate coast and cool, cloudy conditions envelop inland areas.

A special feature of late spring and early summer weather along the Atlantic seaboard is the backdoor cold front. This brings a northeast flow of cool, moist air from the waters of the North Atlantic adjacent to Maine and the Atlantic provinces of Canada. These remain cool at this season while the interior land heats up. During the day the differential heating of land and sea encourages the formation of a sea breeze locally along the immediate coast; this usually penetrates farther inland as the day's heating progresses. The ocean air brings a marked drop in temperature—as much as 10° to 15°F (5° to 8°C) in a few minutes. This is known as a *sea turn* to shore dwellers. The backdoor cold front represents a much greater extension of the maritime influence over the northeastern United States than the local sea breeze. When the pressure alignment is favorable, the seaboard may be overrun by a stream of cool, moist air traveling southwest from New England down the coast as far as the Carolinas. The western edge of the airstream usually reaches the eastern slopes of the Appalachians and may dominate the entire northeastern seaboard for two or three days in May, bringing a throwback to late March or early April temperatures.

The sun increases in altitude by 6°51′ during May, and daylight lengthens by just about one hour. This results in a temperature rise of about 10°F during the month. The warmest stations are still clustered in the southwestern part of New Jersey. Coastal stations, for the first time showing the cooling influence of the ocean, are no longer among the warmest. Shiloh in Cumberland County leads, with a mean of 62.8°F (17.1°C); urban Elizabeth is close behind, demonstrating the heat island effect whereby polluted air over the cities reduces radiational cooling at night. The coolest section lies across the highlands of Morris and Passaic counties rather than to the northwest in Sussex and Warren counties. Charlotteburg has the lowest mean of 57.3°F (14.1°C), followed closely by Long Valley. Since the collection of records began in 1885, the warmest Mays have been in 1896 and 1944, when the state-wide average was 65.3°F (18.5°C). The coolest May occurred in 1917, with an average of 54°F (12.2°C). The absolute recorded range of the thermometer in May goes from 102°F (38.9°C) in 1895 to 18°F (−7.8°C) in 1947.

The amount of precipitation in May shows only moderate increases over April in the northern and southwestern divisions—the gain is only 0.19 inch (5 mm) in each; there is a very slight decrease in the coastal section. The driest station is Atlantic City Airport, with an average of 3.05 inches (77 mm), and it is also dry in the southwest, where Millville reports a May normal of 3.26 inches (83 mm). The wettest area continues to be Morris County: Morris Plains averages 4.32 inches (110 mm) and Boonton 4.20 inches (107 mm). Over the years the state-wide precipitation average has ranged from a high of 8.06 inches (200 mm) in 1948 to a low of 0.59 inch (15 mm) in 1903.

1 / 1963 Traces of snow fell at eighteen stations in central and northern sections.

2 / 1874 Bare ground appeared through the melting snow cover at Newton.

3 / 1861 Snow fell at New Brunswick, Newark, and over the north.

4 / 1774 "We had a smart snow storm and weather colder than ever was known by the oldest man living here, at this season of the year." (*New York Gazette*)

1812 "Gardens and fields covered with snow at noon." (*Newark Centinel of Freedom*)

5 / 1930 Very destructive forest fire in Pine Barrens during high west winds on May 3 to 5; 92°F at Indian Mills; no rain since April 19.

6 / 1937 Landing of the *Hindenburg* at Lakehurst delayed for four hours by thunderstorm; upon dropping of landing lines, hydrogen bags exploded and burned; static electricity or sabotage probable cause.

7 / 1956 Small tornado struck Woodbine, Cape May County, at 1:15 A.M., causing minor damage.

8 / 1803 Famous May snowstorm from Indiana to New England: Gerard Rutgers picked asparagus in snow-covered fields at Belleville in Essex County.

1947 Cold wave brought killing frosts in interior from May 8 to 10: 30°F at Layton, 36°F at New York, 38°F at Philadelphia; traces of snow seen at all three locations.

9 / 1864 Tornado near Culvers Gap in Sussex County.

1977 Traces of snow fell throughout state, south to Atlantic City: an inch reported at Canistear Reservoir in Sussex County.

10 / 1931 Very damaging hailstorm in Burlington County, with hailstones the size of golf balls: auto tops and windshields broken; $300,000 damage.

1947 Late-season cold: 18°F at Layton in Sussex County.

11 / 1966 Very cold in South Jersey: 23°F at Indian Mills, 25°F at Atlantic City Airport, 34°F at Cape May City on May 10–11.

12 / 1881 Early heat wave: 93°F at New York City.

13 / 1867 Tornado from Moorestown to Mount Holly in Burlington County: barns and orchards destroyed.

14 / 1975 Heavy hailstorm over North Jersey: hailstones the size of golf balls accumulated to depth of 12 inches.

15 / 1826 Early heat wave at Woodbury in Gloucester County: 94°F.

16 / 1940 Cloudburst at Hammonton in Atlantic County: 4.89 inches of rain.

17 / 1948 Hailstorm in Bound Brook–South Plainfield area: $50,000 loss; damage to airplanes at Hadley Field.

18 / 1935 Forest fires in Atlantic and Ocean counties on April 18–19 driven by high winds; widespread devastation.

19 / 1780 Famous Dark Day in northeast: smoke from western forest fires filtered rays of sun, producing an eerie, brassy tinge.

20 / 1915 "A remarkably brilliant solar halo was observed from all parts of the State. . . . Five circles were noted . . . displaying the well-known rainbow colors." (*Climate Data*, May 1915)

21 / 1896 Nutley Tornado: three-quarter-mile path in Essex County; light damage.

22 / 1804 Tornado through center of Flemington in Hunterdon County,

crossed Somerset County into Middlesex: funnel seen, roaring noise heard; one person killed.

23 / 1933 Storm of "tornadic proportions" in vicinity of Camden and Moorestown did property damage estimated at $1 million.

1962 Tornado across Mercer County from Washington Crossing through Pennington, Lawrenceville, and Port Mercer to Princeton Junction: minor property damage.

24 / 1877 Snowstorm over the interior from New Jersey to Vermont; four inches in northern counties.

1925 Sudden change: Newton at 96°F on May 23, dropped to 39°F on May 24; hailstorm attended cold-front passage.

25 / 1845 Press reported snowfall in Harlem and the Bronx; not observed at Newark.

26 / 1880 Early heat wave, May 25–27: Newark had 95°F, 95°F, and 96°F.

27 / 1814 Tornado at Troy, Whippany, Bottlehill, and Turkey, all in Morris County.

28 / 1896 Tornado at Allentown, Pennsylvania, and northeast through Warren County, about a hundred yards wide: trees uprooted, barns blown down; damage $100,000.

29 / 1902 Killing frost over southern interior: 33°F at Indian Mills in Burlington County and Woodbine in Cape May County.

1925 Hailstorm at Mullica Hill in Gloucester County: hen-egg-size hailstones remained on ground for three days; storm reached Ocean County.

30 / 1968 Deluge in North Jersey: May 29–31, Canoe Brook in Essex County reported 7.96 inches of rain; Essex Fells had 6.33 inches, Boonton 6.02 inches; flow on Passaic River highest since 1903.

31 / 1895 Hottest temperature for any day in May in New Jersey history: 102°F at Blairstown in Warren County and Paterson in Passaic County.

# June Day-by-Day

June is the month favored by poets and brides, and rightly so. Nature is in full bloom. The atmosphere has warmed to comfortable levels, and the enervating humidity of full summer has not yet arrived. The reason for nature's traditional life-burst in June lies in the high angle of the sun's rays, at their northernmost position when the celestial equator intersects the Tropic of Cancer on or about June 21. The sun is then said to be at the solstice point (from the Latin *solstitium*: *sol*, "sun," and *sistere*, "to stand still"). New Jersey receives its maximum solar input in June, and gardens and fields respond with lush growth. The atmosphere appears fresh and stimulating.

Though Memorial Day supposedly starts the summer season and the beaches are thronged that weekend, there usually are more sunbathers than swimmers, since the ocean remains quite chilly. Water temperatures lag behind their land counterparts. At the beginning of June the normal water temperature at Atlantic City is about 60°F (15.5°C). June is the month when the sea breeze is at its maximum influence, arising almost daily when the pressure distribution is favorable. With the land heating up under the rays of the morning sun, the air is rarefied and rises in convective currents; meanwhile, the denser air over the cool ocean waters moves landward and occupies the place of the rising warm air. The landward flow may attain speeds of 15 to 25 miles per hour (24 to 32 km/h). It is most welcome as the month wears on and the daily heat increases. By the end of June the ocean temperature has risen to about 68°F (20°C).

The high-pressure zones continue their northward migrations in June. An arm of the Pacific high extends northeast over British Columbia, and the Azores-Bermuda high has strengthened, especially in its westward extension, which now dominates the area over the South Atlantic states. The main route for anticyclones runs from the northern plains across the lower Great Lakes and eastward over southern New York and southern New England. Storm paths have moved northward. The track from Alberta now crosses James Bay and Hudson Bay, while that from the northern Plains reaches the upper Great Lakes and continues northeast to the north of the St. Lawrence valley. There is little cyclogenesis in the southern Plains or in Texas, more in the western Caribbean and the Gulf of Mexico, where June marks the beginning of the tropical-storm season. Some years may pass with minor or no storm activity there, but there have been some devastating storms in June—Hurricane Agnes in 1972 is a tragic example.

The sun reaches its northernmost advance at the summer solstice on or about June 21: at noon it stands about 73°30′ above the horizon of central New Jersey. It then produces its maximum solar input to the atmosphere, but it does not exert its greatest influence on surface temperatures until a month later, when the cumulative effect of its heating peaks. The increase in June temperature over May amounts to about 9°F (5°C). In June, the warmest sections of New Jersey are either in the farmland of the southwest or in the urban areas. Both Hammonton, in Atlantic County, and Shiloh, in Cumberland, have means of 71.4°F (21.9°C). Newark and Trenton are very close to that figure. Morris and Passaic counties are on the cool side: Charlotteburg's mean is 65.8°F (18.8°C); Little Valley averages 66.6°F (19.2°C). Sussex County locations are about 0.5°F (0.3°C) warmer. Over the years, 1943 had the warmest June, with a mean of 74.2°F (23.5°C) and 1911 the coolest, with a mean of 63.9°F (17.7°C). The absolute extremes of the thermometer in June over nearly a century of records have been 106°F (41.1°C) in 1923 and 29°F (−1.7°C) in 1938.

Rainfall declines substantially in June from the May peaks in all sections of the state. In the north the drop is almost half an inch (13 mm), in the south about 0.30 inch (8 mm), and in the coastal area about the same. The northern stations are generally the wettest, though Audubon near Camden leads all stations with 3.88 inches (99 mm). Wet spots in the north are Charlotteburg, 3.74 inches (95 mm) and Newton and Belvidere, 3.73 inches (95 mm). Dry locations are both along the coast—Atlantic City Airport averages 2.80 inches (71 mm)—and in the northeast—Newark averages 2.99 inches (76 mm). The wettest June was in 1972, with a state-wide average of 9.36 inches (238 mm); the driest was in 1949—only 0.23 inch (6 mm) fell.

1 / 1907 River Vale in Bergen County had 35°F.

1930 Freeze in South Jersey: 30°F at Belleplain in Cape May County.

1938 Lowest ever in state in June: 29°F at Runyon in Middlesex County.

2 / 1907 Cold continued: Snow flurries at several places during northeast storm.

1915 Snow showers reported by press at Rockaway in Morris County.

3 / 1925 Most intense early June heat wave extended from June 1 to 8: Paterson had maximums of 96°F, 91°F, 99°F, 101°F, 101°F, 101°F, 98°F, 97°F; 103°F at Belvidere in Warren County was record.

4 / 1825 Rare early-June hurricane did extensive damage on land and sea: "it was like a regular and furious equinoctial," according to the *National Journal*, June 7, 1825.

5 / 1903 Yellow Day: heavy smoke which reduced visibility and caused eye irritation resulted from fires in New York State.

6 / 1742 Heavy hailstorm at Amwell in Somerset County killed a boy and damaged roofs.

7 / 1862 Heavy rain caused high flood on Delaware, only three feet below 1841 level at Easton: extensive damage June 6–7.

8 / 1816 Famous "year without a summer" heralded by arrival of cold front on June 6: five consecutive nights with frost as far south as Cape May, but no snow reported in state.

9 / 1933 Six-day heat wave reached a climax with 101°F on June 9 and 105°F on tenth at Elizabeth.

10 / 1930 Severe thundergust at East Windsor in Mercer County upset farm buildings.

1956 Hail did $250,000 damage to crops in Hunterdon and Warren counties: stones varying from mothball to golf-ball size piled up five inches high.

11 / 1958 Strong northwest and west winds swept across the southern part of state: Atlantic City had winds of 40 miles per hour; minor damage.

12 / 1911 Local wind storms spread death and destruction across Passaic, Bergen, and Hudson counties: tornadoes suspected.

13 / 1958 Tornado on Friday, June 13, cut along border of Burlington and Mercer counties: property damage near Bordentown; ninety minutes later tornado and waterspout moved across Barnegat Bay and over Mantoloking.

14 / 1917 Violent thunderstorm struck Jersey City: 1.10 inches of rain fell in fifteen minutes, 3.78 inches in two hours.

15 / 1891 Bergen Point Tornado in Hudson County: path two miles long, with greatest fury on waters of Kill Van Kull; some minor shore damage.

16 / 1806 Total solar eclipse from California to Massachusetts: 98 percent total in Sussex County; clear skies at Elizabeth and Trenton for noontime spectacle; Venus visible.

17 / 1958 Climax of weeklong heat wave: maximum was 100°F at Hammonton and Runyon on June 14.

18 / 1944 Hail did considerable damage to crops in Burlington County, tomato crop hard hit; 100°F at Canoe Brook in Essex County.

19 / 1835 New Brunswick Tornado began near Belle Meade in Somerset County: path of 17.5 miles through center of New Brunswick to Raritan Bay; five people killed, 120

buildings destroyed in New Jersey's worst tornado.

20 / 1919 Hail streak near Montague in Sussex County was five miles long with stones as large as walnuts.

21 / 1923 Hot solstice: 106°F at Belleplain in Cape May County for state record for June; 105°F at Moorestown in Burlington.

22 / 1973 Ex-hurricane Agnes curved over north as a tropical storm: record low June barometer of 29.07 inches at Philadelphia; 5.31 inches of rain at Pottersville in Somerset County.

23 / 1906 Widespread wind and hail damage from Mercer and Burlington counties to Atlantic Ocean; waterspouts with large hail crossed Sandy Hook.

24 / 1926 Hailstorm in Burlington County caused train north of Berlin to stop because of poor visibility.

25 / 1952 Intense three-day heat wave: most reporting stations reached 100°F; highest was 104°F at Runyon on June 26; Atlantic City set its June record of 99°F.

26 / 1943 Longest June heat wave, lasting from June 13 to 28; Newark and Canoe Brook both registered 102°F.

27 / 1921 Severe hailstorm at Trenton, with stones three-quarters of an inch in diameter; much damage.

28 / 1778 Battle of Monmouth: "exceedingly hot and sultry," according to James Parker's diary; heat exhaustion took high toll and discouraged pursuit of retreating foe by Americans; 96°F at New York City.

29 / 1875 Tornado at Little Egg Harbor. Waterspout in bay near Beach Haven.

1892 Tornado at Gloucester: funnel seen, two killed.

30 / 1754 Floods at Woodbridge and Piscataway: dams broken and fields damaged; "greatest quantity of rain for the time fell," according to the *New York Gazette*.

1900 Strong south wind spread flames from pier of North German Lloyd line at Hoboken to vessels: four large liners caught fire and drifted in Hudson River, and three were destroyed; over four hundred people died.

# July Day-by-Day

"When Sirius rises with the sun, mark the dog days well begun." The proverbial "dog days" last from July 3 to August 11; in this time the brightest star in the sky, Sirius (the Dog Star), travels across the sky in conjunction with the sun. The Romans reasoned that the heat of the brightest star added to that of the sun caused July's great warmth. We now know that Sirius radiates only an infinitesimal amount of heat and has nothing to do with the intensity of midsummer heat, but the tradition hangs on. Whatever the reason, July is often characterized by a temperature-humidity index (THI) that makes almost everybody uncomfortable. When the THI is 75, some people are uncomfortable; most become miserable when the THI is 80 or higher.*

"Saint Swithin's Day, if ye do rain, / For forty days it will remain," so goes one version of the lore. Tradition has it that on July 15, 862, it was decided to remove the remains of Saint Swithin, former Bishop of Winchester, from a grave outside the church to a more fitting one inside. To protest this, the saint caused it to rain on that day and for forty days thereafter. So Saint Swithin's Day has taken its place with Groundhog Day as an indicator of weather to come. Of course, it never rains for forty days in the New Jersey area. The longest consecutive rainy-day streak in July is nine, at least according to the 110 years of Central Park records.

During July the atmospheric traffic across the continent reaches its slowest tempo, and the controlling pressure features attain their northernmost locations. The North Pacific high lies in the latitude of Oregon and Washington, and the Aleutian low has migrated northwest to join the Siberian low. In the Atlantic Ocean, the Azores-Bermuda high is expansive in the latitude of the Carolinas and Virginia. The Icelandic-Greenland low has moved into Davis Strait between Greenland and Baffin Island. The jet stream meanders across the continent, entering near Puget Sound, passing north of the Great Lakes, and heading eastward over the Atlantic provinces of southeast Canada. The main continental storm track lies to the north. There are no marked storm paths within the United States, though cyclogenesis may occasionally occur over the northern Great Plains. These travel northeast toward Hudson Bay, where they join the track of northern Alberta lows moving east along the 55°N parallel. With the Bermuda high shifted north, storm activity along its southern periphery picks up; the tropical Atlantic becomes a scene of action with easterly waves

*Dry-bulb temperature plus wet-bulb temperature times 0.4 plus 15 = THI.

moving across the low-latitude waters from the west coast of Africa. Few actually develop into hurricanes during July, but the season is under way and all disturbances in the region must be watched.

The sun retreats southward almost five full degrees in July, reaching a noontime elevation of 68°14′ by July 31. The length of daylight diminishes by forty-six minutes. Atmospheric heat, however, continues to increase gradually, and daily temperatures do not attain the summer's peak until about the twenty-eighth. Mean temperatures for July rise over the June figures by about 4.5°F (2.5°C) inland and about 5.2°F (2.9°C) along the coast. The warmest stations are either urban locations in northeastern New Jersey or rural stations in southwestern areas. Newark has a July mean of 76.4°F (24.7°C); Hammonton in the southern interior has a mean of 76.1°F (24.5°C). The coolest station in the northern highlands is Charlotteburg in Passaic County, with a mean of 70.3°F (21.3°C). Over the years the state-wide averages for July have varied from 79.2°F (26.2°C) in 1955 to 70.1°F (21.1°C) in 1891. The extremes have ranged from 110°F (43.3°C) in 1936 to 33°F (0.6°C) in 1929.

Since thunderstorms frequent the scene, precipitation is considerably greater than in June, about 1.25 inches (32 mm) more in the north, 1.40 inches (36 mm) in the south, and 1.12 inches (28 mm) along the coast. This distribution reflects the more common occurrence of thunderstorms in the interior, where solar heating is more effective. Three stations have a July total of more than 5.00 inches (127 mm); Pemberton, in Burlington County, with 5.12 inches (130 mm), has the most. The extreme southwest is drier than the interior of the south: Shiloh averages 4.00 inches (102 mm) and Millville 4.02 inches (102 mm). Newark and Jersey City are also relatively dry. The wettest July in state records came in 1897, with a state-wide average of 11.42 inches (290 mm). The driest was in the hot summer of 1955, with only 1.13 inches (29 mm).

1 / 1792 *A true and particular narrative of the late tremendous tornado, or hurricane, at Philadelphia and New York on Sabbath-Day, July 1, 1792*: this pamphlet admonished those who sought pleasure on Sundays—about forty young people out boating were drowned when a violent line squall moved across New Jersey and New York Bay.

2 / 1843 Newark had 99.25°F, according to original records.

1945 Tornado funnel seen at Trenton: $50,000 damage, no casualties.

3 / 1929 33°F at Layton in Sussex County, lowest official July reading ever in state.

1966 Heat wave July 2–5: Hammonton in Atlantic County had 100°F, followed by 105°F on next two days.

*A view of the destruction caused by the Cherry Hill Tornado, July 13, 1895. (From the collection of the Bergen County Historical Society)*

4 / 1776 Thomas Jefferson, in Philadelphia, recorded temperature of 76°F at 1:00 P.M., weather cloudy, wind southwest.

1976 Bicentennial Day: after overnight rain, only scattered middle- and upper-level clouds over state; for Operation Sail in New York Harbor, Sandy Hook had a maximum of 79°F, as did Jersey City.

5 / 1900 Bayonne oil fire: lightning struck Standard Oil refinery at Constable Hook; one killed, three injured in explosion; $2 million damage.

6 / 1880 Princeton observer reported cloudburst with 4.44 inches of rain.

7 / 1911 Brief respite in thirteen-day heat: Sussex maximum 87°F after two 100°F days; thirteen stations had reached 100°F on three or more days.

8 / 1900 Severe thunderstorm did "incalculable damage" in Monmouth County; "barns collapsed, roofs were carried off, chimneys blown down . . . corn fields were shredded into ribbons." (*Climate and Crops: New Jersey Section*)

9 / 1945 Cloudburst dumped 8.54 inches of rain at Phillipsburg, almost all within three hours: four killed in building collapse.

10 / 1926 Most damaging lightning stroke in U.S. history hit Naval Ammunition Depot at Lake Denmark in Morris County; sixteen killed, $93 million damage.

11 / 1930 Tornado with forty-mile path from Red Lion in Burlington County to Seaside Park in Ocean, where most damage occurred.

12 / 1818 Woodbury in Gloucester County: According to *Samuel Mickle's Diary*, "hottest day since the Battle of Monmouth, 40 years ago"; thermometer at 103°F.

1977 Severe thunderstorm at Franklin in Bergen County, 5.88-inch downpour.

13 / 1783 Tornado at Morristown "occasioned surprising agitations in the atmosphere"; fifteen houses and barns unroofed or blown down,

trees uprooted.

1895 Cherry Hill Tornado near Hackensack into Hudson County and on to Woodhaven, New York: probable skip action.

1975 Seabrook Tornado in Cumberland County damaged school and packing plant: $10 million loss.

14 / 1958 Tornado hit Pennsauken Township in Camden County, skipped to Moorestown in Burlington: destruction over five-and-a-half-mile path, only twenty yards wide.

1975 Three days of thunderstorms caused flash floods on many streams: Blackwell's Mills near Princeton had 11.48 inches (8.10 inches on July 14); $30 million damage, with New Jersey declared a disaster area.

15 / 862 Saint Swithin's Day: famous in England for forty-day rain delay in reburial of Bishop of Winchester.

16 / 1853 Terrific hailstorm near Newton passed in two veins, ruining crops; vividly described by the editor of the *Sussex Register*.

1966 July heat wave came to an end: New York City had a mean maximum of 90.3°F, highest of July record; 24 percent rise in death rate. Newark Airport had mean maximum from July 1 to 15 of 93.7°F; month was 2.3 degrees above normal.

17 / 1911 Severe local storm at Pleasantville in Atlantic County: buildings unroofed, chimneys demolished; path was three miles long, half a mile wide.

1925 Great hailstorm around Hammonton in Atlantic County did $250,000 damage.

18 / 1936 Hail damage in Mercer and Burlington counties as cold front ended ten days of extreme heat.

19 / 1971 Bergen Tornado: funnel touched down in East Rutherford with minor damage. Morris Tornado: funnel passed over Lake Valhalla and Montville Township, downing trees and damaging roofs.

1977 Heat wave of July 14–22 with climax of 104°F at Chatsworth in Burlington County.

20 / 1930 Broiling heat at shore: 100°F at Asbury Park, with 100°F the previous day and 104°F the following day.

21 / 1930 Hottest day of hot month: 105°F at Elizabeth, 104°F at Somerville.

1975 Mercer County flood: 7.24 inches of rain at Princeton; Assunpink Creek in Trenton at record crest; one thousand people homeless; New York–Washington rail traffic stopped, highways closed; $25 million damage.

22 / 1903 Paterson Tornado: funnel skipped across city; thirty buildings demolished, three hundred houses damaged; $300,000 lost; four people died.

23 / 1803 Bridgeton Tornado: ravages ten to thirty rods wide, structural damage, trees uprooted, crops destroyed, shingles carried nine miles.

1945 Flood in Essex and Passaic counties as result of heavy rains July 15–23: Little Falls 14.22 inches of rain and Cedar Grove 16.02 inches; damage $1 million.

24 / 1926 Thunderstorm did $100,000 damage between Asbury Park and Sea Girt.

25 / 1885 Worst fires ever known raged through the Pine Barrens—they had started on the ninth.

26 / 1892 Waterspout two miles off Barnegat Light, about five hundred or six hundred feet high: "in shape like two funnels joined together by their spouts. The action was rotary and with a swaying motion." (Charles Wood, *Annual Report of the New Jersey Weather Service*)

27 / 1942 Wettest day in wet month: 5.45 inches of rain at Orange in Essex County; month's rainfall 158 percent of normal; thunderstorms occurred on twenty-two days of month.

28 / 1897 Deluge of 8.73 inches at Elizabeth contributed to July precipitation total of 20.80 inches; it rained every day from July 18 to July 29; widespread floods.

1945 Hot day in hottest month in state's records: Plainfield had 99°F, 104°F, 103°F, 102°F on July 27–30.

29 / 1894 Hailstorm at Newton in Sussex County, streak three miles long.

1925 Hail in Burlington remained on ground for three days.

1970 Lightning killed a soldier at Fort Dix.

30 / 1918 Very heavy rainfall: Long Branch had 6.81 inches, Bay Head estimated 8.00 inches.

31 / 1889 Flash floods at South Orange and Plainfield did extensive damage.

1954 Month-end heat wave: 104°F at Hammonton, Phillipsburg, Plainfield, and Belvidere.

*A tree blocks Nassau Street in Princeton after Ex-hurricane David, during the summer of 1979. (Robert P. Matthews photo)*

# August Day-by-Day

July and August are long months, and they can seem extra-long when the atmospheric circulation becomes stagnant. Though dog days are officially over by mid-August, the heat and humidity of July often linger on.

The features controlling North American atmospheric traffic continue at high northerly latitudes in August. The mean jet stream enters the continent over Washington State, then trends east-northeast across the southern Prairie provinces; it continues eastward north of the Great Lakes and leaves the continent over Newfoundland. The jet exhibits its lowest strength and least influence on New Jersey weather during this month.

In the Atlantic Ocean, the Azores-Bermuda high occupies a wide zone across the entire Atlantic Ocean, with the axis of highest pressure along 35°N, the latitude of Cape Hatteras. Its influence may extend inland over the coastal plain from north Florida to the Delmarva peninsula, a strategic position from which to exercise its influence on New Jersey weather. When it is strong, heat and humidity prevail; when it is weak, coastal and tropical storms may move along the seaboard.

The principal storm track across North America lies north of the jet stream, with most Pacific and Alberta cyclones passing over Hudson Bay close to 60°N. Storm generation is infrequent in the forty-eight states—again, the storm action is mostly in the tropics. The route across the Atlantic Ocean from the Cape Verde Islands to the West Indies experiences increasing traffic as the month progresses. Easterly waves in the upper atmosphere move westward; if properly nourished, they can develop into tropical waves, depressions, storms, or even full hurricanes.

During August the sun loses 9°20′ of elevation; its noon position is 58°50′ above the central New Jersey horizon on the thirty-first. Mean temperatures drop about 5°F (2.3°C) during the month. Again, the warmest region is generally the southwest (Shiloh and Hammonton both have means of 74.3°F [23.4°C]); urban Newark is slightly higher, with 74.6°F (23.7°C) and Trenton is slightly lower, with 73.8°F (23.2°C). The coolest means are in the northern highlands: Charlotteburg in Passaic County, 68.5°F (20.3°C) and Long Valley in Morris, 69.2°F (20.7°C). The warmest August came in 1955, with a mean of 76.7°F (24.8°C). The coolest was in 1927, with a mean of 67.1°F (19.5°C). The extremes for August are 108°F (42.2°C) in 1918 and 32°F (0°C) in 1940.

The precipitation regime shows some changes. August is wetter than July by only 0.02 inch (0.5 mm) in the north and drier by 0.21 inch (5 mm) in the south. But the coast is almost 0.50 inch (13 mm)

*Workers at Cape May repair damage caused by tornado associated with Tropical Storm Doria, August 28, 1971. (Special Collections, Rutgers University)*

wetter than in July, showing the increasing influence of tropical storms in the precipitation budget. Only two stations total more than 5.00 inches: Morris Plains, with 5.13 inches (130 mm) and Plainfield, with 5.09 inches (129 mm). Coastal stations are almost as wet: Belleplain, 4.95 inches (126 mm), Atlantic City Airport, 4.90 inches (124 mm), and Long Branch, 4.88 inches (124 mm). Drier conditions prevail in the southwest, as indicated by Shiloh's 4.11 inches (104 mm) and Moorestown's 4.20 inches (107 mm). It is also relatively dry in Essex, Hudson, and Bergen counties. The wettest August resulted from the visits of the tropical storm twins, Connie and Diane, in 1955—the total rainfall that month was 11.85 inches (301 mm). The driest August occurred in 1964, with 0.92 inch (23 mm); during the great drought of the early 1960s.

1 / 1867 Offshore hurricane caused high tides on coast, shipping losses at sea.

2 / 1933 Five-day heat wave ended on night of August 2–3: Runyon had maximums of 96°F, 96°F, 103°F, 101°F, and 101°F from July 29 to August 2.

3 / 1885 Destructive tornado at Camden crossed river near present Walt Whitman Bridge, hit steamer, pounded the river front, crossed back to Philadelphia; five killed; $500,000 damage.

4 / 1915 Urban flooding resulting from 4–5 inches of rain in Plainfield, Bound Brook, New Brunswick, and Elizabeth; South Orange measured 4.89 inches.

5 / 1843 Greatest rainstorm in state's history deluged Newark and lower Passaic valley; Whitehead's 15-inch-capacity rain gauge overflowed—total estimated at 22 inches by bucket survey.

6 / 1918 First of three days of extreme heat: Flemington in Hunterdon County had maximums of 103°F, 108°F, 104°F; Somerville 102°F, 108°F, 104°F.

7 / 1918 South Jersey's stickiest day: Philadelphia had high of 106°F, low of 82°F.

1921 Heavy rainstorm: Trenton had 5.30 inches in nine hours, nine minutes.

8 / 1927 Tornado at West Berlin in Camden County: seven injured; lightning caused fires.

9 / 1949 Start of three-day heat wave at Plainfield: 105°F, followed by 105°F and 106°F on two successive days.

10 / 1952 Tornado at McGuire Air Force Base: 82-mile-per-hour wind damaged planes; path traced northeast to Sandy Hook; farm buildings wrecked, chickens killed.

1977 Tornado hit Leesburg State Prison in Cumberland County, striking buildings, injuring one person.

11 / 1875 Tornado at South Orange: track two hundred feet wide: barns blown down, trees uprooted; "cornfields presented the appearance of heavy rollers having passed over"; 5.10 inches rain caused overflows.

12 / 1831 Blue sun appeared for several days, resulting from volcanic smoke at high altitudes.

13 / 1955 Ex-hurricane Connie moved over central Pennsylvania: Atlantic City had 52-mile-per-hour winds, Trenton 46; heavy rains accompanied—Clinton in Hunterdon County had 9.60 inches, Long Valley in Morris 8.55 inches; damage $200,000.

14 / 1919 Coastal storm produced northeast gales, high tides, excessive rains: Tuckerton in Ocean County, 9.40 inches, Atlantic City 8.64 inches in twenty-four hours.

15 / 1944 Long heat wave: Flemington had 99°F or more for eight days, August 10–17, maximum of 103°F. New York City's longest heat wave.

16 / 1909 Heavy rain: 6.15 inches at College Farm in New Brunswick; 5.15 inches at Oceanic in Monmouth County.

17 / 1876 Tornado at Dyers Creek in Cape May County: two hundred yards wide, one mile long; buildings wrecked.

18 / 1955 Ex-hurricane Diane moved from Camden to Asbury Park on August 18–19: Canistear Reservoir in Sussex County recorded 7.96 inches of rain; greatest flood on Delaware since 1903; five deaths

in New Jersey, ninety in Pennsylvania.

19 / 1788 Tight little hurricane passed northward over length of state between Morristown and New York City about noon: destruction over fifty-mile-wide belt; Philadelphia had 7 inches of rain.

20 / 1955 Ex-hurricane Diane's flood crested at Phillipsburg at 10:00 P.M. on nineteenth, at Trenton about 8:00 A.M. on twentieth; four feet higher than in 1936, many homes flooded.

21 / 1888 Large tornado-waterspout crossed Delaware Bay from the southern part of Wilmington, struck brickworks at Salem: one killed.

22 / 1843 Second great rainstorm of month caused slides in Bergen Cut, blocking railroad; Newark Turnpike washed out.

23 / 1933 Chesapeake Bay Hurricane struck heavy blows across South Jersey: 65-mile-per-hour sustained wind at Atlantic City, with 8.16 inches of rain in twenty-four hours, 10.91 inches storm total; wind and flood did $3 million damage.

24 / 1901 Tornado from Paterson to Staten Island: skip damage—buildings unroofed, $150,000 loss.

1952 Cool: 33°F at Layton in Sussex County, 37°F at Runyon in Middlesex.

25 / 1940 Earliest freezing: 32°F at Layton and at Charlotteburg in Passaic; frost in every month except July.

1941 Violent wind storm struck canning plant at Swedesboro in Gloucester County, doing $300,000 damage and killing one; struck again at Woodbridge in Middlesex, seventy-five miles away.

26 / 1948 Hottest day of weeklong heat wave, August 24–30: 106°F at Clayton in Gloucester County.

27 / 1971 Cape May Tornado: cut length of county south to north: in Cape May City, homes damaged, power lines down; considerable tree damage for forty miles.

28 / 1971 Tropical Storm Doria traveled up state from Delaware Bay to New York Bay: heavy rains—10.29 inches at Little Falls; high floods widespread; Bound Brook, Manville, Elizabeth hard hit; $138.5 million damage; state declared disaster area.

29 / 1953 Extreme late-season heat August 28–31; Newark Airport had 100°F or more each day, with a maximum of 102°F on the thirty-first; several stations hit 103°F.

30 / 1965 Cool wave continued on last three days of August: 34°F at Newton and Sussex in north; 37°F at Pemberton and Indian Mills in south.

31 / 1954 Hurricane Carol, fifty miles offshore, battered state with 60-mile-per-hour gales; storm tides topped by thirty-foot waves; Phillipsburg had 5.05 inches of rain; $250,000 damage, 40 percent of that in Asbury Park area.

# September Day-by-Day

September is often thought of as the month of the harvest moon, the full moon nearest the autumnal equinox. It falls anywhere from about September 9 to October 7, however. Its celebrity lies in the fact that the times between its daily rising each evening are much closer than in adjoining months. This results from the relatively small angle the moon's orbit makes with the eastern horizon at this season. The moon seems to be moving somewhat parallel to the horizon, so at the same hour for several evenings it appears in about the same position.

In September, the path of the prevailing westerlies and the main storm tracks across the continent remain close to their most northerly positions, reflecting the locations of the Pacific high and the Azores-Bermuda high, which both continue at high-middle latitudes, although their strength is not as great as in high summer; by the end of the month they are in retreat. The term *equinoctial storm* used to be used by sailors to describe storms at this time of year, in the mistaken belief that the sun crossing the equator created an atmospheric disturbance.

The jet stream makes its most northerly entrance to the continent over Vancouver Island, British Columbia; it pursues an easterly course close to the 49°N parallel, passing over Lake Superior and on to Canada's Atlantic provinces. The main storm track lies about 10° north of this from the Gulf of Alaska across northern Alberta and on to a rendezvous with the Icelandic-Greenland low, which continues to concentrate over Davis Strait between Greenland and Baffin Island. With the Azores-Bermuda high at a relatively northerly position, tropical disturbances pass along its southern periphery. Sometimes they break through in mid-Atlantic and move northeast between the Azores and Bermuda; at other times they continue westward on a steady course before striking the Greater Antilles, the Bahamas, or Florida. Other tropical storms generate in the Caribbean and Gulf of Mexico after a midsummer lull in these tropical waters.

The principal anticyclonic tracks, too, resemble those of August. The primary still extends in a zone across the northern United States near 45°N latitude. An early portent of autumn appears in the renewal of anticyclogenesis in the Intermountain region and in the tendency of high pressure to stagnate over the upper Ohio valley.

The direct rays of the sun continue to travel toward the equator and beyond this month, losing 11°04′ elevation. At noon on or about September 23 the sun stands just 50° above the central New Jersey horizon, down 23°26′ from its high point at the summer solstice. Daylight is one hour and fifteen minutes shorter, and one can begin to sense the change of season. Temperatures decrease about 2°F inland in the north and south, but along the coast the thermally conservative ocean limits the decrease to 1°F. The warmest areas in September lie along the coast, especially in the southern sector, where the Atlantic City Marina has a mean of 68.2°F (20.1°C). This is one-tenth of a degree warmer than Shiloh in the southwest. The cities also remain warm: Newark's mean is 67.8°F (19.9°C) and Trenton's is 67.2°F (19.6°C). The warmest September occurred in 1931, with a state-wide mean of 70.5°F (21.4°C). The coolest September came in 1917, with a mean of 61.5°F (16.4°C).

There is a marked decrease in precipitation from August to September: 1.04 inches (26 mm) in the north and 1.12 inches (28 mm) in the south. In the coastal region the decline amounts to 1.42 inches (36 mm). This reflects the lessening of thunderstorm activity and also the lack of a big rain month such as August 1955, which distorts the averages. The wettest areas are in the northeast: Plainfield averages 3.97 inches (101 mm) and Paterson 3.92 inches (100 mm). The driest places are in the southeast, where both the Atlantic City stations average below 3.00 inches (76 mm). It is also dry in the western and northwestern sections of the state: Lambertville averages 3.09 inches (78 mm) and New Milford 3.16 inches (80 mm). The wettest September was the hurricane month of 1938, with a state-wide average of 9.67 inches (246 mm). The driest September occurred during a droughty period in 1941, with an average of only 0.28 inch (7 mm).

*Trenton's Pennsylvania Station, September 23, 1882. (Courtesy of Trenton Public Library)*

1 / 1940 Offshore tropical storm deluged Clayton in Gloucester County with 10.52 inches in twenty-four hours; 22.40 inches reported by Soil Conservation Service at Ewan near Glassboro.

2 / 1953 Heat of record intensity and duration for so late in the season continued from August 24 to September 5: 100°F or more August 29 to September 3; 106°F at Paterson on third.

3 / 1821 Cape May Hurricane: calm center moved over peninsula and north along what is now route of Garden State Parkway; enormous storm tide leveled dunes; structural damage at Cape May and Tuckerton; Philadelphia had 7 inches of rain; many shipwrecks.

4 / 1834 Severe hurricane swept northward from Carolinas, damaging shipping offshore.

5 / 1867 Waterspouts on Delaware Bay off New Castle.

6 / 1881 Yellow Day: Michigan forest-fire smoke aloft filtered rays of sun; in Newton "sunrise was accompanied by a yellowish-green fog covering everything and producing wierd effects, for three and a half hours." (*Sussex Register*)

1979 Ex-hurricane David moving north over Pennsylvania caused destructive southeast gales: Trenton had winds of 54 miles per hour, extensive tree damage, and downed power lines; 5.77 inches of rain at Ringwood; one injury.

7 / 1881 Hot: Philadelphia 102°F, New York 101°F, Freehold 100°F.

1888 Early-season frost damaged crops in North Jersey.

8 / 1934 *Morro Castle* wreck: cruise ship caught fire during tropical storm, beached at Asbury Park; Sandy Hook had winds of 65 miles per hour; 6.56 inches of rain in twenty-four hours at Pleasantville in Atlantic County.

9 / 1889 Hurricane stalled offshore, then turned southwest, battered coast for forty-eight hours: half of Atlantic City boardwalk destroyed; 56-mile-per-hour northeast winds on tenth; "highest and most destructive tide in the history of A.C." (Alfred M. Heston, *Absegami: Annals of Eyren Haven and Atlantic City 1609 to 1904*)

10 / 1960 Hurricane Donna moved about a hundred miles east: 58-mile-per-hour west-northwest winds at Atlantic City; 8.2-foot tide, 5.7 feet above normal; barometer at 28.38 inches; Seabrook in Cumberland County measured 8.50 inches of rain; apple crop badly damaged.

11 / 1917 Killing frost: 25°F at Culvers Lake in Sussex County; 23°F in cranberry bogs of Burlington County.

12 / 1882 Tornado at Pleasantville in Atlantic County during passage of hurricane about fifty miles offshore.

13 / 1944 Rahway measured 6.00 inches as major part of three-day hurricane rains of 11.48 inches.

14 / 1944 Atlantic City Hurricane: resort's worst battering in twentieth century; 82-mile-per-hour north winds, 28.73-inch barometer reading; two and a half miles of boardwalk destroyed; storm tide drove over Long Beach Island; damage throughout state over $25 million; eight deaths.

15 / 1895 Killing frost destroyed crops in north; 29°F at Franklin Furnace in Sussex County; 35°F at Woodbine in Cape May County.

16 / 1903 Tropical storm made direct hit on New Jersey coast from the sea: Atlantic City had southeast winds at 47 miles per hour; extensive structural and tree damage over southern counties.

17 / 1876 Hurricane moving north over central Pennsylvania caused 41-mile-per-hour southeast winds at Atlantic City.

1956 Thunderstorm at Atlantic City: winds up to 75 miles per hour; signs, antennas downed; front of house torn off; lightning strikes.

18 / 1945 Tropical storm caused very high tides—moon was at perigee; heavy rain inland, 3.65 inches at Orange.

19 / 1928 Tropical storm passed north over Pennsylvania: Atlantic City had northeast winds of 72 miles per hour; 4.64 inches of rain in twenty-four hours, 5.65 inches storm total.

20 / 1961 Hurricane Esther, performing a loop offshore, approached coast: wind gust to 63 miles per hour early on twenty-first; Tuckerton in Ocean County had 5.65 inches of rain; very high tide on twenty-second.

21 / 1938 Long Island–New England Hurricane: center passed one hundred miles off Atlantic City at 1:00 P.M.: barometer at 28.99 inches, west winds at 61 miles per hour, 7.72 inches of rain; Sandy Hook barometer at 28.71 inches; Long Branch had 6.92 inches of rain; $2 million damage and three lives lost in New Jersey.

22 / 1895 Following frost by a week, late-season heat wave, September 20–23: several stations at 103°F.

1948 Early freeze at Layton in Sussex County: 28°F.

23 / 1882 Tropical storm deluged north: Paterson reported 17.90 inches of rain, September 21–23, resulting in great flood in Passaic valley; Raritan on rampage, Bound Brook inundated.

1904 Killing frost, ice formed: 23°F at Charlotteburg in Passaic County, making only a 142-day growing season.

24 / 1970 Record late-season heat wave: Trenton above 90°F, September 22–26, 93°F, 94°F, 92°F, 92°F, 90°F; Hammonton in Atlantic County reached maximum of 99°F.

25 / 1975 Four-day rains of 7.50 to 11.00 inches caused flooding over north; flash floods on night of September 25–26.

26 / 1950 Blue sun and moon caused by layers of smoke aloft from forest fires in northern Alberta continued for several days.

27 / 1816 Killing frost south to Cape May put an end to growing season; some corn did not mature because of cold nights; wheat and rye harvest in July were good, so no food shortages in New Jersey.

1980 Governor Byrne issued an emergency order mandating water rationing in 114 North Jersey communities; a dry summer with about 50 percent of normal rainfall plus hot weather drained reservoirs; central and southern sections depending on ground or river water were not as seriously affected.

28 / 1947 Hard freeze in north: Layton had 19°F, lowest ever in New Jersey in September; 24°F at Charlotteburg.

29 / 1874 Tropical storm moved very close to Cape May on northeast track: 46-mile-per-hour northeast winds at Atlantic City.

30 / 1943 Tropical storm came ashore on Delmarva Peninsula: Atlantic City had east winds up to 61 miles per hour, 1.61 inches of rain, high tides; 2.00 inches of rain at Toms River.

*Trenton's South Clinton Street and the area around Pennsylvania Station, September 23, 1882. (Courtesy of Trenton Public Library)*

*Trenton's Pennsylvania Station was under water following a tropical storm, September 23, 1882. (Courtesy of Trenton Public Library)*

# October Day-by-Day

October is the transitional autumnal month that starts out summery green and may end with a wintry gray landscape. But often during its course there is a pause in the steady change of the seasons when a brief throwback to summer comes. Several days of soft, pleasant weather prevail, with mild temperatures, light winds, and hazy sunshine. This has long been known as Indian summer, and its existence has intrigued Americans, from dreamers to scientists. Meteorologists have long recognized that Indian summer conditions are brought on by an anticyclone stagnating and remaining over an area for several days. Descending warm air aloft, known as subsidence, creates a temperature inversion that traps haze, smoke, and impurities in the lower atmosphere; sometimes these lead to unhealthful smog conditions. Indian summer may come at any time after the first frost, from mid-October to the end of November.

For the first time since the summer solstice, the atmospheric features that control the circulation across North America, the major high- and low-pressure zones, follow the retreating solar influence and shift southward. In the Pacific Ocean, the large high-pressure area that has dominated all summer migrates a couple of degrees southward, and the Aleutian low moves southeast into the Gulf of Alaska, where it becomes a center of autumn- and winter-storm generation. In the Atlantic Ocean, the Azores-Bermuda high remains with its axis on the latitude of the Carolinas, but its center has shifted eastward, leaving a subcenter over Virginia and the Carolinas.

The jet stream, remaining at its northerly latitude of the previous month, enters the continent over southern British Columbia and traverses the southern Prairies before dipping southeast over the Great Lakes and then on an easterly course to the Atlantic Ocean south of Newfoundland. The main transcontinental storm track now runs about 5° south of its summer position, traversing James Bay instead of central Hudson Bay. A major storm track develops during the month in the lee of the Colorado Rockies where cyclones gather their forces and then move northeast over Lake Michigan and continue over Quebec.

To the south, tropical-storm activity is much less frequent than in the peak month of September. The main Atlantic track lies farther off the coast, crossing New Jersey's latitude of 40°N about 500 miles (805 km) to the east. The Caribbean Sea revives as a breeding ground in October and has sent some strong tropical storms northward over the southeastern states and along the Atlantic seaboard.

Anticyclonic movement is more evident than in September. From the Pacific, high-pressure centers enter the continent over Oregon, cross the northern Rockies and Plains, drop southward just below the Great Lakes, and move across Pennsylvania and southern New England. A more southerly branch dips into Oklahoma and Arkansas, then swings to the northeast and passes over North Carolina. The cold-season track from the Canadian Northwest reappears and takes on increasing importance as the month progresses. During October anticyclones often stagnate over the upper Ohio valley and the Middle Atlantic states. These are designated *West Virginia highs* and become influential factors in regulating autumn weather in New Jersey.

The sun recedes about 11° southward during October. The solar elevation at noon along New Jersey's central line of latitude declines to about 39°N above the horizon by October 31. Daylight decreases by one hour and fifteen minutes during the month. Average temperatures during October drop about 10°F (5.6°C), and each day is that much colder than on comparable dates in September. The coastal strip continues to be the warmest section because of its proximity to the ocean waters, which cool less rapidly now than the interior land surfaces. Atlantic City Marina reports an October mean of 58.9°F (14.9°C), the highest in the state. Atlantic City Airport at Pomona, ten miles (16 km) inland, is 2.2°F (1.2°C) degrees cooler than the Marina location on the bay. In the southwest, Shiloh, Hammonton, and Glassboro report means above 57°F (13.9°C), as do urban Newark and Elizabeth. The northernmost stations experience rapid seasonal cooling, with means falling very close to 52°F (11.1°C). The all-time warmest October state-wide average was 60.4°F (15.8°C) in 1947. The coolest was 49.1°F (9.5°C) in 1925. The temperature range stretches from 97°F (36.1°C) in 1941 to 9°F (−12.8°C) in 1936.

October's rainfall is again lower than the summer maximum, decreasing from the September totals by 0.50 inch (13 mm) in the north, 0.34 inch (9 mm) in the south, and 0.19 inch (5 mm) along the coast. Near the ocean, Toms River reports an average of 3.57 inches (91 mm) and Atlantic City Airport 3.46 inches (88 mm); it is also relatively wet in the north, where Charlotteburg reports 3.57 inches (91 mm). It continues drier in the west and south: Lambertville in Hunterdon County averages 2.68 inches (68 mm) and Audubon in Camden averages 2.74 inches (70 mm). The northeastern counties from Union to Bergen are also relatively dry. Over the years, the wettest October came in the big flood season of 1903, with a state-wide average of 8.92 inches (227 mm). The driest was during the droughty autumn of 1924, with 0.31 inch (8 mm).

1 / 1924 Heavy rains September 29–30 (5.86 inches at Layton and 4.85 inches at Phillipsburg) put Delaware River in highest flood since 1903 at Phillipsburg and since March 1914 at Trenton.

2 / 1913 Very heavy rains at Bayonne in Hudson County (7.00 inches): local flooding.

3 / 1841 October Gale of '41 in New England ended with snowflakes mixed with rain at New York and New Brunswick.

4 / 1869 Saxby's Storm in Bay of Fundy: offshore hurricane combined with low-pressure trough aloft produced 5.00-inch average deluge over New Jersey; high floods in north on all rivers.

1885 Westwood Tornado in Bergen County demolished church-school building just before classes; other structural damage along path.

5 / 1786 Pumpkin Flood: heavy rains caused freshets on all rivers, ripe pumpkins from fields along river banks floated downstream.

6 / 1941 Very warm: 97°F at Tuckerton in Ocean County, highest of record in state for month.

7 / 1902 Well-formed waterspout off Cape May visible for three minutes.

8 / 1749 Tornado associated with hurricane cut through Cape Henlopen on Delaware Bay: trees torn up by roots, small craft ashore.

9 / 1903 Great Deluge and Flood of October 1903: twenty-four-hour rains of 11.45 inches at Paterson, with storm total of 15.51 inches; worst floods ever known on Delaware and Passaic rivers; highways and railroads washed out.

10 / 1925 Northwest gales carried cold and snow flurries to north: extensive wind damage, 53-mile-per-hour winds at Sandy Hook; 30°F at Layton in Sussex County, 32°F at New Brunswick.

1979 Snow fell all day in central and north sections: accumulations to 5 inches; earliest measurable at many stations; tree damage and power outages.

11 / 1949 Heat wave: Runyon had 93°F after 92°F on tenth; Rutherford had 94°F on tenth; many stations above 90°F on tenth and eleventh.

12 / 1846 Great Hurricane of 1846 on "Hazel" path over Pennsylvania: southeast wind backed up Delaware Bay, demolishing buildings.

13 / 1906 11°F at Layton, 19°F at Charlotteburg, record cold for so early in season.

14 / 1977 Coastal storm caused damage at Monmouth Beach and Sandy Hook: 50-mile-per-hour winds; high tide; heavy rains.

15 / 1954 Hurricane Hazel moved north over Pennsylvania: 66-mile-per-hour southeast winds at Atlantic City, 57-mile-per-hour south winds at Trenton; extensive property damage, especially to old farm buildings; five deaths.

16 / 1955 Tornado in Red Bank–Oceanport area: high winds moved across state, assuming "tornadic characteristics" (*Climatological Data: New Jersey Section*); $25,000 damage.

17 / 1791 Enough snow fell near Springfield in Union County for sledding at the Scudder family farm.

18 / 1927 Heavy rains: flash floods, especially on Millstone in Somerset County; Trenton had 5.18 inches, New Brunswick 5.44.

19 / 1972 Record early snow depths across central New Jersey: 2.5 inches at

Trenton.

20 / 1940 Early snow in central and southwestern sections: 3.1 inches at Merchantville in Camden County.

21 / 1930 Trace of snow at Culvers Lake in Sussex County.

22 / 1819 Woodbury in Gloucester County: "violent snow squall at noon." (*Samuel Mickle's Diary*)

1925 Second snowfall of month across northwest.

23 / 1878 Strong hurricane moved over Washington, D.C., and north over Pennsylvania: winds up to 65 miles per hour at Cape May, 56 miles per hour at Barnegat; great damage at Cape May.

1930 Early cold in south: 12°F at Belleplain in Cape May County; in contrast, Sandy Hook's minimum was only 41°F.

24 / 1897 "Worst northeaster in the history of Atlantic City" (Heston, *Absegami*); tide 6 inches higher than in September 1889; 53-mile-per-hour northeast winds on twenty-fifth; no trains until twenty-seventh.

25 / 1925 Severe windstorm caused damage in south and on coast; south winds up to 53 miles per hour at Atlantic City.

26 / 1859 Earliest substantial snowfall of record in northeastern part of state: 3 inches at Newark, 4 inches in New York; sleighing on Staten Island.

27 / 1943 Tropical storm dropped very heavy rains, October 25–29: 11.33 inches at Lakewood, 10.13 inches at Toms River; high tides.

28 / 1936 Record October cold: 9°F at Layton in Sussex County; 12°F at Runyon in Middlesex; 13°F at Canoe Brook in Essex.

29 / 1973 Heavy rains caused floods in the north: Essex Fells 6.31 inches, West Wharton in Morris County 5.62 inches, Bernardsville in Somerset 5.20 inches.

30 / 1925 Snow fell throughout the state from dawn to dusk: 1 inch in south to 5 inches in north, "heaviest in October since 1859." (*Climatological Data: New Jersey Section*)

31 / 1925 Cold ending of coldest October: 12°F at Layton, 13°F at Sussex, 20°F at Belleplain in Cape May County, 32°F at Cape May City.

*West Street, Paterson during the flood of October 1903. (Courtesy of Paterson Museum Archives)*

# November Day-by-Day

The leaves are usually gone from most New Jersey hardwoods by the end of the first week in November, and the limbs stand stark and bare against the sky. In November winter-type storms begin to stir in the atmospheric conflict between the still-warm southern latitudes and the increasingly cold northern latitudes. Some of the mightiest wind forces have swept over New Jersey this month, for example on November 25, 1950, when the Great Appalachian Storm struck on Thanksgiving weekend, and at the end of November 1898, when two mighty snowstorms covered the entire state with an average fall of 14.7 inches. November is also the month when winter northeasters take over from tropical storms the task of battering New Jersey's eroding coastline.

During November the large dominating high- and low-pressure systems that control the circulation over North America move into their winter positions, and the pace of cyclonic and anticyclonic development and movement quickens. The jet stream displays increased vigor. After speeding across the Pacific Ocean, it enters the continent in a mean position over Vancouver Island, then continues eastward in an undulating fashion, with a southward curve carrying as far as the Ohio valley before taking a northeast trend over New Jersey and southern New England.

Anticyclonic activity increases over the West, with high pressure prevailing frequently from Idaho southeast to western Colorado. When fully developed, these are known as Intermountain highs and make up a principal feature on many autumn and early-winter weather maps. Anticyclones of Pacific Ocean origin move inland, reinforce the Intermountain highs, then break off southeastward as far as Oklahoma and Arkansas before recurving northeast to West Virginia and offshore over New Jersey. The polar anticyclonic track from the Canadian Northwest increases in activity and may transport chilling arctic air all the way to New Jersey to introduce the first touch of winter.

Two areas in the West are prominent in storm generation. Pacific troughs, after crossing the western mountains, often become disorganized, but once to the lee of the mountain barrier in Alberta they regenerate into active cyclonic systems. The main storm track dips southeast from Alberta to the Great Lakes. Another cyclogenetic area lies to the lee of the Rocky Mountains in Colorado, with activity increasing over October. A storm track leads northeast to the Great Lakes, where it joins with the Alberta track for a passage down the St. Lawrence valley. There is also a renewal of activity in the Gulf of

Mexico and along the South Atlantic coast, where secondary disturbances occasionally form in long north-south troughs of low pressure and drive up the Atlantic seaboard with winterlike fury.

The sun continues to slip lower and lower toward the southern horizon. At noon on November 1 it stands at an elevation of 38°; by the end of the month it will have declined 7°. The period of daylight between sunrise and sunset decreases by fifty-four minutes. Temperatures respond to the declining insolation with a fall of 12°F (6.7°C) below the October figure. The warmest areas are either along the immediate coast, in the southwest, or in the cities of the northeast. The Atlantic City Marina has a mean of 48.4°F (9.1°C), 2.4°F (1.3°C) warmer than at the more inland airport. Hammonton has the highest mean in the southwest, 47.0°F (8.3°C). The higher-elevation stations in the north turn in the lowest November means: Newton 41°F (5°C), with Sussex, Charlotteburg, and Little Valley close to that figure. The warmest November occurred in 1931, with a state-wide average of 50.3°F (10.2°C). The coldest was in 1901, with a state-wide average of 38.5°F (3.6°C). The extremes experienced in November over the period of official record since 1885 are 88°F (31.1°C) in 1950 and −7°F (−21.7°C) in 1938.

After the early-autumn decrease in precipitation, November reverses the trend: there is 0.98 inch (25 mm) more in the north, 0.78 inch (20 mm) more in the south, and 0.72 inch (18 mm) more along the coast. The wettest area is the northeast, mainly in Morris and Passaic counties; Charlotteburg reports 4.79 inches (122 mm). The dry places are in the central and southwestern sections: Moorestown and Millville average 3.46 inches (88 mm). The wettest November in state records came in 1972, with 9.26 inches (232 mm); the driest was in 1917, with 0.56 inch (14 mm). Little significant snow falls in most Novembers, but occasionally the last week brings substantial amounts, as occurred in 1882, 1898, and 1938.

1 / 1950 Record heat wave: 88°F at Elizabeth; 87°F at Chatsworth in Burlington County.

2 / 1810 Snowstorm of 6–8 inches at Newark, heaviest of record so early in season.

3 / 1861 Late-season hurricane hit at time of perigean high tide on November 2–3.

4 / 1970 Heavy hailstorm at Point Pleasant Beach in Ocean County: 2.5-foot accumulation.

5 / 1879 Snow and cold over north: 23°F and 1.5 inches of snow at New York City.

6 / 1953 Big coastal storm and early snow: 69-mile-per-hour northeast winds at Atlantic City; 9 inches of snow at Bridgeton, 4.2 inches at Trenton; very high tides.

7 / 1951 Easterly storm: 52-mile-per-hour winds at Atlantic City; 3 inches of rain at Clinton in Hunterdon County.

8 / 1892 Wet snow fell overnight into the next day: Newark received 3 inches; wires down.

1977 Weak tropical storm: 50-mile-per-hour winds, tides 2–5 feet above normal; 8 inches of rain; floods in north did $100 million damage.

9 / 1932 Coastal storm: 60-mile-per-hour east winds at Atlantic City; 3.38 inches of rain; high tides broke through near Sea Bright; $400,000 damage.

10 / 1962 Second coastal storm in a week: high winds and tides caused additional destruction along the coast.

11 / 1820 Early November snowstorm dropped 6 inches over north; rain in south.

12 / 1810 Heavy rains caused floods: at Bound Brook water was five feet higher than known before; Paterson Bridge swept away; Hackensack Meadows causeway inundated.

13 / 1833 Great meteor shower viewed under clear skies in early morning.

1904 Deep coastal storm: 43-mile-per-hour north winds; 28.74-inch barometer reading at Atlantic City; wires down; "worst since '88." (*Climate and Crops: New Jersey Section*)

14 / 1972 Second heavy rainstorm within week caused widespread urban flooding in south: Tuckerton had 3.04 inches.

15 / 1973 Heat wave: 78°F at Long Branch, Cherry Hill, Pemberton, and Tuckerton; 77°F at Newark and New York City.

16 / 1917 Widespread forest fires during dry month when only 0.56 inch of rain fell.

17 / 1977 Heavy hail across Mercer County: Trenton State College damaged; 73-mile-per-hour winds at Mercer Airport; Princeton had 6 inches of hail.

18 / 1924 Extreme cold: 1°F at Runyon in Middlesex County; 7°F at Layton and Sussex; 8°F at Belleplain in Cape May.

19 / 1957 Late-season tornado hit business district at Washington in Warren County, doing considerable structural damage.

20 / 1798 Greatest November snowstorm: gale and heavy snow, November 19–20; "no less than 18 inches fell" in New York City. (Hugh Gaine's diary).

21 / 1944 Snowstorm in northwest: 7 inches at Newton and Charlotteburg.

22 / 1931 Four-day late-season heat wave: at Hammonton in Atlantic County

maximums were 75°F, 78°F, 78°F, 76°F, November 20–23.

23 / 1880 Early three-day cold wave: Philadelphia minimums of 14°F, 10°F, 16°F, November 22–24; New York City minimums of 13°F, 14°F, 14°F still stand as date records.

24 / 1812 "A tremendous wind," strong southwest gale did damage at Woodbury and throughout South Jersey. (*Samuel Mickle's Diary*)

1938 First snowstorm of month dropped 8.8 inches at New York City on Thanksgiving day and night.

25 / 1950 Great Appalachian storm: southeast and east gales swept entire state; 108-mile gust at Newark; Burlington had 9.01 inches of rain; thirty-two fatalities; $30 million damage.

26 / 1888 Full-fledged late-season hurricane offshore: Atlantic City had 38-mile-per-hour north winds on previous day, and 29.21-inch barometer reading.

27 / 1898 Severe snowstorm dropped average of 11 inches over state: 17 inches at Oceanic and 16 inches at Asbury Park.

28 / 1783 Heavy snowstorm at Morristown, left 11-inch accumulation, according to Joseph Lewis's diary.

29 / 1882 Snowstorm dropped 9.0 inches at New York City.

1945 Strong coastal storm: northeast winds at 68 miles per hour, barometer 29.49 inches at Long Branch; 3.56 inches of rain in twenty-four hours at Brooklawn in Camden County; up to 5 inches of snow in northwest.

30 / 1875 Record cold: 5°F at New York, 8°F at Philadelphia.

1963 Coastal storm with low barometer: 28.70 inches at New York, 28.80 inches at Philadelphia; 50-mile-per-hour winds at New York; tides three feet above normal.

*Asbury Park after a coastal storm, November 6, 1953. (Special Collections, Rutgers University)*

# December Day-by-Day

"Dark December" is New Jersey's gloomiest period. As seen from 40°N, the sun at noon on December 21 rises only to 26°30′ above the southern horizon; that is, the sun stands only 29 percent of the way from the southern horizon to the zenith, in contrast to its June 21 position, when it is 82 percent of the way to the zenith. The low solar elevation reduces the duration of daylight to a minimum of about nine and a half hours; there are about fifteen hours of daylight on June 21. Not only is the duration of daylight at its shortest, but cloudiness is at its peak in December. The hours with sunshine drop to as little as 50 percent of the possible at most stations; at coastal Atlantic City the figure falls to 43 percent. Everything in the meteorological and astronomical realm seems to combine to cause New Jersey's darkest hours during December. The frequency of destructive winter storms increases, reaching a seeming climax during the last week of December. The post-Christmas Snow of 1872, the Christmas night storm of 1909, the snowstorm of 1947, and the year-end blow of 1962 are examples. Christmas week is also famous for cold waves of arctic severity. The coldest period in the twentieth century came in late December 1917 and early January 1918; a frigid period of almost equal severity struck in late December 1933. Christmas Day in 1980 proved the bitterest ever; the temperature fell from 24° to 0° during the morning, with strong northwest winds.

The main Pacific jet stream follows much the same path across the continent as in November, except that it continues directly east from the Ohio valley, passing south of New Jersey and making an exit over Virginia. A new feature in the upper-air circulation becomes evident in the form of a tropical jet that enters the continent over Baja California, moves east to Texas, then sweeps northeast to near Cape Lookout in North California on its way to join the northerly jet over the Atlantic south of Nova Scotia.

The large semipermanent pressure zones assume their full winter stature during the opening days of December. The Aleutian low moves into position over the northwest Gulf of Alaska and the Aleutian peninsula and attains its full power as a storm-generating region. In the Atlantic Ocean, too, the Icelandic-Greenland low takes up a stance in the waters southeast of Greenland and exercises a powerful influence over cyclonic activity across the North Atlantic.

The high-pressure zones over the oceans are found in about the same latitudes as in November, but their positions have shifted laterally.

The Pacific high is centered more than a thousand miles west of San Diego, now joined to an active anticyclonic area over southern

Idaho and northern Utah, the Intermountain high. When this feature expands eastward to the crest of the Rocky Mountains and beyond, it encourages a strong northwesterly flow of cold Canadian air into the Mississippi valley and the East, greatly affecting New Jersey weather. The main anticyclonic track in December reflects this flow, from the Canadian Northwest into the central Mississippi valley and eastward through Kentucky and Virginia. A secondary track from Canada develops at this time of year, leading from northern Ontario to southern Quebec and Maine.

The principal cyclone routes are much the same as in November, running from British Columbia or Alberta through the southern Prairie provinces to Lake Superior. The southerly track from Utah and Colorado now crosses Lake Huron in its northeastward travel. From the south there is increasing traffic from the Gulf of Mexico overland to Cape Hatteras and then northeast off the New Jersey shore to Long Island and Cape Cod.

The sun continues its decline toward the southern horizon until the solstice is reached on or about December 21. In approaching its annual nadir, the sun lowers by 1°36′ after the first of December and regains 0°20′ by the year's end, resulting in only a slight variation in total insolation during the month. Surface temperatures continue a steady decline; Trenton's mean drops from 40°F to 32°F as the month progresses, and each December day is about 11°F (6.1°C) colder than its November counterpart. The range of mean temperatures over the state extends from 37.7°F (3.2°C) at the Atlantic City Marina to 28.7°F (−1.8°C) at Newton and Sussex. As for extremes, the mercury has been as high as 75°F (23.9°C) in 1951 and as low as −29°F (−34.0°C) in 1917.

December is drier than November by 0.29 inch (7 mm) in the north and 0.13 inch (3 mm) in the south, and just equal to November in the coastal zone. The wettest area lies in the northeast, in Passaic and Morris counties, where four stations average 0.85 inch (22 mm) wetter than the four driest stations in the west. Charlotteburg receives 4.26 inches (108 mm) compared to Newton's 3.29 inches (84 mm)—they are only 17 miles (27 km) apart. The wettest December came in 1973 with a state-wide average of 7.85 inches (199 mm). The driest was in 1943, with 1.41 inches (36 mm).

Snowfall becomes a factor in December, with an average fall across the state of about 5.0 inches (13 cm); the greatest amount—21.1 inches (54 cm)—fell in 1904. The least occurred in several years when only a trace was observed.

1 / 1831 Start of coldest December of record, with snow on ground throughout: persistent cold, no great extremes; only four days above freezing in New York City, maximum 38°F there.

2 / 1942 Deep cyclonic storm over state: 28.74-inch barometer at Trenton, 28.75 inches at Long Branch, 28.84 inches at Atlantic City; west winds at 56 miles per hour at Long Branch.

3 / 1925 Rare December hurricane lost energy off New Jersey coast: 55-mile-per-hour winds at Atlantic City; huge waves caused enormous beach erosion.

4 / 1786 First of the month's great snows: 18 inches fell at Morristown December 4–5, according to Joseph Lewis's diary.

5 / 1927 Heavy sleet storm: 1–4 inches of ice pellets accumulated on the ground, hampered traffic and blocked sewers; 2.77 inches of precipitation in twenty-four hours at Trenton.

6 / 1962 Lightning struck transmitter and put Trenton radio station off air.

7 / 1914 Severe coastal storm did much damage to shore installations: Atlantic City had northeast winds of 32 miles per hour, with highest tide since 1903.

1951 Record warmth: 75°F at Belleplain in Cape May County and Lakewood in Ocean; 74°F at Chatsworth and Pemberton in Burlington County.

8 / 1786 Second snowstorm of month: 8 inches at Morristown December 7–8.

9 / 1786 Third snowstorm of month: 15 inches at Morristown December 9–10; snowfall totalled 39 inches in a week.

10 / 1946 Heat wave: 74°F at Lambertville in Hunterdon County, Chatsworth in Burlington, Canoe Brook in Essex.

11 / 1878 Passaic River flooded Paterson, washed out Erie Railroad, broke canal banks; also great damage at Delaware Water Gap.

12 / 1960 Prewinter snowstorm: 20.4 inches fell at Newark in about twenty-four hours, 20.5 inches at Paterson, 20.0 inches at Plainfield; Atlantic City had 7.5 inches.

13 / 1847 Heavy rains and floods: dams and bridges out in West Jersey.

14 / 1881 Warmest so late in the season: Trenton 71°F, Newark 66.5°F.

1956 Ice storm swept across north, Sussex hardest hit: telephone and power lines down; four killed in accidents.

15 / 1916 Heavy mid-December snowfall: 16 inches at Pompton Plains in Passaic County.

16 / 1835 Famous Cold Wednesday when northwest gales drove temperature down to 4°F early on seventeenth while great fire raged in New York City.

17 / 1973 "Howling storm of snow and freezing rain" affected most of state; "damage to trees astronomical"; Monmouth and Ocean counties suffered most. (*Climatological Data: New Jersey Section*)

18 / 1919 Early severe cold: −18°F at Culvers Lake; −4°F at New Brunswick.

19 / 1832 Philip Freneau, New Jersey's early journalist and author, perished in a snowstorm near Middletown Point in Monmouth County.

20 / 1948 Sunday snowstorm: 16 inches at Trenton, 18 inches at Paterson, 23 inches on Staten Island; Eagles and Bears played for National

Football League championship at Philadelphia on snow-covered field.

21 / 1942 Cold wave dropped mercury to −17°F at Layton; Trenton at −2°F had its lowest so early in the season.

22 / 1916 Coastal storm with thunderstorms: 2.00 inches of rain at Bridgeton in Cumberland County, where temperature range was from 45°F to 32°F; Long Branch had northwest winds up to 66 miles per hour.

23 / 1972 Five successive high tides at Cape May, centered on twenty-third: "worst since March 1962"; considerable beach erosion. (*Climatological Data: New Jersey Section*)

24 / 1912 Big day-before-Christmas snowstorm: 11.4 inches fell at New York City, ending at 3:40 P.M.

1966 Big Christmas Eve snowstorm: from 4.5 inches at Cape May to 19 inches at Layton and High Point in Sussex County produced the deepest Christmas snow cover ever.

25 /1909 Christmas night snow: Central New Jersey's greatest snow, when storm center deepened to 28.57-inch barometer reading at Cape May; Moorestown had 21.6 inches of snow, Plainfield 21 inches.

1964 Warmest Christmas: 70°F at Elizabeth and at Pemberton in Burlington County, but only 38°F maximum at Layton in Sussex.

1980 Coldest Christmas day: Newark thermometer dropped from 28°F at 10:00 P.M. on December 24 to 0°F at 10:00 A.M. next morning; afternoon maximum 6°F; wind averaged 24 miles per hour, producing severe wind chill; Trenton mimimum 2°F, Atlantic City 9°F, New Brunswick 1°F.

26 / 1947 Big Snow of '47: coastal storm produced the most paralyzing snow of twentieth century; 30 inches fell at Long Branch and 26 inches at Newark within twenty-four hours; all-time records for snow intensity and depth.

27 / 1913 Damaging coastal storm, first of winter series: massive beach erosion, with Sea Bright and Long Branch especially hard hit; highest waves in twenty-five years; Long Branch had winds of 70 miles per hour; ten seamen lost.

28 / 1917 Year-end cold wave of record intensity: New York City dropped from morning 37°F to midnight 8°F; Philadelphia from 40°F to 10°F; Boonton, in Morris County, 34°F to 2°F; Trenton, 34°F to 7°F.

29 / 1933 Cold wave dropped minimum at Charlotteburg to −17°F; below zero for four nights, December 28–31.

30 / 1917 Another cold day: maximums of 4°F at Newton and Newark; record state December minimum, −29°F at Culvers Lake on thirty-first.

1962 Cold wave dropped temperatures from mid-twenties to below zero; winds of 40–55 miles per hour, gust to 81 miles per hour at Newark; power lines down; windows smashed; lowest tide in Delaware River for years.

31 / 1947 Ice storm following big snow by a week brought the worst New Year's Eve driving conditions ever.

1965 Warmest New Year's Eve: 67°F at New Monmouth in Monmouth County and Pemberton in Burlington; other stations at 66°F.

CHAPTER 4

# New Jersey's Weather Types

## Hurricanes and Tropical Storms

Hurricanes and their other tropical relatives have been called the greatest storms on earth. They can be massive, with great vertical height, cover enormous geographic areas, and have lifespans of many days, even weeks. Great natural disasters taking huge tolls of life and inflicting great property damage can result when a mature hurricane strikes populated areas.

New Jersey's 123-mile coastline lies fully exposed to the hurricane threat, although its geographical alignment on a north-south axis makes it less vulnerable to the intrusion of a hurricane center from the sea than the southward-facing shores of Long Island and New England. Only once—in September 1821—has the eye of a great hurricane passed directly over part of the Garden State. But the entire coast is exposed each season to the dual onslaught of wind and wave from passing offshore hurricanes.

The once-deserted barrier beaches of the early nineteenth century are now crowded with resort settlements connected to the mainland only by narrow causeways that are often crowded with automobile traffic. In 1944 and 1962 the tidal surges of Atlantic Ocean storms swept completely across parts of these sandy islands from ocean to bay and destroyed much unprotected property.

With the population of the coastal exposures increasing annually, the problem of evacuating such a large number of people appears most difficult unless warnings can be provided long in advance by the National Weather Service and everyone has been trained in what to do.

A *hurricane* is a rotating wind system, developing over tropical waters and having a warm central core, whose wind force attains speeds of 74 miles per hour (119 km/h) or more. Otherwise, the cyclonic whirl is designated a *tropical storm*, with wind speeds between 39 and 73 miles per hour (61 to 117 km/h), or a *tropical depression*, with wind speeds of 38 miles per hour or less. The word *hurricane* is derived from the Spanish *huracan*, a term thought to have originated from similar words employed by Caribbean Indian tribes for "storm god," "evil spirit," or "deity."

Tropical storm activity varies from month to month throughout the season. In June and early July the area of most frequent tropical-storm generation lies in the western Caribbean and the Gulf of Mexico. These storms often make a landfall on the Texas or middle Gulf coasts and usually lose their organization and wind energy after passing a hundred or so miles inland. The dying circulation, however, may drift northward, causing heavy rains over the Appalachians and along the coastal plain. Occasionally the amount of moisture brought northward by an ex-hurricane can result in heavy precipitation, such as occurred in June 1972 when ex-hurricane Agnes caused devastating floods from Virginia northward to central New York and total damages of $2.1 billion.

The second phase of the hurricane season begins in late July or early August when the scene of most frequent storm generation shifts eastward to the tropical waters of the Atlantic Ocean between 10°N and 25°N. The principal area of storm formation now lies in the waters near and to the east of the Lesser Antilles and to the east of the Bahamas. Activity picks up after August 15 and continues through September, with the first two weeks of that month being the high season for large hurricanes. The area of hurricane generation extends eastward all the way to the coast of West Africa. Some of the mightiest hurricanes have first been detected in the vicinity of the Cape Verde Islands and have taken a week to ten days to travel westward in the easterly flow at low latitudes before striking a land area in the West Indies or on the coast of North America. These are known as Cape Verde types; the Long Island–New England Hurricane of September 1938 was of this breed.

Tropical-storm activity decreases by the end of September or early October, then increases slightly in mid-October. This is attributed to the renewal of storm generation in the Caribbean Sea and Gulf of Mexico after a midsummer lull. These storms move almost directly northward, striking the eastern Gulf coast or crossing the Florida peninsula. Occasionally they continue northward along the Atlantic coastal plain and threaten New Jersey.

Tropical storms and hurricanes pursue three main paths north to New Jersey and its offshore waters. The most frequently traveled follows a course over water from the West Indies to the vicinity of Cape Hatteras. Then it generally curves northeast and heads over the ocean in the direction of Cape Cod or the open Atlantic to the east. The alignment of the upper-air troughs and ridges is an all-important determinant of whether the storm poses a threat to New Jersey. If a trough of low pressure with a north-south axis exists over the Appalachians or along the seaboard, the storm center may enter the trough and speed directly north from Cape Hatteras, with the storm center passing within 100 miles (161 km) of the New Jersey coast. Severe hurricane lashings of this type occurred in September 1938 and September 1944, when the centers struck Long Island and southern New England.

A second track runs inland after a hurricane center has made a landfall in Georgia or South Carolina. Striking directly north, the center races over land, passing near Raleigh, North Carolina, Washington, D.C., and Harrisburg, Pennsylvania, all well west of New Jersey. This places the Garden State in the dangerous eastern semicircle of the storm circulation where southeast gales drive huge breakers onto the beaches and cause a storm tide to surge up the bays and estuaries. Hurricane Hazel in October 1954 was an example of this type, and in September 1979 ex-hurricane David gave the state a severe wind lashing that caused major power outages.

The third path involves part-land and part-sea trajectories. The storm center moves north-northeast from Florida or the Gulf states over the coastal plain. Most frequently it passes out to sea well south of New Jersey in the vicinity of the Outer Banks of North Carolina or the Virginia Capes. If the circulation is large and vigorous, or the path brings the center within 200 miles (322 km) of Cape May, it may cause considerable damage to South Jersey and the coastal strip northward. Hurricane Donna in September 1960 performed in this manner. Even if the storm center remains well offshore, it can create high tides, topped by huge waves, that damage shore installations and cause serious erosion of beaches.

Only one tropical storm in the past hundred years has made a landfall directly on the New Jersey coast from the sea. This occurred in September 1903 when a vigorous tropical storm tracking north-northwest from the mid-Atlantic passed about two hundred miles east of Cape Hatteras and came ashore in the Atlantic City area. Considerable damage resulted to shore installations and across much of South Jersey from the gales, which were clocked at a peak of 47 miles per hour (76 km/h) at Atlantic City.

An important aspect of tropical storms for New Jersey concerns the accompanying rainfall; it may vary from a few hundredths of an inch to a deluge of as much as 15 inches (381 mm) in two or three days. On several occasions such tropical deluges have resulted in severe floods causing huge property destruction. Yet rainfall from a tropical storm can be very beneficial. Since September is among New Jersey's driest months, the frequency of tropical storms can be very important to agricultural interests. Along the southeast coast as much as 40 percent of September's rainfall is attributable to tropical storms; the figure is 30 percent as far north as southern Monmouth County. For the entire year's rainfall budget tropical storms contribute about 6 percent in the southeastern part of the state, lowering to about 3 percent in the northwest. Some of the state's worst summerlong droughts have been relieved by the timely arrival of a tropical storm carrying a copious supply of moisture.

Until ex-hurricane David came along in early September 1979, the last major hurricane to affect New Jersey occurred in September 1960, when Donna passed just offshore. This marked the conclusion of a thirty-year period that witnessed a number of damaging wind storms striking at some part of the state from Cape May to High Point; these visitations from the tropics took place in 1933, 1938, 1944, 1954, 1955, and 1960. There were a number of other threats, but none inflicted major wind damage. In the thirty years prior to 1930, however, no New Jersey storm qualified as "major" in terms of destruction, though the tropical storm of 1903 was quite severe in South Jersey. From 1871 to 1900, there were several damaging tropical storms and hurricanes, especially in the 1870s and 1880s. Still further back, the period from 1847 to 1870 proved rather uneventful in this storm category, in contrast to the years from 1815 to 1846, when activity was frequent.

In the tropical arena of storm generation some years are very productive and others are not. In some seasons the disturbances move directly westward from the Atlantic through the Gulf of Mexico or the Caribbean and strike Texas, Mexico, or Central America. It requires a special alignment of the upper-air flow contours to permit a tropical storm to recurve northward and travel along the Atlantic seaboard. The Bermuda-Azores high must have migrated to a northerly latitude and lie somewhat east of its normal longitude. The westerlies must also cooperate by carrying eastward a trough of low pressure which possesses a greater latitudinal depth to the south than usual. A favorable combination for generating a tropical storm threat for New Jersey is the movement of an easterly wave across the tropical Atlantic while a trough in the westerlies arrives on the eastern coast of North America. The low pressure of the trough supplies a congenial channel for a tropical storm to recurve and come northward to threaten the seaboard of the Middle Atlantic states and New England.

## The Cape May Hurricane of September 1821

The center of a fully developed hurricane passed over the Cape May peninsula and then traversed the coastline northward during the afternoon of September 3, 1821. It became known locally as the September Gale, not to be confused with New England's September

Gale of 1815, celebrated by Oliver Wendell Holmes. Perhaps it might be best to redesignate this storm the Cape May Hurricane of September 1821, since its impact on New Jersey was greatest in the area between the waters of Delaware Bay and the Atlantic Ocean. This is the only instance of a full-fledged hurricane's retaining its tropical eye structure while passing over a New Jersey land area.

The first indication of the hurricane's presence came from Turks Island on September 1, when shipping reported gales and rough seas. Before dawn on the third the mighty hurricane raced over the Outer Banks of North Carolina and was raging at its height in the vicinity of Norfolk, Virginia, just before noon. The next checkpoint of the northward-rushing whirl came at Cape Henlopen at the mouth of Delaware Bay, where the gale had begun from the east-southeast, then shifted to the east-northeast until a thirty-minute calm ensued as the eye passed over. At Cape May, fifteen miles across the bay, the wind started from the northeast, then veered southeast and blew with great violence. A fifteen-minute calm prevailed at Cape May until the gale started again and blew strong for another two hours. The eye's exact path cannot be determined without minute-by-minute wind reports, but it appears that the center passed directly over Cape Henlopen and just west of Cape May, where the calm was shorter and the winds had previously been from the southeast.

The storm, now racing north-northeast at over 50 miles per hour (80 km/h), roared through southern New Jersey only a short distance inland from the coast. At Tuckerton, fifty-five miles (88 km) northeast of Cape May, the main blow struck at 2 P.M.; a violent gale from the southeast continued for two hours. There was extensive structural damage at the small port on Little Egg Harbor and at other communities north along the coastal strip into Monmouth County. The storm track northward lay very close to the present route of the Garden State Parkway.

The New York metropolitan area lay directly in the path of the onrushing hurricane. The editor of the *Newark Centinel of Freedom* supplied a meteorological summary of conditions in North Jersey. Rain started at 9:00 A.M.; wind was fresh from the south to southeast all day. About 5:00 P.M. a shift to northeast took place, and it "blew violently" until 6:30 P.M., when the gale was at its peak. There was little diminution until about 7:30 P.M. when "the wind suddenly veered to northwest and quickly swept away the clouds, and presented the stars brightly twinkling in the face of heaven."

Even the northwest corner of the state felt the force of the blow. Newton's *Sussex Register* reported a "very severe gale of wind from the S.E. accompanied with heavy rain, visited this place last Monday afternoon—prostrating the fences to the ground, uprooting and twisting from their trunks the largest trees, and leveling the corn and

*Destruction of Octagon Hotel, Sea Bright, January 1914. (Moss Archives)*

buckwheat with the earth. The farmers have sustained considerable injury in the destruction it occasioned in their apple orchards."

The mention of southeast winds at all New Jersey locations during the morning and early afternoon suggests that a marked trough of low pressure existed just to the west, but with the approach of the actual center of the hurricane the winds backed into northeast and eventually into northwest after the center had passed north of a locality's latitude.

The impact of wind and tide at the neck of Cape May in New Jersey was related by Charles Ludlam, of South Dennis, who witnessed the hurricane passage at that exposed point:

> The morning of September 3d, 1821, commenced with a light wind from the west, there was nothing in the looks of the atmosphere that indicated bad weather. At about 9 o'clock the wind hauled round to the southeast, steadily increasing. At 11 o'clock it might be called a gale, at 12 it was blowing a hurricane with intermittent gusts that drove in doors and windows, blowing down outbuildings, trees, fences and overflowing the marshes between the beach and mainland several feet. At this time it was diffi-

cult to stand without some support; no clouds were to be seen, but in their place was a universal haze like a thick fog. The salt spray of the sea was driven inland some miles so as to kill vegetation. At about 10 o'clock [Ludlam in error here; 1430 approximately correct] it fell perfectly calm for about fifteen minutes, then the wind suddenly burst out from the northwest the directly opposite quarter, and blew with increasing violence for about three hours, then gradually subsided, and by six o'clock had nearly ceased and cleared off at sundown. The evening was as clear as the morning, but oh dire was the devastation it left in its progress. Vessels foundered, driven ashore, or dismasted, woodland nearly ruined by being broken down or blown up by the roots, the writer of this had a favorite weeping willow that made three-quarter of a cord of wood that was blown down by the southeast wind and when it came out, northwest blew it over to the opposite. Cape Island lost from 16 to 20 feet of its bank, and what is most singular, a ship anchored that evening immediately opposite the present breakwater that carried top gallant sails all day and knew nothing of the hurricane. The vortex or center of this cyclone as laid down in Blunt's Coast Pilot, struck our continent at or near the point of the Cape and passed over the center of the county and could not have exceeded 50 miles in width as it was but partially felt in Bridgeton and Salem. It was a providential circumstance that it was low water and a low run of tides, otherwise it would have been calamitous in the extreme in the loss of life and property.

On our bay shore the tide was higher than on the seaside of the Cape by several feet; persons who witnessed the overflow said it came like a perpendicular wall some five feet high driven by the wind when it changed to the northwest and came in an overwhelming surge. From the formation of the land in the cove in our bay, in the vicinity of Goshen and Dias Creek and Cedar Hammocks, the water was concentrated as a common center and the tide was higher there than anywhere along the shore; drift was lodged in the tree tops at the Cedar Hammocks nine feet high; in all probability the heave of the sea had something to do in this.

The day of this September gale Elijah Miller lived in the southern end of Dias Creek on the farm now owned and occupied by David Compton. The elements were so threatening that he walked north to the school house and asked for his children, Vincent and Mary. The teacher replied "Can't you stay a little while for we all will be going out soon. But Mr. M. replied, "No, I wish my children immediately and advise you to dismiss all the pupils at once and not wait until the regular closing hour." This advice was heeded. One of Mr. M.'s children started to go home a short cut through the woods but as the limbs and tree tops were breaking off, fearing they might be killed thereby, hustled them homeward by the main road as fast as their feet would carry them. Looking backward as they went up the hill south of Dyers Creek causeway, they saw great waves capped with foam rolling where they had walked but a few minutes before.

*D. M. Ludlum,*
Early American Hurricanes,
*quoting from Charles Tomlin,*
Cape May Spray

# The Atlantic City Hurricane of September 1944

"The hurricane which lashed the eastern coast of the United States on September 14, 1944, took a toll of at least eight lives in New Jersey and was, from the standpoint of property damage, the most destructive storm in this State for more than half a century. In fact, neither weather records nor old newspaper accounts reveal another storm as damaging since the Civil War." Thus, A. E. White, the state's climatologist at the time, described its impact.

A storm circulation was first spotted on September 9 near 60°W and 21°N, or about 600 miles (966 km) east-northeast of Puerto Rico. It moved west-northwest for the next several days to 75°W at a point east of Jacksonville. Here recurvature to the north took place on a parabolic course which took the center of the now large and vicious storm slightly to the east of Cape Hatteras at 9:20 A.M. on the morning of the fourteenth. The barometer dropped to a record 27.97 inches (94.7 kPa) and the wind peaked over 100 miles per hour (161 km/h).

Turning slightly east of north, the center sped by the New Jersey coast from about 5:30 to 9:00 P.M., standing about 50–75 miles (80–121 km) offshore. The lowest pressure at Atlantic City, 28.73 inches (97.3 kPa), occurred at 6:00 P.M.; an hour later 28.93 inches (98.0 kPa) were registered at Long Branch. The center, now tracking northeast, crossed the eastern tip of Long Island about 10:00 P.M.

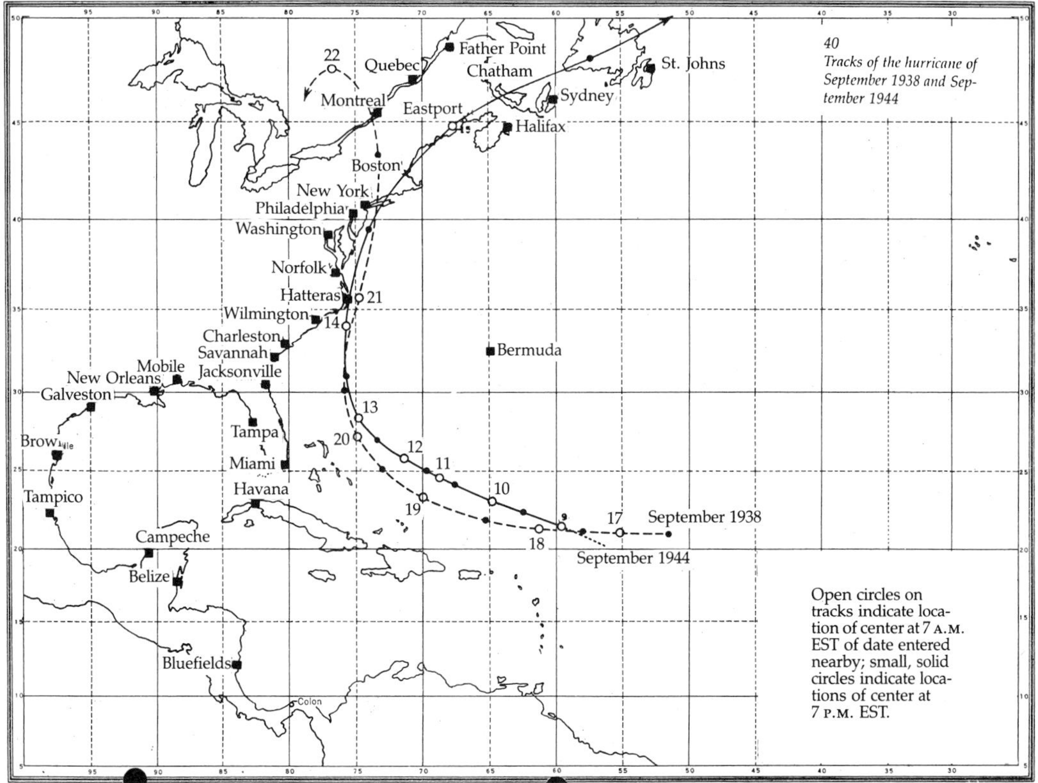


*Tracks of the hurricanes of September 1938 and September 1944*

A maximum wind speed of 82 miles per hour (132 km/h) was registered at Atlantic City at 5:30 P.M. Long Branch recorded 74 miles per hour (119 km/h) from the north and Trenton 49 miles per hour (79 km/h), also from the north.

Rainfall was very heavy throughout the state, with the greatest amounts in the northeast: Rahway reported 11.40 inches (290 mm) and Elizabeth 11.62 inches (295 mm) for the four-day rain period. The greatest single-day amount fell on the thirteenth, when Rahway measured 6.00 inches (152 mm).

Property damage throughout the state has been estimated conservatively at $25 million. Compilations by authorities indicated that 460 homes were destroyed and more than 3,000 others damaged. A total of 217 other buildings of various kinds were reported destroyed and 635 damaged. Scores of small boats were lost. Boardwalks were generally completely destroyed, and about two and one-half miles of the famous Atlantic City esplanade were demolished. The huge piers were also severely damaged. Flooding along the shore took a high toll. Water was several feet deep in Atlantic City and Ocean City streets. At the great Atlantic City Convention Hall water stood eight feet deep in the basement on the day after the storm. The greatest wreckage of homes occurred on Long Beach Island, where more than 300 seasonal or permanent homes were destroyed and as many more rendered unfit for habitation. Damage to roofs and chimneys was heavy in all shore communities.

Throughout the rest of the state there was great destruction among shade and orchard trees. Many thousands were uprooted from soil that had been softened by the rains preceding the hurricane winds. Approximately 700,000 bushels of apples were blown from trees. Agricultural losses were estimated at $3.5 million. Damage to communication and power lines proved heavy. An official of the New Jersey Bell system estimated losses to property at $450,000, with considerable anticipated revenue not received as a result of interrupted service.

Eight persons were known to have lost their lives: five drowned on Long Beach Island and one at Sea Isle City. Two deaths resulted from injuries at Atlantic City where 121 others were injured. Seventy-five were hurt at nearby Brigantine, and on Long Beach Island 50 persons were treated by physicians.

*Lighthouses provide superb vantage points for observing New Jersey's weather. Navesink Light is shown here. (Special Collections, Rutgers University)*

# Hurricanes and Tropical Storms of the Late Nineteenth Century*

1876 SEPTEMBER 17 Hurricane center traveled north over Pennsylvania: "most destructive in 30 years" in New Jersey; Atlantic City anemometer broke after recording 41-mile-per-hour winds; extensive beach erosion, severe at Barnegat Inlet; hotels unroofed at Cape May; farms along Delaware Bay flooded, as were Hackensack Meadows.

1878 OCTOBER 23 Hurricane passed near Washington, D.C., and Harrisburg: raised winds to 58 miles per hour at Cape May, to 44 miles per hour from east at Atlantic City; extensive destruction in South Jersey; hotels damaged at Cape May; serious beach erosion.

1879 AUGUST 18 Hurricane passed about 120 miles southeast of Cape May on track carrying near Cape Cod: northeast wind to 47 miles per hour at Atlantic City.

1882 SEPTEMBER 23 Tropical storm moved short distance offshore, producing rains up to 11.00 inches; severe floods in Passaic River valley.

1888 NOVEMBER 24–25 Strong late-season hurricane passed well offshore: winds of 31 miles per hour at Atlantic City; huge waves caused serious damage to shore installations and boardwalks; extensive beach erosion.

1889 SEPTEMBER 10–11 Hurricane, "most severe in past 40 years," stalled 180 miles off Maryland and turned southwest while dissipating: highest storm tide since 1846 hit New Jersey; wind 56 miles per hour from the northeast at Atlantic City; vast structural damage and beach erosion along coast; 31 vessels wrecked with loss of forty lives.

1893 AUGUST 23–24 Hurricane center moved about forty to fifty miles offshore, making landfall on western Long Island: 41-mile-per-hour winds from northeast at Atlantic City; 3.15 inches of rain in 12 hours at Oceanic; several ships ashore.

1896 SEPTEMBER 29 Ex-hurricane moved north over central Pennsylvania, causing southeast winds of 32 miles per hour at Atlantic City.

1897 OCTOBER 24–25 Tropical storm performed loop off Virginia, then moved east: Atlantic City had 40-mile-per-hour winds on twenty-fourth, 42 miles per hour on twenty-fifth.

*Wind speeds recorded prior to 1928 are corrected to current 3-cup standards. The Atlantic City anemometer from 1873 to 1902 was located at elevations of 26.5, 40, 50, and 76 feet; after 1902 it was at 172 feet on Absecon Lighthouse.

# Hurricanes and Tropical Storms of the Twentieth Century

1903 SEPTEMBER 16 Ex-hurricane made landfall near Atlantic City: wind at 47 miles per hour; extensive damage at shore locations and throughout central and southern sections.

1915 AUGUST 4 Tropical storm moved from near Trenton to Bergen County: heavy rains north of track: Somerville had 7.86 inches in four days; urban flooding in Somerset, Middlesex, and Union counties; Long Branch had winds up to 60 miles per hour.

1924 AUGUST 26 Hurricane passed about 150 miles east of Cape May; 56-mile-per-hour winds at Atlantic City; barometer 29.30 inches; little damage.

1925 DECEMBER 3 Ex-hurricane turned southeast off Maryland: wind at Atlantic City 54 miles per hour; extensive structural damage along coast and beach erosion from huge waves.

1932 NOVEMBER 9–10 Late-season hurricane well offshore pounded beaches with waves of long fetch: total damage $300,000–400,000; 60-mile-per-hour wind at Atlantic City.

1933 AUGUST 23–24 Hurricane moved inland over Chesapeake Bay: Atlantic City winds peaked at 65 miles per hour from east; four-day rain total of 10.95 inches; flooding and wind damage estimated at $3 million.

1934 SEPTEMBER 8 "Morro Castle Storm": tropical storm winds peaked at 65 miles per hour at Long Branch on the day the cruise ship S.S. *Morro Castle* caught fire and beached at Asbury Park; Northfield, in Atlantic County, measured 6.56 inches of rain on eighth.

1938 SEPTEMBER 21 Long Island–New England Hurricane passed about one hundred miles east of Atlantic City about 1:30 P.M.: lowest pressure at Sandy Hook, 28.71 inches; maximum wind 61 miles per hour at Atlantic City; 6.21 inches of rain at Lakewood; three killed; $2 million damage.

1939 AUGUST 19 Tropical storm caused very heavy rains over state: Tuckerton reported record 14.81 inches in twenty-four hours, August 18–19; four drowned; $1 million flood damage.

1940 SEPTEMBER 1 Tropical storm about 150 miles east of Cape May produced torrential rains inland (Clayton reported 10.52 inches) but none at Atlantic City and other coastal locations.

1944 SEPTEMBER 14 Atlantic City Hurricane; center was 50–75 miles off Atlantic City at 6:00 P.M.; lowest barometer 28.73 inches; maximum wind 82 miles per hour at 5:30 P.M.; 11.40 inches storm total at Rahway; $25 million damage; eight lives lost, 320 injured: later crossed southeastern New England with very heavy damage.

1954 AUGUST 31 Hurricane Carol passed about fifty miles east of Atlantic City: wind at 60 miles per hour; thirty-foot waves lashed beaches with damage to shore installations; rains up to 5.00 inches helped alleviate drought; two killed; total damage $250,000.

1954 SEPTEMBER 11 Hurricane Edna sped by about one hundred miles east of Cape May: winds reached 65 miles per hour at Atlantic City; rain ranged up to 5.70 inches at Jersey City; damage minor.

1954 OCTOBER 15 Hurricane Hazel traveled overland from North Carolina to Pennsylvania: peak gusts to 66 miles per hour from southeast at Atlantic City; rains generally less than an inch; property damage $7.5 million; apple crop suffered heavily; five deaths.

1955 AUGUST 13 Ex-hurricane Connie moved north over central Pennsylvania: 9.16

inches of rain at Clinton; wind 52 miles per hour at Atlantic City; eight deaths; $200,000 damage.

1955 AUGUST 19 Ex-hurricane Diane crossed New Jersey from near Camden to Asbury Park: excessive rains north of track; greatest flood known in Delaware valley; two deaths in New Jersey, ninety on tributaries of Delaware in Pennsylvania.

1960 SEPTEMBER 12 Hurricane Donna passed about eighty miles east of Atlantic City: Long Branch had one-minute sustained wind of 72 miles per hour, Atlantic City 58 miles per hour; precipitation over 8.00 inches; damage to shore installations; minor flooding; crops suffered; nine deaths.

1961 OCTOBER 21 Hurricane Gerta well offshore sent high seas onto coast, causing extensive flooding.

1971 AUGUST 27–28 Tropical storm Doria moved from Cape May to Bergen County: tornado in Cape May County; very heavy rains and severe flooding throughout state, the worst since 1955; Princeton reported 10.15 inches in forty-eight hours.

1972 JUNE 22 Ex-hurricane Agnes curved northwest over southern New York; rains heavier over New York and Pennsylvania, with amounts two to three times the 5.00 inches in New Jersey, where damage was relatively slight.

1976 AUGUST 9 Hurricane Belle lost force over cool waters east of Maryland and New Jersey before crossing Long Island: Atlantic City had gust of 62 miles per hour with 40-mile-per-hour sustained winds; general rainfall of about 3.00 inches; little damage.

1979 SEPTEMBER 6 Ex-hurricane David, pursuing a track northward over central Pennsylvania, caused southeast gales: extensive tree and power line damage; tornado in South Jersey; Trenton had 54-mile-per-hour southeast wind and 1.56 inches rain, September 5–6.

*Waves caused by Ex-hurricane David hit houses on the Boardwalk at Atlantic City. (Special Collections, Rutgers University)*

# Tornadoes

A full view of the funnel of a mature tornado is one of nature's most awesome spectacles. No refuge above the ground assures full protection from its wrath. Property destruction can be almost complete in a limited area when a well-developed funnel sweeps the surface of the earth; human life is placed in great jeopardy from devastating wind blasts, flying objects that become deadly missiles, and collapsing buildings.

A tornado's distinguishing feature is a pendant cloud in the form of a cone or column narrowing down from top to bottom. It is almost always associated with a cumulo-nimbus cloud that is in turn associated with a thunderstorm. The visible funnel is formed by the condensation of water vapor around the lower pressure within the whirling column. It normally turns in a counterclockwise direction, though anticyclonic circulations have been documented. The funnel may assume various forms from a thin, writhing, gray-white rope to a thick, amorphous, whirling mass of black cloud. Many tornado formations in the Northeast are imbedded in heavy cloud areas and not distinctly visible to the observer.

When the funnel reaches to or just above the ground, great destruction of surface objects takes place and the tornado formation becomes filled with dust and whirling debris. The massive destructive power is caused by: blast effect from high wind speed; explosive effect from greatly reduced atmospheric pressure; aerodynamic lifting of roofs and objects through differential pressure; and impact of flying debris and airborne missiles.

There are other less violent local circulations with tornadic characteristics. *Twister* is a popular name usually reserved for whirls of small dimension that do relatively minor damage. *Waterspouts* have similar though less violent tornadic circulations, with added marine aspects. *Whirlwinds* and *dust devils* are also relatively small in dimension and violence but differ in that they derive their energy from direct contact of the air with a heated ground surface.

Tornadoes may occur at any time of year. They are rare in autumn and winter, but the tempo of formation increases in March; the center of most frequent outbreak migrates northward from the Gulf states into the Great Plains and the Midwest in spring. Summer is the time of their greatest frequency in New Jersey. This results from the fact that most tornadoes are associated with cumulo-nimbus clouds of a prefrontal thunderstorm, and July and August are the height of the season for the production of these thunder and lightning storms. A recent study of 19,312 tornadoes has shown that 75 percent of all tornadoes are associated with temperatures between 65°F and 84°F (18°C and 29°C) and with dewpoints greater than 50°F (10°C).

Tornadoes favor the warmer part of the day for formation; again, this is the time of greatest thunderstorm activity. A national survey showed that 82 percent occur between noon and midnight and 42 percent between 3:00 and 7:00 P.M. local time.

Based on almost six thousand tornadoes observed between 1930 and 1958, a movement from southwest to northeast predominated. But tornadoes have been known to move from any direction, to change directions abruptly, to follow a zigzag course, and to perform loops and complete circles. Most New Jersey tornadoes, however, do not endure long enough to perform these antics.

No wind-measuring instrument has ever survived the full impact of a tornado. While much damage can be inflicted by winds of 125 miles per hour (201 km/h), it is probable that winds in an extreme tornado can exceed 200 miles per hour (322 km/h).

New Jersey is not in prime tornado-producing territory. The requisite ingredients for creating tornado funnels—airstreams of contrasting temperature and humidity in close proximity accompanied by a sharp wind shear aloft—do not come together along the Eastern seaboard to the degree or frequency they do in the Mississippi valley, the homeland of massive, killer tornadoes. In the early decades of the twentieth century, about two reports of tornadoes each year were normal, but now, under the stimulus of public awareness programs, the number of tornado sightings has increased. Tornado alerts covering sections of New Jersey are issued several times a year by the National Weather Service.

Most New Jersey tornadoes are short-lived, with time spans of a few minutes; they have narrow tracks only a few yards wide and cover limited distances measured in tenths of a mile. Yet some tornado occurrences in the state have caused substantial destruction. The New Brunswick Tornado on June 19, 1835, moved along a track at least 17.5 miles (28 km) long through the heart of the town, killing five persons and doing extensive structural damage. The Camden-Philadelphia Tornado on August 3, 1885, tore a two-block-wide swath through densely populated areas, destroying or damaging about five-hundred buildings and killing five persons.

Though most tornadoes have short paths within the Garden State, there are records of some rather lengthy tracks. The Burlington-Ocean Counties Tornado on July 22, 1930, spread an extended path of destruction for 40 miles (64 km) between Red Lion and Seaside Park. The Gloucester-Middlesex Counties Tornado on August 25, 1941, did damage over 75 miles (121 km) from Woodbury to Woodbridge. After the Gloucester-Monmouth Counties Tornado on March

10, 1964, there were damage reports from locations 58 miles (93 km) apart. The Cape May Tornado on August 27, 1971, pursued a path northward the length of the county for at least 28 miles (45 km) before dissipating in Atlantic County. Some of these, perhaps all, may have skipped along their paths when the deadly funnel lifted from the ground for some distance, as small tornadoes often do.

# Major New Jersey Tornadoes Described in the Contemporary Press

## The New Brunswick Tornado of June 19, 1835

The city of New Brunswick was the scene, on Friday afternoon last, of a most desolating tornado, which swept over its western section, causing much destruction of property, and, we regret to add, depriving several individuals of life.

As far as we have been able to learn, the whirlwind or tornado first made its appearance with a falling of ice in the township of Amwell, near a place called Ringgold's [Ringoes], and taking an erratic zig-zag course, spent its fury over Staten Island, in the neighborhood of Rossville, and on the bay, by another fall of large irregular shaped pieces of ice. Its first approach to New Brunswick was from the north west, passing over Middlebush, about three miles from that place, where the dwelling and barn of John French were laid prostrate with the earth. It thence passed over the farm of David Dunn, about two and a half miles from New Brunswick, whose dwelling was unroofed, and the barn and other out-buildings were razed to the ground. The out-houses attached to the premises of J. G. Wyckoff, in the same vicinity, were also destroyed. The next building which felt its effects was the dwelling of Theophilus Holkham, about one mile from New Brunswick, the roof of which was blown off. The barns of James Fisher and Abraham Blauvelt, in the outskirts of the city were next blown down, and a small dwelling belonging to Mr. Prevost was nearly destroyed, and the wife of Tunis Silcocks badly injured.

New York Gazette,
*June 23, 1835*

The tornado had now reached the hill, "where," according to the *New Brunswick Times,*

> it remained apparently fixed for a minute or two, presenting the appearance of a pillar of fire—its base resting on the earth, and its top reaching a mass of black clouds. It then took an eastern course, threatening Albany and Church streets, but suddenly changed its direction, swept across the town lot towards the dwelling of Mr. B. Myer, Mrs. Deare, professor McClelland, rev. John Croes, L. Kirkpatrick, esq. Mrs. Kirkpatrick and rev. Dr. Janeway, tearing the roofs off some, making literal wrecks of the barns and out-houses, and either uprooting or twisting off the largest trees—in some instances carried the latter 20 or 30 paces. It then crossed to the buildings at the head of Paterson, Liberty, Bayard and Schureman streets, unroofing the house of Mrs. Harrison, levelling the store of Mr. Little, and burying beneath the falling timber Nicholas Booraem, esq. and his eldest son Henry. Both were extricated a short time after—the son in a dying state, in which he lingered until 9 o'clock, when death relieved him from his suffering—the father is not dangerously hurt. A young lad of about 8 years of age, son of Capt. Baird, was also killed near this spot, a rafter from the blacksmith's shop having struck him immediately above the eyes, and almost severed his head.
>
> The tornado now swept with increased force across George street, down Liberty, Shureman and New streets, crossing Nelson to Burnet street, a quarter of a mile distance, down to the river, unroofing or tearing off the tops of the houses, and sweeping the lower floors and windows from their fastenings. Schureman and Liberty streets, from top to bottom, may be said to be a complete mass of ruins, as is likewise part of Burnet street. The Methodist church, a brick edifice, is damaged beyond repair, having been unroofed, and the eastern and southern walls blown down; and the rear wall of the Catholic church, also of brick, is drove into the body of the building.
>
> New Brunswick Times,
> *June 23, 1835*
>
> After leaving New Brunswick, the tornado passed down the river a short distance, then took a course across the river, and passed over the farm of James T. Dunn, tore up several trees by the roots, laid all his out buildings in ruins, without doing the slightest damage to his dwelling. It then passed down to the farm of Joel Randal, and carried away part of the roof and gable end of his dwelling.

Thence its course was over Piscataway, a small town, containing about a dozen houses, situated two miles from New Brunswick. Here, every building except two in the place, including the Episcopal church, was demolished. We regret to add, that Mr. Thomas W. Harper, of New York, was killed by being struck on the head by a beam. We understand that Mr. H. had just received the deed of some property which he had been purchasing, and that his visit to Piscataway was for the purpose of making some arrangements respecting it. He was a silversmith, residing at 31 Rose street, and has left a large family.

The tornado then passed on towards Perth Amboy, where one building was destroyed, and spent its fury on Staten Island as above stated.

Among the extraordinary occurrences which took place on this melancholy occasion, the fate of the son of Wm. G. Dunham (a small lad) was the most singular. He was taken off the piazza of the house, corner of New and George streets, carried in the air a distance of 300 yards, and landed on the wharf in Burnet street, having only sustained a slight injury in one of his arms. On being questioned as to his feelings, he stated that he recollected passing through the top of a willow tree, and that the sensation produced by being carried up in the whirlwind was like that of being pulled in contrary directions.

A bedstead was taken from the third story of a house in Schureman street, carried a distance of 200 yards, and landed in Burnet street, without having sustained the slightest injury. A carpet bag and some bedding were carried from the garret of Dr. Janeway's house to the river, a distance of nearly half a mile.

New York Gazette,
*June 23, 1835*

## The Camden-Philadelphia Tornado of August 3, 1885

The cyclone was first observed advancing at a marvelously rapid rate across the Delaware River from Greenwich Point. It looked first like a dark rain cloud, from which a heavy rain was pouring upon the earth so dense that everything around it looked black. Dark clouds were approaching at the same time from the southeast, and at a point directly over the roofs of the property of the Pennsylvania Salt Company at Greenwich Point, the rain column and the black clouds from the southwest seemed to meet. Immediately the tall column began to whirl with a frightful velocity, accompanied by the roar of a hurricane that could be heard in the distance. Buildings at the salt works were demolished in the space of a minute, and fragments of them and even whole roofs were carried high in the air and scattered around like shavings. From here it passed in a northeasterly direction toward Kaighn's Point, Camden, catching in its train at an unlucky moment the steamboat Major Reybold, and spreading havoc and devastation over the decks of the steamer in a way that could not have been more complete if it had been raked with the fire of a cannon. Old river men who witnessed the sight say they never saw anything to equal it in their lives. It is almost a miracle that the loss of only one life is to be recorded in the disaster to the steamer. Five persons were more or less severely injured. The sweeping demon in the air whirled to the banks of the Jersey shore, and everywhere havoc, ruin and devastation were strewn in its path. Houses were demolished, trees carried into the air, and property destroyed. At least three persons lost their lives, eight were injured, and one missing.

The cyclone kept along the Jersey side of the river until it reached a point opposite Port Richmond. Here it swept across the stream again driving vessels from their moorings, unroofing houses, demolishing buildings, resulting in the loss of one life and the injury of sixteen persons. All the work of ruin along the length and breadth of the cyclone's track was all done probably in the space of a quarter of an hour. There was no rain at the time, and only a light breeze blowing.

The rush of the cyclone was estimated to be 500 feet wide. Its appearance was that of a dense black cloud revolving at terrific rate. In the heart of it the gloom was like the darkness of midnight, and eye witnesses describe the air as so black that they could not see their hands before their faces. The bottom of it moved over the river like a rolling ball of smoke. The phenomenal force of the wind can only be imagined from the visible evidence of its destruction, and its power seemed to be almost supernatural. In the recollection of no one in this city has a phenomenon of such character and ruinous results ever visited the neighborhood of Philadelphia, and by those who were the victims of its work it will never be forgotten. After the cyclone passed, a heavy rain storm set in, which lasted during the early part of the evening, with frequent sharp flashes of lightning.

Philadelphia Inquirer,
*August 4, 1885*

## A View from Above

### How the Cyclone Looked as Seen from a High Building— An Awful Sight and the Terror it Created

As seen from a high window of the Pennsylvania Railroad Company's building on Fourth street, the cyclone was a great but terrible sight. Its course could be traced from Greenwich Point until it reached nearly to Port Richmond. It came along in the shape of a huge black cloud, driving before it a lighter funnel-shaped mass that seemed like spray or a densely compacted snow squall. Its course was not directly up the river, but across it in a diagonal line, which included two or three miles of the river in its course. The cloud rushed along with terrible velocity, but never at the same height. It alternately sank so low as to touch the earth and then rose again to a considerable height, the alternate dipping and rising occurring with the course of perhaps three or four hundred yards. Whenever the cloud dropped there was sure to be an upheaval, and with it a roof would go flying off. With a clear view across the river this could be plainly seen. At first the lighter or misty cloud which seemed to precede the darker one, would come into view after having taken a downward course, and then with the shadow of the other, which followed closely in its wake, all flying debris was given a darkened appearance.

### An Awful Sight

A roof, when struck would be lifted straight up for quite a distance, resembling a piece of black felt, and then, after being twisting around and around and hurled along with frightful rapidity, would break into a thousand pieces. In their fall the pieces resembled the breaking up of a barrel, the staves tumbling in every imaginable shape. It was noticed that whenever the outward line of the dark cloud sank below the roofs a crash of some kind was bound to follow. This lifting of roofs seemed to continue all along the Jersey shore from a point somewhere near Kaighn's Point avenue to Cooper's Point, after which it moved to the eastward crossing again into Port Richmond. The clerks in the railway office seemed to be terror-stricken for a time. They rushed to the windows and with breathless awe gazed intently on the mass of broken materials whirling in the cyclone's bosom. At other time fences, roofs, and trees went sailing aloft and circling around like so many feathers. Several tin roofs stripped bodily from the houses in the southern part of Camden, were noticed sailing about with the rest. The awful sight lasted less than ten minutes, but will never be forgotten by those who witnessed it.

Philadelphia Inquirer,
*August 4, 1885*

## Cherry Hill Tornado of July 13, 1895

Shortly before 4:00 P.M. on Saturday, July 13, 1895, a massive black cloud gathered over Cherry Hill near Hackensack in Bergen County and let loose a storm of hail and rain followed by a tornado funnel. Three local residents died, eleven were injured (six of whom had to be hospitalized), and most of the sixty or more dwellings in the village were damaged, some of them completely destroyed.

The general path and destructive characteristics of the tornado were described by a reporter for the *New York World*:

The path of the tornado is plainly marked from where it struck at Waldwick, in the northwestern corner of Bergen County, until it passed over the Palisades, twenty miles away. It landed in a great piece of woods near Walwick and mowed a wide swath through them, tearing the trees out by the roots. Rounding along in a southeasterly direction it passed the villages of Ridgewood and Spring Valley, levelling everything in its path. Then it swirled around

*The Cherry Hill Tornado damaged or destroyed most of the houses in the village. The Cherry Hill Reformed Church is in the background of this photograph. (Courtesy of Mrs. Robert Dickie.) (From the collection of the Bergen County Historical Society)*

Cherry Hill, where the greatest destruction was done, ten miles from the start.

Fences and crops were cut down for three miles more until Teaneck. The magnificent estate of William Walter Phelps was struck. A hundred trees were blown down and part of the greenhouses wrecked, but none of the buildings was damaged. The tornado sailed over the Palisades and passed above Harlem, just touching the city with its lower strata. It then dropped again with destructive force on Woodhaven [Long Island, where it claimed another life].

New York World,
*July 15, 1895*

Blacksmith John H. Jones witnessed the approach of the dense black cloud from the west at about 2:30 P.M. He was in the Reformed church at the time and was astonished at the dense blackness that descended on the village. He ran out into the road, found a heavy wind blowing and a strange-shaped cloud that seemed to be full of yellow light approaching from the northwest.

"I ran across the street to Friedman's Hotel," said Jones to a *New York Times* reporter, "and cried, 'Look out, there's a heavy gale coming.' I was so excited that I threw my tools on the floor, and went out to the door again to watch the storm. Just then something struck me on the head, and I was lifted up bodily and thrown into the ditch on the opposite side of the road.

"I did not lose consciousness, but crouched down in the ditch clinging to the grass. The big cloud that seemed full of yellow light spun round and round. Everything seemed to go round—dirt, bricks, wood; everything. I could see all that happened. I saw Friedman come flying out of the window of his hotel. I waited until there was a lull, and then rushed out on the railroad track, and lay there till the blow was over.

"As I lay flat on my stomach I glanced around, and saw that my own house had been blown from its foundations and tilted back like a rocking chair with half the hind part of the rockers torn off."

New York Times,
*July 15, 1895*

## Paterson Tornado of 1903

At about 3:00 P.M. on the afternoon of July 22, 1903, a fully developed tornado funnel swept across the width of the city of Paterson at the Great Falls of the Passaic River, from Lambert Castle to Hawthorne. Four people were killed, twenty-five hospitalized. Thirty buildings were demolished, three hundred damaged. About $300,000 in damages was reported. The disaster was covered in great detail by the metropolitan press by experienced reporters. The following excerpts from the *New York Times* are good examples of the coverage.

> A dense black cloud, assuming the shape of a cone, and whirling with furious rapidity, loomed up over the top of Garrett Mountain, just southeast [southwest?] of Paterson, at 3 o'clock this afternoon. In less than ten minutes it swept over that section of the city known as South Paterson, killing four persons, seriously injuring fifteen, and hurting more than a hundred, and wrecking six buildings and damaging more than 200 others. Then it passed over the Passaic River, across the meadows, and disappeared in the air.

> Shortly after 2 o'clock the clear sky became cloudy. Steadily it grew darker and darker, until it became necessary to turn on lights in the business houses and homes.
>
> Then dimly outlined against the dark sky appeared the still blacker funnel-shaped cloud. Few beheld it, as almost everybody, fearing the storm, had sought shelter indoors. The cloud was suspended for a moment some distance above the mountain, then descended with fearsome rapidity and swirled across the part of town lying north and east of it.
>
> Roofs of houses were wrested from their fastenings and blown around and around by the force of the wind; other buildings in the path were twisted on their foundations, out-buildings were picked up and carried great distances and were dashed to pieces against other objects or fell when the storm had passed. Trees were uprooted, huge boards and timber from a lumber yard were sent whirling in the air and trolley and telephone and telegraph wires fell beneath the debris that was strewn about in the roughest manner imaginable.

In Chestnut Street the rise of the tornado from the earth can be plainly traced. The limbs of trees are twisted off higher and higher, until at last the storm marks cease entirely where the apex of the tornado had risen above them. The path of the storm was about 1,000 feet wide.

The storm, after rising, seems to have swerved somewhat to the south, and then, having traveled about a half mile without doing damage, although its course can be plainly followed by the debris which dropped on to houses, streets, and yards, it again struck in the vicinity of Madison and Market Streets.

There it caught the General Hospital buildings. It had not settled to the ground, but tore off a portion of the roofs of the main building and broke some windows on the upper floors. A few feet beyond the main building was the boiler house, and this appears to have received the full force of the storm. The roof of this structure was twisted into a spiral and carried away. In the hospital building there was a repetition of the scenes in St. Joseph's a few minutes earlier. The wind seemed to spend its greatest force at this strike around the hospital, and trees and shrubs in the yard and in the vicinity were torn and broken by the swirl. A house on Madison Street not far from the Hospital was considerably damaged.

The storm again leaped into the air, only to settle again in the vicinity of Park Avenue and twenty-second Street, and it again bounded into the air at about Twenty-sixth Street. Park Avenue for four blocks is almost stripped of the trees which made it one of the finest streets in the city. The houses in the path of the storm suffered considerably, but none was seriously damaged, except the grocery of Henry Westhoven, at Twenty-fourth Street, which had the roof blown off.

The storm landed again, but only for a second, at Park and Twelfth Avenues, in the vicinity of the residence of ex-Attorney General John W. Griggs. There a number of trees were blown down and uprooted.

The tornado, after passing over that part of the town, swerved toward the river, striking Public School 13 and doing much damage to dwellings in the vicinity. Then it whirled about, and, crossing the Passaic, between Twelfth Avenue and Warren Point, swept across the low meadows, wrecking farmhouses and leveling standing grain.

At Fairlawn, a hamlet about five miles east of Paterson, it lifted the roof and mow of a barn, leaving cattle and horses standing uncovered in their stalls.

Then the cloud which had gradually been losing its compactness, seemed to rise and lose itself in the air. A moment after the tornado swept over the city almost a deluge of rain fell. The streets became torrents for a few minutes and houses that had been unroofed were drenched. The precipitation in the ten minutes was almost unprecedented here.

*The* New York Herald *reports on the tornado that swept over Paterson on July 22, 1903. (Courtesy of Princeton University Library)*

NEW YORK HERALD, FRIDAY, JULY 24, 1903.—EIGHTEEN PAGES.

## Views of the Tornado Swept District at Paterson, N. J.

HORSE SHOE DISTRICT OF SANDY HILL LOOKING TOWARD STATE & CLAY STREETS FROM CHESTNUT STREET PATERSON, N.J

VIEW ON CLAY STREET BETWEEN CHESTNUT AND STATE STREETS. PATERSON, N.J

## SUBWAY JOINED TO BIG BUILDINGS

Many Obtain Permission to Build Short Cuts to Tunnel Stations.

DEPARTMENT STORE PLAN

Hotels and Office Buildings to Have Entrances to Underground Tracks.

At the suggestion of Mayor Low William Barclay Parsons, chief engineer of the Rapid Transit Commission, was authorized yesterday by the commission to issue tentative permits allowing owners of private property to connect their buildings with the subway stations. The permits are to be issued with the understanding, however, that the rate of compensation established by the Rapid Transit Commissioners for the privilege will be agreed upon later and with the provision that the Interborough Rapid Transit Railway Company does not object to the connections.

This action was taken to enable the owners of large buildings now in course of construction to arrange for the connection at once.

Controller Grout said that the rate of compensation would probably be three and one-half per cent of the assessed valuation of the land.

This action was brought about by the application of John Wanamaker for permission to connect his store with the station at Eighth street. After some discussion the permit was granted upon the basis that the applicant pay the expense of the increased size of the station and pay the city three and one-half per cent of the assessed value of the land.

The trustees of the Mercantile Library, at Astor place and Broadway; the owners of the Young Men's Christian Association Building, at Fourth avenue and Twenty-third street, who are about to build a new

## ARITHMETIC PLAN OUT-EUCLIDS EUCLID

Mrs. Charlotte Roddy Sues Another Woman to Whom She Imparted Secret.

OLD FORMULAS ABOLISHED

Circles Squared, Roots Extracted and Highest Powers Furnished Instantaneously.

Declaring that she had a wonderful system for reducing higher mathematics to forms of simple arithmetic, and that her system had been appropriated by Mrs. Julia Van Tassel, a teacher in Miss Dana's school, at Morristown, N. J., Mrs. Charlotte Roddy, of New York, yesterday brought suit against Mrs. Van Tassel to recover $210, the price of twenty-one lessons in higher mathematics.

## EXPLOSION BLOCKS EVERY "L" LINE

Angry Patrons Crowd Stations and Threaten to Cause Trouble.

JUST AT THE RUSH HOUR

Fuses Blow Out and All Power Is Turned Off for Forty-Five Minutes.

Traffic on all the elevated lines was blocked for forty-five minutes last evening, owing to a serious explosion at the main power house, at East Seventy-fourth and Seventy-fifth streets and the East River.

Great inconvenience to residents of Harlem and the Bronx was caused by the blockade.

The cables used for conveying the electric current from the power house to the ele-

## MRS. POILLON HAS A WOMAN ARRESTED

Annie Ornwitz Is Charged by Her with Threatening to Take Her Life.

ACCUSATIONS ARE DENIED

Woman Who Is Suing W. Gould Brokaw Declares Vitriol Was Ready for Her.

Annie Ornwitz, thirty-three years old, of No. 169 East 123d street, was arrested yesterday on a warrant sworn to by Mrs. Katharyn Poillon, who is suing W. Gould Brokaw for $250,000 for breach of promise.

Mrs. Poillon in obtaining the warrant from Magistrate Hogan in the West Side Police Court said it was for a woman who had on several occasions threatened her life. She declared that on Wednesday evening the

# Other Significant New Jersey Tornadoes

1742 APRIL 24 "We hear from Newark in East New-Jersey that sometime last week they had a most violent Hurricane, the extent of which was about 40 Rod, and tore up every Thing in it's way, particularly a Barn, and some Timber near it which it carry'd to a very great height and distance." (*American Weekly Mercury* [Philadelphia], May 6, 1742)

1783 JULY 13 "At Morristown, on the Sabbath of the 13th instant, between five and six o'clock P.M. a heavy gust that came out of the Southwest, in a seeming direct course to the town, was providentially met within a quarter of a mile from the town, with another from the East, with thunder and rain, which turned its course to the Northward, and which occasioned a surprising agitation in the atmosphere and dismal in its effects, scattering fences, twisting off sturdy oaks; tearing up trees by the roots and almost some whole orchards, and carrying the trees to a considerable distance, blowing down some houses and barns, unroofing others to the amount of 15: unhousing some, taking up others and carrying them to a considerable distance whereby they were much bruised, but through a kind providence no bones were broken or lives lost." (*New Jersey Journal* [Chatham], July 16, 1783)

1804 MAY 22 Flemington: earliest tornado fatality in state history; reported as "tornado or whirlwind" in press; funnel observed, rumbling noise heard; woman killed by falling tree; further damage reported at New Brunswick.

1835 JUNE 19 First reported in Amwell Township of Somerset County; then skip damage in Middlesex County east of Millstone River; moved through downtown New Brunswick just west of Albany Street; 120 buildings either destroyed or badly damaged in city, perhaps 25 more in rural districts; continued over Raritan Meadows, last sighted over bay from Tottenville, Staten Island; total length of path about 17.5 miles, 200–400 yards wide; property damage $61,000; five reported killed.

1838 AUGUST 15 Twin whirlwinds passed over the Musconetcong valley at the same time about one mile apart: paths from southwest to northeast; each about one hundred yards across; damage to trees and barns.

1842 APRIL 26 Newton area: two funnels, seven miles apart, did extensive damage to fields.

1865 MAY 11 Trail of destruction from Philadelphia to New York City, possibly from skip tornadoes: Newark suffered considerable structural damage; wagons blown into tops of trees, people lifted off their feet, but no serious injuries.

1871 JULY 17 Vineland: evening tornado destroyed Episcopal church, two railroad depots, two dwellings; several injuries reported.

1882 SEPTEMBER 12 Pleasantville, Atlantic County: tornado associated with hurricane about seventy-five miles southeast of Cape May; trees uprooted, fences blown down; house moved from foundation.

1885 AUGUST 23 Camden: large funnel crossed river from Philadelphia near Walt Whitman Bridge; damaged two steamships; moved north along river streets of Camden; crossed river again to Port Richmond area of North Philadelphia; more than five hundred buildings damaged; $500,000 loss in Camden and Philadelphia; six killed, more than one hundred injured.

1895 JULY 13 Cherry Hill Tornado: struck one and one-half miles north of Hackensack; four dwellings and a depot destroyed; twenty-six other buildings damaged; three killed.

1901 AUGUST 24 Jersey City: two-block-wide strip of the lower city on the river plain devastated; churches, theater, and parks wrecked; over 200 homes damaged; loss estimated over $100,000; three injured, none killed.

1902 AUGUST 10 Trenton: funnel imbedded in thunderstorm hit downtown area; second stories of six houses ripped off; lumber yard and railroad carpentry shop demolished; ten other houses unroofed or damaged; damage estimated at $100,000 from wind, $25,000 from flooding.

1903 JULY 22 Paterson Tornado: funnel skipped across city from near Lambert Castle to Hawthorne; thirty buildings demolished, three hundred damaged; four deaths; twenty-five hospitalized; $300,000 damage.

1911 JUNE 12 Suspected tornadoes did extensive damage in Paterson, Hackensack, Jersey City, and Bayonne; confirmed tornadoes in New York State and Pennsylvania; one killed in New Jersey.

1912 APRIL 2 Camden: probable tornado crossed Delaware River from Philadelphia; nearly two hundred buildings in Camden wrecked or seriously damaged in densely populated area; one killed, several injured; $100,000 damage; path continued eastward doing tree and structural damage.

1921 MARCH 28 Somerville: "fairly well developed form swept over a portion of the county and city, and did considerable damage," according to state climatologist; accompanied sharp cold front passage.

1929 APRIL 1 Warren County: tornado crossed Delaware River at Portland near Water Gap; superstructure of a wooden bridge damaged; two houses and a number of barns demolished along path toward Blairstown; three killed in Pennsylvania, one in New Jersey.

1930 APRIL 1 Tornado damage along forty-mile path from Red Lion, Gloucester County, to Seaside Park, Ocean County, with greatest loss at latter location.

1941 AUGUST 25 Destruction along 75 miles from Gloucester to Middlesex County: $400,000 damage, mainly to packing plant at Swedesboro and housing development at Hopelawn near Woodbridge; one killed, twenty-five injured.

1952 AUGUST 10 Narrow path of damage through Burlington and Monmouth counties from Wrightstown to Leonardo: airplane damaged at McGuire Air Force Base; chicken farms wrecked near Cookstown; barns and garages damaged at Leonardo; passed out to sea over Sandy Hook.

1957 NOVEMBER 19 Washington in Warren County struck by tornado in two-block business area; skipped to housing development; roofs blown off, many windows out.

*The Statue of Liberty Tornado, as photographed from the Battery in Manhattan, July 7, 1976. (Robert T. Mahoney photo)*

1971 AUGUST 27 Cape May County: tornado associated with Tropical Storm Doria moved from Delaware Bay over Cape May City and north the length of the county; width about forty yards; roofs damaged, trees felled, power outages.

1975 JULY 13 Seabrook, Cumberland County: path 1.5 miles long, width seventy-five yards; $10 million damage.

1976 JULY 7 Bicentennial Tornado at Bayonne and Jersey City touched down near Marine Ocean Terminal in Bayonne: trailers picked up, buildings damaged; moved north over river.

1982 JUNE 29 A tornado touched down in the western section of Silver Ridge Park near Rutland Drive in Berkeley Township in Ocean County near Toms River. It moved in a gently curving east-northeast direction which twisted its way through two New Jersey retirement villages. At least one hundred homes were torn apart by the swirling wind; fifteen were totally destroyed; forty had major damage. Seven autos were damaged and four totalled. The vicious tornado with devasting winds and rain also bent flagpoles, downed power lines, and turned cars upside down. It was followed by torrential rains causing heavy flooding. Only minor personal injuries were reported.

*Wreckers at work at Barnegat Light, January 25, 1868. (Courtesy of* Harper's Magazine*)*

# Snowstorms

People of different ages and predilections react in different ways to the coming of a snowstorm. Most children view the first flakes with expressions of delight and imagine the landscape transformed into a winter wonderland of sledding, sliding, and snowballing. To many adults engaged in the working world, thoughts are less enchanting with anticipation of slippery roads, stalled cars, and long delays. To the elderly, the flakes evoke nostalgic memories of wintry scenes long ago. A snowstorm is a great initiator of conversation between people of all ages, whether friend or stranger, with everyone wishing to express his or her personal reactions to the all-encompassing snowstorm.

A snowstorm consists of the descent of myriads of minute ice crystals that have formed aloft in a subfreezing stratum of the atmosphere. At the core of every ice crystal is a tiny condensation nucleus consisting of a microparticle of solid matter around which moisture clings. Liquid water droplets and free ice crystals cannot coexist in the same cloud space, because under saturated conditions the vapor pressure of ice is less than that of water. Hence the ice crystals rob the liquid water droplets of their moisture and grow continuously by accretion. Sizable ice crystals form rapidly. Some adhere to each other and create snowflakes in a variety of beautiful arrangements (usually hexagonal). Most flakes found in a snowstorm, however, consist of broken fragments or clusters of adhering crystals.

The moisture needed for New Jersey snowstorms comes from the south, while the required coldness comes from the north. When the two ingredients meet in the proper quantity or degree and the necessary structure of the atmosphere prevails aloft, major snowfalls—four inches or more—result. A high-pressure area or anticyclone to the north or northeast with a low-pressure center or cyclone to the south or southwest of the region is the usual pattern. From the high pressure flows a stream of cold air from the northeast that assures surface temperatures at or below freezing; the circulation around the low-pressure center draws a flow of moist air from the Gulf of Mexico or the adjacent Atlantic Ocean. The forced ascent of the moist air over the cold air overlying New Jersey results in cooling, condensation, and the formation of snowflakes. It is essential that the storm center pass to the south and east of the locality in order to keep temperatures aloft in the below-freezing range and prevent the descending snowflakes from melting into raindrops.

Classic snowstorms result from the formation of a low-pressure center somewhere in a crescent-shaped zone running from Texas through the northern Gulf of Mexico to the Atlantic Ocean waters off Georgia and the Carolinas. The storm centers moving northeast pass near Cape Hatteras and continue over the ocean toward Cape Cod and Nantucket. The trajectory of the storm center, whether it passes close to the New Jersey coast or at a distance, largely determines both the intensity and the duration of the snowfall over the state. Also very influential in the behavior of a snowstorm is the upper-air structure of the atmosphere. Usually an elongated north-south trough prevails aloft, serving to guide the path and to support and intensify the storm center.

A Rutgers University study of heavy snowfalls in New Jersey found that six main storm types arising from different weather-map situations were responsible for the state's major snowstorms.

1. The storm system develops over the southern Plains, usually in Texas or the Oklahoma panhandle, then moves to the Ohio valley. The original center dissipates or *fills*, as meteorologists describe a rise in barometric pressure in a storm center. A secondary low-pressure center forms along the Atlantic seaboard somewhere from Long Island southward.
2. The storm formation is the same, but high pressure to the north forces it to follow a more southerly path that carries out to sea south of New Jersey over Virginia or the Carolinas.
3. A storm circulation originates in the Gulf of Mexico, and its center moves northeast along the Atlantic seaboard.
4. The original development takes place in the western Gulf of Mexico, with the storm center tracking west of the Appalachians; later a secondary forms on the Atlantic seaboard.
5. The low-pressure center first appears in the mid-Mississippi or Tennessee valley with or without secondary development along the Atlantic seaboard.
6. A low-pressure system from the northern Plains or the Great Lakes region moves steadily southeast, instead of the more normal east or northeast direction, and moves out to sea south of New Jersey.

As usual with things meteorological, numerous additional situations that do not have distinct surface features can produce snowfalls, too: overrunning warm air, upper-air troughs of low pressure, and the backlash of deepening storms offshore.

The zone of heaviest snowfall across New Jersey usually occurs in a southwest-to-northeast strip about 50 miles (80 km) wide, approximately parallel to the path of the storm center and about 125 to 175 miles (210 to 282 km) northwest of it. If the center passes well offshore, only South Jersey will receive a substantial snowfall. When the track passes close inshore, warm air from the ocean is drawn into the surface circulation, resulting in rain falling over South Jersey and snow or rain over the rest of the state. Sometimes a passing storm center brings rain to the south, mixed precipitation to central sections, and snow to the north.

The depth of the snow depends primarily on the moisture supply available for snowmaking and on the duration of the snowfall. Most snowfalls are limited to six to eight hours. Since the rate seldom exceeds one inch per hour, the accumulations are not great. But if the forward progress of the storm system is slowed, the snow period may be extended by twelve to twenty-four hours and the depth of the fall increases accordingly.

The classic situation for a heavy snow over New Jersey places a concave ridge of high pressure to the north over Canada stretching from Quebec to the Atlantic provinces, with an arm extending southward over the ocean toward Bermuda. This creates a blocking situation in which the advancing low's progress northeast is slowed and then halted for six to twelve hours or more. The barometric center usually intensifies during this process, creating severe conditions with heavier precipitation and higher winds. Such an extended period can result in snowfalls from twelve to twenty inches (30 to 51 cm) accumulating over parts of New Jersey.

Seasonal snowfall in New Jersey varies from an average of about 15 inches (38 cm) at Atlantic City to about 50 inches (102 cm) in Sussex County. There is great variability from year to year. The largest total in any one season was 108.1 inches (275 cm) at Culvers Lake in 1915–1916. On the other hand, Atlantic City received as little as 0.4 inch (1 cm) during the entire season of 1972–1973, and some stations in the south reported no measurable snow that winter.

February is the month with the greatest total snowfall and the time of year when maximum accumulations on the ground are usually reached. During the snowy month of February 1961, after three major snowstorms over the winter, depths accumulated to 40 to 50 inches (102 to 127 cm) on the ground in the highlands of the north and northwest. The maximum depths ever measured at the three first-class weather stations near urban areas were: Atlantic City Airport, 27.9 inches (71 cm), Newark Airport, 26.0 inches (66 cm), and downtown Trenton, 30.0 inches (76 cm).

The greatest amount of snow to fall in a single storm since record keeping began in 1885 came on February 11–14, 1899, when, in blizzard conditions, record amounts fell over the south and near-record amounts in the north. The state-wide totals for February 1899 averaged 31.3 inches (80 cm), the greatest of any month of record. This resulted from two minor storms on February 4–5 and 7–8 and the great storm on February 11–14. A total of 34 inches (86 cm) was reported at Cape May Lighthouse in the big storm, after which the depth on the ground there measured 41 inches (104 cm).

## The Blizzard of '88

Nothing in the folklore traditions of colonial America or the formally recorded meteorological history of the northeastern United States equals the storm that enveloped the area from Virginia to Maine on March 11–14, 1888. No other storm possessed to such a degree all the requirements for an eastern blizzard: penetrating, gale-force winds; near-zero cold; and deep, drifting snowfall. The Blizzard of '88 attacked New Jersey with unprecedented fury and achieved a historical reputation unrivaled by any other storm.

The alignment of the weather map features on the morning of Saturday, March 10, presented nothing unusual to cause forecasters to issue warnings for the Atlantic seaboard. An ordinary-appearing trough of low pressure extended from the Great Lakes southward over the Mississippi valley, with the areas of lowest pressure near Green Bay, Wisconsin, and St. Louis.

During the next twenty-four hours the trough continued eastward to the Appalachian Mountain ridge. As often happens at this stage, the northern centers faded out and a new center of action developed

*Trains could not get through during the blizzard of March 11–14, 1888. This derailment occurred on March 13 at Whitehall, near Andover, on a Newton to Waterloo run of the Sussex Railroad. It took the rescue crew two days to clear the wreck. (From the original photograph owned by Mrs. William Hendershot. Collection of the New Jersey Historical Society)*

in the southern end of the trough. On the morning of Sunday, March 11, it was located near Augusta, Georgia, with a moderate pressure of 29.86 inches (101.1 kPa). Continuation on a normal northeast track for another twenty-four hours would have taken the storm center east of Cape Hatteras and to the vicinity of Cape Cod and Nantucket.

On Sunday evening, however, factors operating many miles distant from the low-pressure center entered the situation. The blocking influence of the slowly retreating high-pressure center to the north and east began to slow down the forward momentum and change the direction of movement of the storm center off the South Atlantic coast. At the same time, intensely cold northwest airstreams from Canada were drawn into the widening storm circulation.

As a result of these influences, the storm center progressed only to a position over the ocean east of Cape May and south of Long Island by the morning of the twelfth. Now the southerly flow in the trough aloft was carrying vast quantities of moisture over New York and New Jersey, while the easterly flow at the surface ahead of the low-pressure center was carrying a cool current of maritime air. These continued to do so and kept the precipitation process going for another twenty-four hours over northern New Jersey and for much longer over southern New England.

At the same time a strong northwest flow with near-zero temperatures in the western sector of the storm began to circle around to the south of the storm center and out over the ocean in a dynamic clash with the warmer air overlying the Gulf Stream.

During the daylight hours of Monday, March 12, the storm area continued north-northeast offshore at an ever-slowing pace, and by nightfall had consolidated over the waters lying between Block Island and Cape Cod. After remaining stationary, or nearly so, overnight, the now circular center appeared to perform a counterclockwise loop on the thirteenth over the adjacent land areas of Rhode Island and southeast Connecticut.

While the center remained in this area, the southern end of the trough of low pressure with its embedded cold front pivoted eastward far out over the Atlantic Ocean and then swung northward until it lay on an approximately west-east axis south of eastern New England and the offshore waters. North of this line of sharp temperature difference, east and northeast winds had a long fetch over the ocean waters; upon reaching the shore and encountering the northern end of the trough of low pressure still stalled over the Connecticut valley, the moisture-bearing flow was forced to glide up over the cold wedge of air overlying western New England and the Hudson valley. Extremely intense precipitation resulted.

The full gale blowing most of the twelfth and thirteenth made it difficult to measure the snowfall accurately. The Newark observer, Frederick W. Ricord, reported: "The exact depth of snow which fell upon this occasion cannot be given. We place it at nineteen inches, and have reason for believing that this is not far from correct." The observer at Union caught 25 inches (64 cm) in his gauge. New Brunswick estimated snow "between two and three feet deep." The Trenton recorder gave the figure of 21 inches (53 cm). The Freehold observer "measured 20 inches [51 cm] in the woods." His total precipitation from rain and snow storms was 3.35 inches (85 mm). The Atlantic City weather bureau reported 7.0 inches (18 cm) of snow, and the observer at Cape May Court House had 10 inches (25 cm). The official Philadelphia measurement downtown was 10 inches, and this was probably representative for most of the lower Delaware valley.

The observers of the New Jersey State Weather Service reported the storm for their localities in the *New Jersey Weather Chronicle*. P. Vanderbilt Spader of New Brunswick observed: "It was the worst I have any record of. It was impossible to measure the depth of the snow. One remarkable thing about the storm was, that although the temperature was low and the snow dry, still the wind blew so violently that the snow was packed together so solidly that it could only be removed by the shovel. Snow ploughs were of no use." H. Y. Postma of Egg Harbor City said: "On the 11th rain began falling at 11:20 A.M., the wind gradually increasing to a terrible gale, which continued until 2 A.M. of the 12th; the rain turned to snow, while the wind blew with a force of a hurricane at intervals, doing considerable damage to property. The instrument shelter was completely demolished and all the instruments rendered unserviceable. On the 13th frequent snow squalls, wind diminishing in force. All communication cut off. The snow is piled in drifts of from eight to ten feet." George H. Larison of Lambertville reported: "On the 11th, a light rain commenced falling which continued until 11:40 P.M., when it came down quite heavily and shortly thereafter turned into snow, which continued until 3 P.M. of the 12th, and was accompanied by high wind, mostly from the northwest. All railroad and telegraphic communication cut off from Sunday night to Thursday noon. Great banks of snow one mile west of Ringoes. Funerals were delayed three days, owing to the impassable condition of the roads."

New Jersey's newspapers gave much space to reporting the storm and supplied some meteorological details for their localities:

> Rain on the 11th, commencing at 3 P.M. and increasing after nightfall, changing during the night to snow and continuing heavily throughout the 12th, the wind rising to

a gale, and the snow drifting so that the depth could not be estimated. The snow ceased during the night of the 12th, but the gale continued throughout the 13th, the snow filling the air continuously like a driving storm.

[Temperature: Sunday, eleventh, maximum 44°F (7°C), minimum 10°F (−12°C); Monday, 13th, maximum 13°F (−11°C), minimum 4°F (−16°C).]

Monmouth Democrat
*(Freehold), March 15, 1888*

All through the day the storm continued, the snow falling and the wind blowing, until at night the ground was covered with a white mantle two feet deep on a level, piled up in spots to ten and even fifteen feet.

[Temperature at noon Sunday was 44°F (7°C), at noon Monday 20°F (−7°C), at noon Tuesday 14°F (−10°C). The lowest reported was 8°F (−13°C) at 7:00 A.M. on Tuesday.]

New Jersey Courier
*(Toms River), March 14, 1888*

It was a real northwestern blizzard. The storm began on Sunday noon with a light rain, which soon turned to snow, melting as it fell. About 5 p.m. the mercury dropped below the freezing point and the snow began to accumulate. By midnight an eighty-mile hurricane was blowing with relentless fury, and the wind hurled the snow through the air in blinding clouds, making it impossible to see any distance. The gale continued with unabated force till Tuesday forenoon. The temperature dropped to 16 degrees above zero at 7 a.m. on Monday; at 12 o'clock it was 12 deg. above; at 6:00 p.m. 7 above, and on Tuesday morning 1 deg. below zero, and no rising above 9 deg. during the day. At 6 p.m. it was 5 deg. above, and on Wednesday morning 19 above zero, with snow still falling.

The snow was drifted in huge heaps, and packed so solidly as to bear a man's weight. It was useless for man or beast to brave the fury of the gale and the frozen particles of snow cut the pedestrian's face with acute pain. It did not take many hours to effectually block travel by rail.

Sussex Register
*(Newton), March 14, 1888*

The blizzard played havoc in South Jersey, the principal damage being along the lines of the railroads, where telegraph poles and wires were blown down and the roads blocked by great snow-drifts. . . . Shortly before dark on Sunday, rain began falling with a strong southeast wind, and continued in torrents until quarter of one on Sunday morning, when the wind veered and the temperature fell rapidly, changing the rain to snow. The air was thick with snow, and the frame buildings were groaning and trembling as if they were ready to fly apart. Few people slept. The storm increased in fury until it bordered on a hurricane, and the falling snow was whirled in immense banks, which in some instances covered the fence tops.

Cape May County Gazette,
*March 17, 1899*

The blizzard of March 10 & 11, 1888 [sic] was accompanied by but 10 inches of snow.

Cape May County Gazette,
*March 17, 1899*

From 2 o'clock Monday morning until Tuesday afternoon the storm raged with an unabated fury. The snow fell continuously and was drifted and whirled into every sheltering nook. Banks were formed on the east side of buildings nearly to the top of the first story windows and in some places on the streets were as high as the street lamps. The doors of the post office and First National Bank were blockaded for 48 hours, but as little business could be transacted few suffered any inconvenience.

Asbury Park Journal,
*March 17, 1899*

The blizzard that struck this city on Sunday night beats anything on record, and has completely cut off the town from the outside world both by rail and telegraph. The roads to the country are unbroken and obstructed by fallen trees and telegraph poles, and the rural districts are as unexplored regions. Part of the city's population succeeded in getting around after a fashion yesterday, braving the wintry blasts and ploughing their way through the deep snow-drifts. Paths have been beaten here and there and through them the people make their way. The snow has drifted in banks six and eight feet deep in the thoroughfares, completely blocking and obstructing many of them and compelling the people to walk in the road in snow up to their knees in many places.

Daily State Gazette
*(Trenton), March 14, 1888*

The snow storm which set in on Sunday night and which continued until a late hour last evening was, according to the oldest inhabitants, "the worst which has visited this city within their memories." The railroads are completely blocked, but two trains having arrived from New York and one from Trenton. The two former trains are still at this depot and the passengers are staying at the different hotels in the city, the railroad company bearing the expenses. The halted train started out and is snowbound at Rahway [10 miles toward New York City]. No newspapers have been received in this city since yesterday morning and they came from New York. Mr. P. Van Derbilt [sic] Spader states that this is the worst storm that has visited this locality within his recollection, taking all things into consideration. The snow is between two and three feet deep on a level, that it would be if a level could be found, which it cannot for the high winds have piled the snow in heaps varying from four to ten feet in depth.

New Brunswick Times,
*March 13, 1888*

The storm continued all day Monday and the drifts grew deeper and broader. It was impossible for anyone to get out of town, or for anyone out of town to get to Red Bank. The early morning train from New York got to Red Bank, giving people their mail and newspapers. The train got as far south as Little Silver [1.5 miles], where it got stuck in a drift and could get no further. The early train to New York got as far north as Red Bank, and then got stuck. The engineer loosened the locomotive from the rest of the train and tried to force his way through the drifts, expecting then to return for the rest of the train. He succeeded in getting about a hundred yards and then could go no further, and on starting to return to the train found that the snow had drifted in behind him so much that he could not get back.

This was about eight o'clock. There were ten or twelve passengers board, all men. They stayed in the cars all night and got their meals in the restaurants near the station. Yesterday their money ran out and Superintendent Blodgett telegraphed to Red Bank to have the men get their meals and have the bills sent to him.

Red Bank Register,
*March 14, 1888*

## The Official Record of the Blizzard

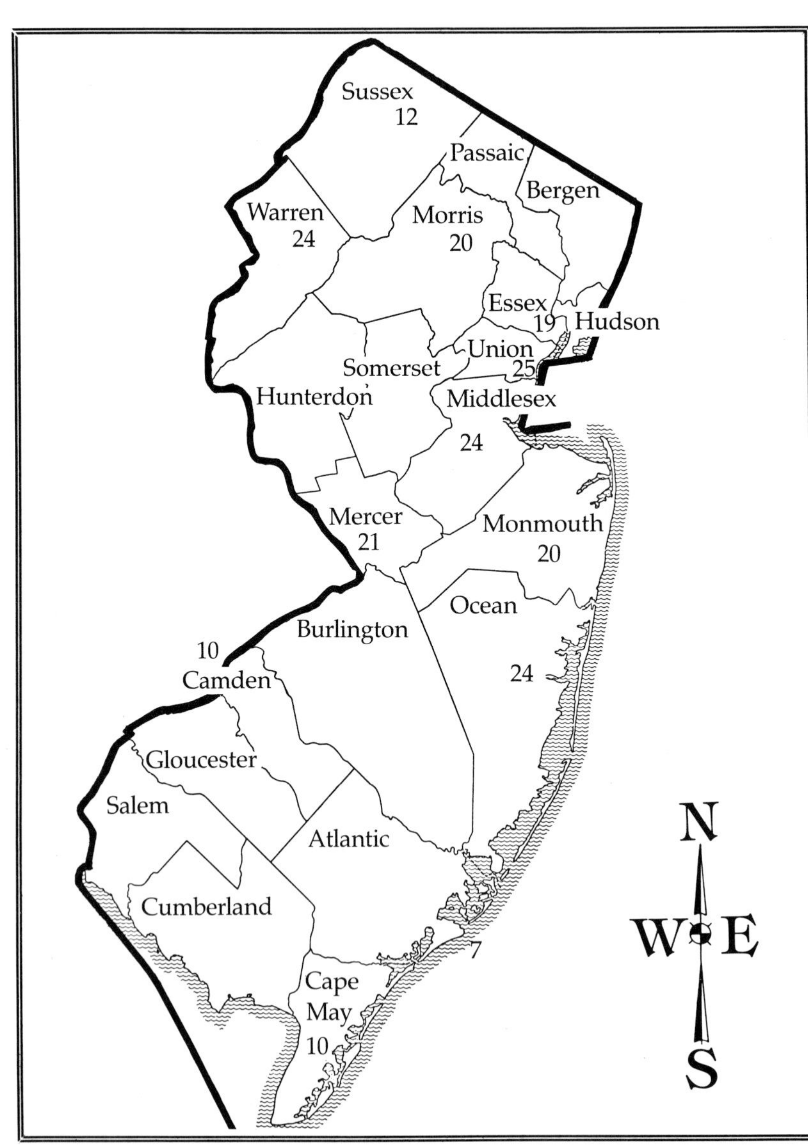


*Blizzard of March 11–14, 1888*

### New York City

March 11. Cloudy during the morning; light rain began at 12:50 p.m. and ended at 2:50 p.m.; began again at 3:25 p.m. and ended at 4:57 p.m.; began again at 6:45 p.m. and continued.

March 12. The light rain turned into snow at 12:10 a.m. and continued through the day, with high northwesterly winds reaching a maximum velocity of 48 miles an hour (38 corrected).

The high winds began during the early morning. At 3:00 a.m. the anemometer wires were blown down, and owing to the cold weather and severe driving snow it was not possible to get them up and in working order until 10:00 a.m., and only then with the greatest effort. The highest velocity is evidently recorded by the self-register.

The storm is the most severe ever felt in this vicinity. The high winds and fine cutting snow made it almost impossible to travel. Travel by street railway was entirely suspended by 7:00 a.m., and by 8:00 a.m. nearly all business suspended. Railway trains and ferries ceased to run; all vehicles snowbound in the streets and abandoned. Many accidents and one fatal collision occurred on the elevated railroads. At some points the snow had drifted to an elevation of 15 to 20 feet. Snow ploughs that had started to clean the railway tracks were abandoned and buried.

All telegraph and telephone wires in the city were down, and at night the city was left in total darkness.

Trees, signs, and awnings were blown down and light structures scattered in all directions.

The streets are deserted and only a few of the hundreds of thousands that are seen daily on the streets made their appearance. During the night, receiver of standard rain gauge, pattern of '85, was blown away and could not be found.

Snowfall 16.5 inches.

Cloudy sunset.

March 13. The light snow ended at 5:55 a.m.; began again at 1:55 p.m. and ended at 7:05 p.m.; began at 8:15 p.m. in flurrys and continued. High westerly winds throughout the day.

Halyards frozen, impossible to display flags.

People crossing East River on congealed ice.

Railroad still blocked and navigation at a stand still.

Business almost suspended.

Office constantly filled with reporters and the public in general seeking the latest information.

Snowfall 3.0 inches.

Cloudy sunset.

March 14. The light snow ended at 3:40 a.m.; began again 6:25 a.m. and ended 7:15 a.m.; began again 10:40 a.m.; and ended 2:50 p.m.

Fresh to brisk northwesterly winds throughout the day.

Ice floating in North and East rivers.

Business reviving; railroads still blocked by snow, but clearing tracks rapidly.

Ferries running regularly.

Snowfall 1.4 inches.

Yellow sunset.

Philadelphia: 11th, light rain began at 8:45 a.m. and during the evening changed to heavy rain; wind, northeast; barometer falling rapidly; at 11:15 p.m. the heavy rain changed to snow, wind north. The storm continued with great severity during the night of the 11–12th, the fierce north wind, blinding snow, and rapidly falling temperature causing suspension of street railway traffic. Throughout the day the wind ranged from 30 to 60 miles per hour, the maximum occurring at 10:30 a.m. The most enterprising street railway companies were unable to resume traffic until noon of the 13th.

At the Breakwater, out of forty vessels in the harbor on the 11th, only thirteen escaped damage or destruction, and thirty or more lives were lost. The damage sustained at the Breakwater and to marine interests is estimated at half a million dollars, but, vast as is this sum, it became inconsiderable when compared with the losses sustained by the several railroad companies, the least part of which, being the interruption to travel. This storm is considered the most disastrous that has ever visited this locality.

# South Jersey's Greatest Snowstorm: The Blizzard of '99

The weather map became very active in early February 1899, with successive surges of arctic air pouring south from Canada and storm systems forming over the southeastern states and moving northward. Two coastal storms moved close enough to the New Jersey coast, one on the fifth, and one on the seventh-eighth to drop moderate-to-heavy snows. Accumulations ranged from about 8 inches (20 cm) in the north to over 12 inches (30 cm) in the south.

Following these wintry visitations, bitter arctic airstreams powered by high pressure of great magnitude over central Canada drove the mercury below zero in all parts of New Jersey. On the tenth, thermometers ranged from −17°F (−27°C) at Sussex to −3°F (−19°C) at Cape May. It was probably the coldest morning, state-wide, ever experienced.

The anticyclone over the plains and prairies increased to 31.15 inches (105.5 kPa) on the morning of the eleventh. At the same time a wave on an old front in the Gulf of Mexico was throwing a canopy of snow along the Gulf Coast, while another disturbance off north Florida was producing a mixture of precipitation types along the Georgia and Carolina coasts. These two storm systems moved northeast during the next forty-eight hours to positions north and south of Cape Cod, giving New Jersey heavy precipitation over a 52-hour period.

Snow depths were generally heavier in southern and central sections than in northern. Amounts of 20 inches (51 cm) or more fell south of a line from Hightstown to Asbury Park, with totals of 24–26 inches (61–66 cm) being common. The greatest depths were in the extreme south, where reports were in excess of 30 inches (76 cm).

The United States Weather Bureau station at Cape May reported a total fall of new snow of 34 inches (86 cm) as follows: 9.0 on February 12, 20 on the thirteenth, and 5.0 on the fourteenth. The snow started at Cape May at 7:45 P.M. on the eleventh and ended at 2:00 A.M. on the fourteenth.* The total depth on the ground at the end was 41.0 inches (104 cm). The barometer dropped to 29.48 inches (99.8 kPa) at 8:00 P.M. on the thirteenth and the maximum wind was 40 miles per hour (64 km/h) (corrected).

The *State Gazette*'s dispatch from Cape May read:

> The snow storm after raging fifty-two and one-quarter hours, ceased early this morning, after forty-one inches had fallen. The wind blew from the northwest last night

*Snowfall was measured daily at 8:00 P.M. The 5.0 inches attributed to the fourteenth fell mainly in late evening of the thirteenth.

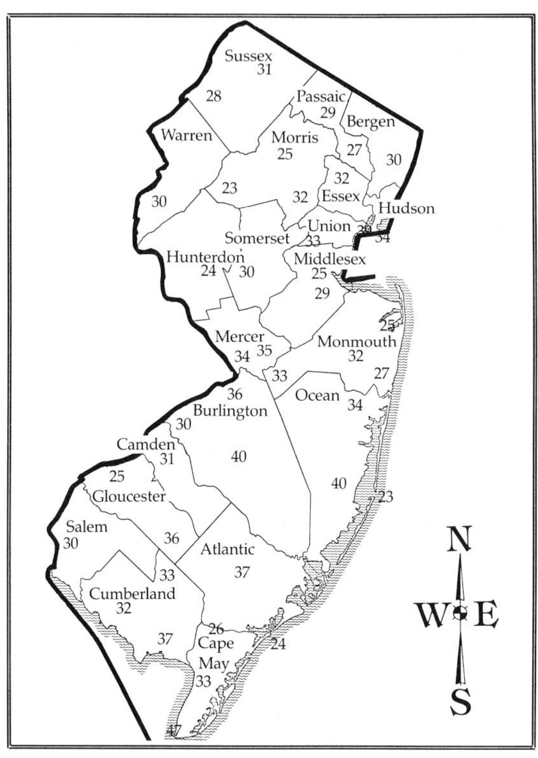


*The greatest snow depths state-wide on record, February 6–7 and February 12–14, 1899*

at fifty miles per hour. No trains in; one started out but reached only 0.75 mile from Cape May. Pier at Cape May Point completely destroyed; other damage confined to broken-down roofs. . . .

The edge of the ocean as far as the eye can see is a mass of ice.

# North Jersey's Deepest: The Post-Christmas Storm of 1947

At noontime on Christmas Day 1947 the northeastern United States lay under a ridge of high pressure; a trough of low pressure extended south from the Great Lakes. Skies over northern New Jersey were sunny and the temperature hovered just above freezing. All appeared serene on the weather map with the exception of a small storm center off the Georgia coast. The New York City forecaster on duty that holiday afternoon looked for "increasing cloudiness, some snow likely after midnight. . . . Friday—light snow ending in forenoon followed by partial clearing."

During the afternoon and evening there were several developments. The high pressure over New York and New England continued slowly eastward, as did the upper-air trough over the Great Lakes. The latter increased greatly in depth and developed a strong southerly flow aloft along the Atlantic seaboard. This steered the low-pressure center off the South Atlantic coast northward, rather than on a normal northeast track, and stimulated its development into an energetic storm center. After passing near Cape Hatteras, the deepening center was off the Virginia Capes at midnight, heading on a track that would pass about 150 miles (241 km) off the South Jersey coast soon after sunrise.

During the daylight hours of December 26, the center came under the influence of the high pressure to the northeast, which began to exert a blocking influence on its forward progress. This first slowed and then stalled the forward progress of the storm center while causing it to deepen eventually to a pressure of 29.24 inches (99.0 kPa). When it was south of Long Island the center spread out in an elliptical form with a west-to-east axis. This kept the moisture-laden wind with a long ocean fetch blowing over the metropolitan area and North Jersey during the afternoon and early evening hours, continuing the heavy snowfall many hours longer than normal in a coastal storm.

The first flakes filtered down in New York City at 3:20 A.M. on Friday and continued for twenty-three hours forty-five minutes until 3:05 A.M. on the twenty-seventh. By 7:00 P.M. on the twenty-sixth the depth of the new snow amounted to 24 inches (61 cm); thereafter the fall became light, with only another 1.8 inches (4.6 cm) being added. The snow fell at the heavy rate of 2.0 inches (5.0 cm) an hour during midafternoon.

The temperature during the storm ranged from 24°F (−4°C) at 7:00 A.M. on the twenty-sixth to 30°F (−1°C) at 11:00 A.M.; thereafter it remained near 29°F (−2°C) until the end of the storm. The lowest sea-level pressure at New York City reached 29.41 inches (99.6 kPa). The prevailing wind came from the north and northeast until 1:00 P.M. on the twenty-sixth, when it shifted to northwest as the storm center reached the latitude of New York City in the waters off Long Island. The maximum wind speed during the storm period was 36 miles per hour (58 km/h) from the northwest at about 8:53 P.M. on the twenty-sixth.

The zone of heaviest snow—20 inches (51 cm) or more—covered all New Jersey's northeast counties and extended westward in a strip that included Hackettstown, High Bridge, and Phillipsburg; to the north and northwest amounts diminished. South of New Brunswick there was also a sharp drop-off: Trenton, 8 inches (20 cm), Mount Holly, 7 inches (18 cm), Hammonton, 7 inches (18 cm), and Atlantic City, 6 inches (15 cm). The greatest amounts were concentrated in northeast Monmouth County close to New York harbor and the ocean, where 30 inches (76 cm) were measured at Long Branch, Keyport, and Red Bank.

# The Spring "Blizzard" of 1982

During its transcontinental journey in the first week of April 1982, a storm system from the Pacific Ocean earned the title of "a multitalented storm" from weathermen. A variety of weather extremes attended its passage from California through the Ohio Valley, and across Virginia on the fifth. It began to influence New Jersey soon after midnight on the sixth when precipitation started to fall in the western counties.

Upon reaching the Virginia–Maryland coast, the deepening center "turned the corner" to the northeast and drew increasing energy from the relatively warm waters of the Atlantic Ocean. The light precipitation became moderate to heavy, and rain over the north-central section turned to snow as a strong northeast air flow brought in colder air. The storm center underwent great intensification during the sixth, reaching a very low barometer reading of 28.56 inches (96.7 kPa) when off the coast of Maine. Near blizzard conditions developed and continued for forty-eight hours.

*Ashland Avenue, looking toward William Street in East Orange on December 26, 1947, after New Jersey's deepest snowfall. (From the collection of the East Orange Public Library)*

The depth of snowfall in New Jersey was influenced by a number of factors—latitude, elevation, nearness to the ocean, type of surface, and soil temperature. The southern counties had only rain below 40°N latitude, roughly from Philadelphia to Barnegat. McGuire Air Force Base reported 1.0 inch (2.5 cm) of snow and Lakehurst 2.0 inches (5.0 cm). To the north and east most of the precipitation fell in the form of snow with little surface melting. The top figure reported in the state, 14.0 inches (36 cm), was from the cooperative station at High Point. The New Jersey Weather Observers, a group of weather fans, reported 13 inches (33 cm) or more at Glen Rock, Elmwood Park, Parsippany, North Caldwell, and Verona, and over 12 inches (30 cm) at Lodi and Harrison. Newark Airport measured 11.0 inches (28 cm) and Central Park in New York City, 9.6 inches (24 cm).

# The Snowiest Winter of the Twentieth Century: 1960–1961

## The Prewinter Storm of December 1960

The snowstorm of December 11–12 brought from 7 to 21 inches (18 to 53 cm) of snow to New Jersey, with winds from 28 to 55 miles per hour (45 to 89 km/h). This was the greatest state-wide snowstorm so early in the season. In some localities it was the greatest snowfall of record for any month during a period of twenty-four hours or less. Persistently strong winds caused much drifting of the snow. Bitterly cold weather followed the snowstorm. Fifty-two deaths were attributed to the storm, most of them due to exposure, exhaustion, and heart attacks from overexertion. Only one traffic death was reported during the storm, although a few traffic fatalities resulted from accidents on icy roads after the storm. Pre-Christmas shopping was halted; banks, stores, and industrial plants were closed. Some schools remained shut for the entire week.

Snowfall was heaviest in a southwest-northeast band across the central part of the state, with 15 to 21 inches (38 to 53 cm) falling from Burlington northeast to Bergen. The greatest amount was reported at Newark, with 21.4 inches (54 cm), and there were 20-inch (51 cm) reports in Union and southern Passaic counties. Millville in the south had only 6 inches (15 cm) and Atlantic City 7.5 inches (19 cm).

# The Kennedy Inaugural Storm of January 1961

The snowstorm of January 19–20 dumped up to 14 inches (36 cm) over the southern and central portions and from up to 26 inches (66 cm) over the northern part of the state. A few places in the extreme south reported less than 10 inches (25 cm); in the extreme north maximum readings of 26.4 and 24.0 inches (67 and 61 cm) were reported in unofficial records. Winds exceeding 35 miles per hour (56 km/h) in most localities caused considerable drifting. Bitter cold weather followed the storm, with minimum temperatures dropping to near zero nearly every night during the following week. Maximum temperatures remained below freezing until early February, making for the most prolonged cold spell since the turn of the century. One traffic fatality occurred during the storm. Several deaths and injuries were indirectly attributable to the storm.

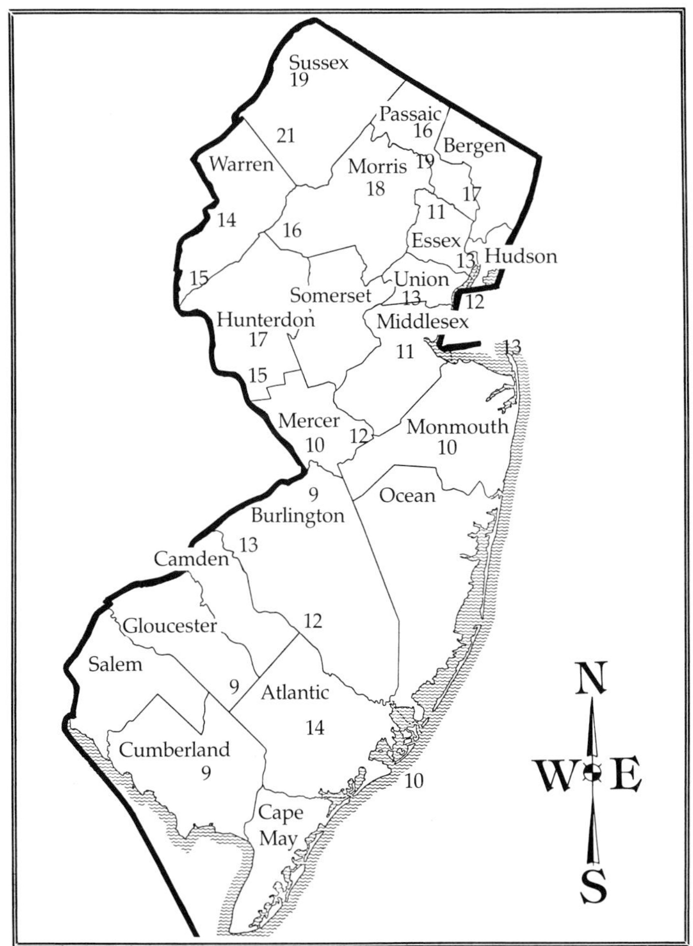


*Kennedy inaugural storm, January 19–20, 1961*

## February 1961

The third major snowstorm of this snowiest of modern winters was the most disruptive. Strong gale-force winds caused great drifting. The dividing line between heavy and overwhelming snowfall ran from north of Trenton to New York Bay. Though Trenton reported only 8 inches (20 cm), New Brunswick had 20.8 inches (53 cm) and Newark 22.6 inches (57 cm). Amounts farther north ranged up to 24 inches (61 cm) at Flemington, where the cover on the morning of February 5 was 48 inches (122 cm). Even greater depths were reported at Layton (50 inches, or 127 cm) and Canistear Reservoir (52 inches, or 132 cm); these were the greatest snow depths of record at these stations.

Newark's total snowfall of 73.5 inches (187 cm) for the 1960–1961 season was the greatest of record at Newark Airport and was exceeded in old city records only by the 75.0 inches (191 cm) that fell in 1867–1868.

# Early and Late Snowfalls

Early and late snowfalls elicit particular interest from the public, often raising questions as to whether the climate is changing. Records over the years show that a measurable snowfall in October or May is a rarity indeed. In the very recent past, however, New Jersey received a May snowfall in 1978 and an October one in 1979.

*A dramatic view of Broad Street in Newark during the fire and snowstorm of February 4–5, 1846. (Collection of the Newark Museum)*

## Early Snowfalls

1703 OCTOBER 8 The earliest snowfall of record dates back to 1703, when an apparent coastal storm spread a covering of white from southeast Pennsylvania to Boston. Isaac Norris's diary told of the storm at Philadelphia on September 27 (Old Style) or October 8 (New Style): "We have had a fall of snow and the northwest wind blows very hard." No amount was mentioned, nor has any report of its occurrence from a northern New Jersey source been found. At Boston "from three to four inches" fell, according to Samuel Sewall's diary.

1859 OCTOBER 26–27 The Great October snow of the nineteenth century occurred in 1859, when northern sections received a substantial covering. In New York City the depth was given as about four inches, while William Whitehead in Newark reported his measurement at three inches. The Erasmus Hall record in Brooklyn gave some details: "Snow from eight in the evening, wind west light, continuing quite moderately until eight next morning, about four inches in depth." The appearance of sleighs was reported on Staten Island.

On five occasions during the period of coordinated weather records in New Jersey memorable October snows have fallen in some part of the state.

1925 OCTOBER 30 "The weather of October 1925 in New Jersey will go into the records as being the stormiest since the systematic compilation of data. . . . To produce a sensational climax to what was already a notable month, snow fell practically throughout the State on the 30th from morning to early night, amounting from a trace to five inches. The 31st dawned showing trees and shrubs in full foliage draped under a spectacular snow covering. The snowstorm probably exceeds all October records back to that of October 1859. In northwestern counties there was sufficient snow on the 22d to arouse comment," wrote the state climatologist. Layton and Culvers Lake in the north reported 4.0 inches, Bergen Point in the central section 3.5 inches, and Indian Mills in the south 3.0 inches. Shore points had only a trace.

1940 OCTOBER 19–20 "The snow cover in central and southwestern New Jersey accumulated to a depth of one to three inches on exposed objects, though it was much less on the ground because of soil warmth. Evergreens and trees had the appearance of midwinter. This was the heaviest snowfall ever recorded in these parts so early in the season. Oddly enough, the snowfall was much lighter in the extreme north with most stations recording only a trace," reported the state summary. Merchantville near Camden had the greatest measurement—3.1 inches. Amounts of 2.0 inches were general over the south. Philadelphia had 2.2 inches, Trenton 0.5 inch, and Newark only a trace.

1952 OCTOBER 20 Measurable snow fell over the northern counties: Charlotteburg had 1.0 inch, Morris Plains 1.3 inches, Newton 1.0 inch. At Trenton "the snow continued for nearly two hours and was very heavy part of the time." (*Climatological Data: New Jersey Section*)

1972 OCTOBER 18–19 Snowfall reported in all counties during the night. Canistear Reservoir, in Sussex County, measured the greatest amount—3.5 inches. Snowfall was also substantial in the Trenton area, where one station reported 2.4 inches. Long Valley in Morris County had 2.0 inches, as did Woodstown in Salem County.

1979 OCTOBER 10 A snowstorm spread northward over the interior from West Virginia to central New England. All locations except the coast and southeastern New Jersey received measurable amounts. It was heaviest in the north: Oak Ridge Reservoir had 5.5 inches, Long Valley 5.0 inches, and High Point 4.0 inches. In the central section, Hightstown reported 1.6 inches and Pemberton 1.0 inch. Trenton had 0.1 inch and Cape May a trace.

## Late Snowfalls

1774 MAY 4 New York City: "Wednesday Last [4th] we had a smart snowstorm and the weather colder than ever was known by the oldest man living here, at this season of the year; which we are afraid will be very destructive to peaches, apricots, etc." (*New York Gazette & Weekly Mercury*, May 9, 1774)

Woodbury: "In 5 mo 1774 a snow fell somewhat similar to this (1803) but not so great." (*Samuel Mickle's Diary*)

1803 MAY 8 Woodbury: "Trees and bushes bending under weight of a wet snow. Many boughs broken down, and had to saw off many broken ones, Trees mostly in large leaves and blossoms." (*Samuel Mickle's Diary*)

Belleville: "This morning cut a mess of asparagus—the beds covered with Snow." (Gerard Rutgers's diary)

1812 MAY 4 Newark: "We mention it as a circumstance uncommonly rare, that yesterday noon the gardens and fields were covered with snow. The snow commenced falling in the morning and continued to 5 o'clock P.M. Had the weather been so cold as to prevent the snow's melting, (in part) it would have probably been 5 inches deep. Some kinds of vegetation and peach trees in particular, (which are in blossom) will be materially injured if it should blow off freezing cold." (*Centinel of Freedom* [Newark], May 5, 1812)

1874 APRIL 25–29 April 1874 was the coldest fourth month in the history of New York City's thermometer records, dating from 1822. The mean of 41.3°F was 7.8°F degrees below the long-term normal. A major storm raged over New Jersey from April 14 to April 17, with heavy snow falling over central and northern sections. This was followed by another extended storm from the twenty-fifth to the twenty-ninth. The *Sussex Register* took notice: "The storm of 1874 began on April 25th with a mixture of snow, hail and rain, which reached an equivalent of 15 inches. On the 28th and 29th this was followed by a storm which left over two feet of snow, notwithstanding the shrinkage when it reached a warmer atmosphere than that at which it was formed. It froze hard on the night of the 30th. Sleds and sleighs were running on the 29th and 30th, but it wasn't first-class traveling. Spots of bare ground were seen on May 2d, and on May 10th the mercury stood at 89 degrees in the shade."

1977 MAY 9 "Rain, sleet and snow reported on the afternoon of the 9th especially northern counties up to 4 inches was reported in north east Sussex County," according to the *New Jersey Weekly Digest* of the Department of Agriculture. The following were reported in *Climatological Data:* Canistear Reservoir, 1.0 inch; traces at Charlotteburg, Newark, Plainfield, Atlantic City Airport, Hightstown, New Brunswick, Trenton, Long Branch, Tuckerton, Woodstown, and New York City. Philadelphia reported none. Minimum of 23°F at High Point State Park.

# The Winter of Little Snowfall: 1918–1919

Sandwiched between two winters of outstanding severity came the winter of 1918–1919, with the least snowfall since records were started in 1885. The average total for the entire state was only 4.6 inches (12 cm). The greatest amount reported at any station in one month was 9.1 inches (23 cm) at Culvers Lake in February. The temperature for the winter, December through March, averaged 4.5°F (2.5°C) above normal; the departures for the individual months were: December +4.6°F (2.6°C), January +4.3°F (2.4°C), and February +3.5°F (1.9°C). March, too, ran well above normal, with a departure of +5.7°F (3.2°C).

# The Winter of the Least Snow: 1972–1973

South of a line from Trenton across to Asbury Park, the winter of 1972–1973 was practically snowless. In some locations more snow fell in October than in all the remaining months of the winter combined. Trenton had a record 2.5 inches (6 cm) in October, but only 0.7 inch (1.8 cm) afterward. Newark's winter total was only 1.9 inches (5 cm) and New Brunswick's 3.4 inches (9 cm). In the south, Millville, Moorestown, and Toms River reported only a trace for the entire winter. The greatest amounts for 1972–1973 were in the north, where Oak Ridge Reservoir led all stations with a season's total of 25.5 inches (65 cm). Canistear Reservoir and Sussex each reported 22 inches (56 cm). The only substantial snowstorm of the entire winter came on January 29, when about 12 inches (30 cm) fell over the northern highlands. For the state as a whole, snow for the winter averaged 3.9 inches (10 cm), of which 2.0 inches (5 cm) came in January.

# Old-Fashioned Winters

Newark possesses the longest snowfall records in the New York metropolitan area. They were started by William Whitehead in 1843 and continued to his death in 1884. Frederick Ricord, George Sonn, and William Weiner carried on through 1924. A gap in the official records from 1924 to 1931 has been filled by the Elizabeth observations taken at nearby Newark Airport. Since 1931 the records have been made at Newark Airport.

Was it snowier in the "good old days" of the mid-nineteenth century? If the Newark records are representative, the answer is yes. From 1843 through 1870, the Whitehead estimates for snowfall at Newark show an annual average fall of 43.8 inches (111 cm); the modern average for Newark Airport is 28.4 inches (72 cm), 65 percent of the earlier figure.

Over the years, the snowiest times were the two decades from the winter of 1850–1851 to 1869–1870, with an average of 46.6 inches (118 cm). Only four winters had more than 70 inches (178 cm): 1853–1854, 1867–1868, 1906–1907, and 1960–1961. In the past decade, the snowiest winter was that of 1977–1978, with 64.9 inches (165 cm).

The two decades from 1920–1921 to 1939–1940 were the least snowy period, with an average of only 25 inches (64 cm). Warm winters marked much of the first half of the present century. In fact, for the five winters from 1927–1928 to 1931–1932, the average was only 9.8 inches (25 cm). Other periods in recent years with little snowfall extended from 1949–1950 to 1954–1955 and from 1970–1971 to 1975–1976.

*Commuters fight snow and slush in Newark. (Courtesy of Newark Public Library)*

## Newark Snowfall: 1843–1982

| Snowiest months | | | Snowiest seasons | | Least snowy seasons | | Biggest storms | |
|---|---|---|---|---|---|---|---|---|
| Inches | Month | Year | Inches | Season | Inches | Season | Inches | Date |
| 3.0 | October | 1859 | 75.2 | 1867–1868 | 1.9 | 1972–1973 | 26.0 | December 26–27, 1947 |
| 23.0 | November | 1898 | 73.5 | 1960–1961 | 4.5 | 1918–1919 | 23.9 | March 16–19, 1956* |
| 29.1 | December | 1947 | 71.0 | 1853–1854 | 7.3 | 1931–1932 | 22.6 | February 3–4, 1961 |
| 35.7 | January | 1925 | 70.0 | 1906–1907 | 9.6 | 1900–1901 | 20.4 | December 11–12, 1960 |
| 31.7 | February | 1926 | 68.0 | 1872–1873 | 10.7 | 1949–1950 | 20.0 | February 4–5, 1845 |
| 26.0 | March | 1956 | 65.0 | 1855–1856 | 10.9 | 1950–1951 | 20.0 | January 5–6, 1856 |
| 15.8 | April | 1915 | 64.9 | 1977–1978 | 11.0 | 1936–1937 | 20.0 | December 20, 1875 |
| Trace | May | 1977 | 63.5 | 1898–1899 | 11.1 | 1937–1938 | 20.0 | February 4–5, 1907 |
| | | | 63.0 | 1851–1852 | 12.2 | 1877–1878 | 19.6 | February 6–7, 1978 |
| | | | 62.5 | 1866–1867 | 13.7 | 1954–1955 | 19.0 | March 12–14, 1888 |
| | | | 62.5 | 1947–1948 | | | | |

*5.7 inches fell on March 16–17, and 18.2 inches on March 18–19, with a break of no snowfall between these two dates.

## Newark Airport Snowfall: 1931–1982

| Snowiest months | | | Snowiest seasons | | Least snowy seasons | |
|---|---|---|---|---|---|---|
| Inches | Month | Year | Inches | Season | Inches | Season |
| 0.3 | October | 1952 | 73.5 | 1960–1961 | 1.9 | 1972–1973 |
| 14.2 | November | 1938 | 64.9 | 1977–1978 | 7.3 | 1931–1932 |
| 29.1 | December | 1947 | 62.5 | 1947–1948 | 10.7 | 1949–1950 |
| 27.4 | January | 1978 | 58.3 | 1957–1958 | 10.9 | 1950–1951 |
| 26.4 | February | 1934 | 57.3 | 1966–1967 | 11.0 | 1936–1937 |
| 26.0 | March | 1956 | 43.2 | 1963–1964 | 11.1 | 1937–1938 |
| 11.0 | April | 1982 | 42.1 | 1933–1934 | 13.7 | 1954–1955 |
| Trace | May | 1977 | 41.2 | 1948–1949 | 13.9 | 1941–1942 |
| | | | 40.2 | 1955–1956 | 13.9 | 1967–1968 |
| | | | 39.0 | 1940–1941 | 14.0 | 1953–1954 |

NOTE: The only winter in records prior to 1931 to exceed the 1960–1961 figure is that of 1867–1868, with 75.2 inches. The least snowy winter prior to 1931 was 1918–1919, with 4.5 inches. Normal, 1942–1978 = 28.4 inches.

## Trenton Snowfall: 1866–1982*

| Snowiest months | | | Snowiest seasons | | Least snowy seasons | | Biggest storms | |
|---|---|---|---|---|---|---|---|---|
| Inches | Month | Year | Inches | Season | Inches | Season | Inches | Date |
| 2.5 | October | 1972 | 63.0 | 1867–1868 | 2.0 | 1918–1919 | 22.0 | February 12–13, 1899 |
| 14.0 | November | 1898 | 61.0 | 1898–1899 | 3.3 | 1972–1973 | 21.0 | March 12–13, 1888 |
| 21.5 | December | 1960 | 54.0 | 1966–1967 | 3.8 | 1949–1950 | 18.0 | December 26, 1872 |
| 20.8 | January | 1978 | 51.7 | 1957–1958 | 5.1 | 1930–1931 | 17.8 | March 19–21, 1958 |
| 34.0 | February | 1899 | 51.3 | 1977–1978 | 5.2 | 1931–1932 | 16.6 | December 11–12, 1960 |
| 22.5 | March | 1888 | 48.5 | 1960–1961 | 5.6 | 1950–1951 | 16.0 | April 3–4, 1915 |
| 16.0 | April | 1915 | 42.5** | 1887–1888 | 7.3 | 1937–1938 | 16.0 | February 6–7, 1978 |
| Trace | May | 1977 | 40.9 | 1922–1923 | 7.6 | 1905–1906 | 14.3 | March 3–5, 1956 |
| | | | 40.1 | 1933–1934 | 8.7 | 1929–1930 | 14.0 | January 25, 1905 |
| | | | 38.8 | 1955–1956 | 8.9 | 1941–1942 | 13.8 | February 20–22, 1922 |
| | | | | | | | 13.8 | February 6–7, 1967 |

NOTE: Normal 1941–1980 = 23.5 inches.

*The years 1881 to 1887 are missing from the Trenton record. A comparison with New Brunswick data shows that only December 1883, with 25.0 inches, exceeds any of the above figures.

**Does not include October–December 1887.

**Atlantic City Snowfall: 1884–1958, and Atlantic City Airport (Pomona) Snowfall: 1958–1979**

| Snowiest months | | | Snowiest seasons | | Least snowy seasons | | Biggest storms | |
|---|---|---|---|---|---|---|---|---|
| Inches | Month | Year | Inches | Season | Inches | Season | Inches | Date |
| Trace | October | 1972 | 46.9 | 1966–1967 | 0.4 | 1972–1973 | 18.0 | February 16–17, 1902 |
| 16.7 | November | 1898 | 40.4 | 1904–1905 | 0.7 | 1949–1950 | 17.0 | February 18–19, 1979 |
| 17.5 | December | 1935 | 38.1 | 1963–1964 | 1.5 | 1918–1919 | 16.2 | February 28–March 1, 1941 |
| 22.3 | January | 1905 | 37.3 | 1933–1934 | 2.4 | 1937–1938 | 16.0 | January 25, 1905 |
| 35.2 | February | 1967 | 34.0 | 1892–1893 | 2.7 | 1950–1951 | 15.1 | February 11–13, 1899 |
| 23.6 | March | 1914 | 33.7 | 1901–1902 | 3.0 | 1948–1949 | 14.7 | January 12–13, 1964 |
| 6.0 | April | 1915 | 33.5 | 1913–1914 | 3.3 | 1941–1942 | 14.0 | February 13–15, 1885 |
| | | | 33.5 | 1957–1958 | 3.8 | 1944–1945 | 14.0 | November 26–27, 1898 |
| | | | 32.3 | 1960–1961 | 3.9 | 1931–1932 | 13.1 | February 9–10, 1967 |
| | | | 29.8 | 1935–1936 | 4.7 | 1920–1921 | 13.0 | December 21, 1900 |

NOTE: Normal 1945–1980 = 16.0 inches.

# Ice Storms

To the extent it can disrupt modern living, winter's worst menace is a freezing rain that coats all objects in a sheath of ice. The power outages such an ice storm can cause mean inconvenience, even hardship and suffering; often a severance of normal communications adds to the malaise of the situation.

An ice storm occurs when rain droplets from aloft in an above-freezing layer of air fall through a shallow below-freezing layer near the surface of the earth. The vertical depth of the lower layer determines just what form the ice will take. If the layer is relatively deep, the descending rain droplet will have time to freeze into a solid pellet. This is known, technically, as a *sleet storm* or *ice-pellet storm*. A storm of this type is accompanied by the rattle of pellets on windows or other objects. They may accumulate on the ground and eventually adhere to each other in an icy mass.

A true ice storm occurs when the rain droplets fall through a relatively shallow depth of freezing air and do not freeze until they touch an object such as a tree, pole, or structure. A clear icy sheath, known technically as *glaze*, forms around branches and wires; if the accumulation continues, the increasing weight of the ice may cause branches and wires to break and entire trees or poles to fall. Heavy ice loads have been known to topple high utility- and radio-and-television-transmission towers.

Sometimes both snow pellets and glaze occur during the same storm, and often snowflakes are intermixed with the falling precipitation. Then very thick diameters of frozen material may cling to outdoor objects and greatly increase the ice load, creating fantastic forms and shapes. Despite the damage and inconvenience resulting from a clear ice storm, it can present a most spectacular scene when the rays of a rising sun cause thousands of spangles to glitter from each ice-coated tree and shrub.

Freezing rain can develop under a variety of weather-map situations. Usually there is an anticyclone to the north or northeast and a cyclonic disturbance at the surface to the south or southwest. The upper-air trough of low pressure lies west of New Jersey, with a flow of warm, moist air at intermediate levels supplying one of the main needed ingredients—a layer of above-freezing air aloft. This overruns the cooler air at the surface and initiates the precipitation process. Freezing rain has occurred with the surface temperature as low as 11°F (−12°C).

All sections of New Jersey, from High Point to Cape May, have been subject from time to time to the rigors of an ice storm. Their occurrence depends on the distribution of the pressure systems regionally and the structure of the atmosphere locally. The prevailing temperature, of course, is the chief determinant. The state is often divided into several zones with different types of precipitation present in each. A cold rain may be falling over the southern portion of the state, freezing rain over the central section, and snow over the northern counties as a coastal storm moves northeastward not far offshore. The distance from the passing storm center is often the crucial factor in determining the temperatures of and type of precipitation from a winter storm.

Having normally a lower temperature on most winter days, the north has a greater chance of an ice storm occurring. Elevation, too, plays a role in lowering the temperature to just below freezing to cause ice to form on hilltops while valley locations remain above freezing. Often a difference of only one or two hundred feet can make the difference between liquid rain and adhering ice. Essex County's Orange Mountains, with an elevation of only two hundred feet above the valley, have on occasion been locked in an icy sheath while valley residents have experienced nothing except wet rain.

Severe ice storms seem to occur somewhere in the state about once every ten years, but hardly a winter goes by that an area does not have some ice forming that causes minor inconveniences. Damaging ice storms have occurred somewhere in New Jersey on the following dates during the past thirty years:

December 31, 1947–January 1, 1948
January 8–11, 1953
December 16–17, 1956
February 13–14, 1960
February 19, 1962

December 30–31, 1969
December 12–13, 1970
April 7, 1972
December 16–17, 1973
January 3–4, 1974
February 2–4, 1974
January 13–14, 1978

## The Ice Storm of January 5, 1873

The storm's severity was noted even in the metropolis across the river:

> The storm in New Jersey caused great damage. The trees in some of the finest streets and parks in the State were almost entirely ruined, and the damage to fruit trees throughout the State is irreparable. A few accidents from falling branches are reported, but none of a serious character. In the parks of Jersey City and Newark broken branches and prostrated trunks quite cover the ground in many places. The walk from Orange Valley to Newark, which many were compelled to perform, was said to be like tramping through an old forest. By far the greatest injury was done to the telegraph companies, whose wires in many places were thrown down, covered with a sheeting of ice, poles broken, and communication generally suspended. The police and fire-alarm telegraphs in Jersey City were out of order yesterday and last night.
>
> New York Times,
> *January 6, 1873*

## The Ice Storm of February 21–22, 1902

> The ice and sleet storm of the 21st and 22nd was the most destructive we have any record of. All telegraph, telephone, traction and electric light wires were prostrated for several days, and thousands of shade and fruit trees were seriously injured by having the top branches broken off by the weight of ice. The rivers, too, overflowed their banks, and did great damage in the vicinity of Paterson, Bound Brook, and other points.

### Observers' Notes

Bergen Point.—Severe storms of snow, sleet and rain, accompanied by strong gales, characterized the month. Great damage done to trees, telegraph and telephone lines.

Roseland.—On 22nd the trees were covered with ice, which was not entirely off until noon of the 24th; many trees broken.

Lambertville.—Severe ice storm 21st and 22nd did serious damage to telegraph, telephone and electric light wires, and seriously interfered with traffic on railroads.

New Egypt.—The heavy storm of sleet on 21st did great damage to all kinds of trees.

Chester.—The snowstorm of 17th filled the roads full of snow, and on the 21st and 22nd the sleet did great injury to trees, fences and telegraph poles; many of the latter broken down.

Somerville.—The town wore a sorrowful look this morning (22nd); so many of our beautiful shade trees with their top branches broken off by the heavy sleet. Telegraph and telephone lines suffered severely.

Trenton.—The sleet of 21st did great damage to all kinds of trees.

Rancocas.—There were three remarkable storms during the last half of the month. The heavy snow on 17th drifted badly, blocking the roads; that of 21st broke trees down with the weight of ice—such devastation has never been seen here before. The town looked as though a tornado had struck it. Pine forests suffered great damage. The storm of 28th was a tropical thundershower, the rainfall measuring 1.12 inches.

Plainfield.—The storm of 21st was disastrous in this section of the State. Trees, telephone, telegraph and electric light wires down and badly tangled.

Dover.—Great damage done by sleet on 22nd.

Climate and Crops:
New Jersey Section

# The Ice Storm of January 8–10, 1953

In the Pocono Mountains of Pennsylvania ice accumulations were generally from 1 to 2.5 inches (25 to 64 mm), with extremes reported at 4.37 inches (111 mm). A length of wire 15 inches (38 cm) long weighed nearly two pounds (0.9 kg) and circumferences reached 10 to 13 inches (25 to 33 cm). In the Catskills of New York ice accumulated to 2 to 3 inches (51 to 76 mm). Accumulations in Sussex County probably approached these figures, though no actual measurements appear to have been made.

> Except for mildness, the most unusual feature of the weather in January was the severe glaze storm of the 8–10th over the northern one-third of the State. Though there was some sleet on the 8th, the heavy glaze was mostly due to freezing rain which began in some areas on the 8th and continued to the 10th. There were many traffic and other accidents. Very heavy damage was caused to communication and power lines. 70,000 homes and business places were reported without electricity, and approximately 30,000 telephones were out of use. It took more than a week to completely restore utilities to service in all localities. Damage to utility companies was estimated at $1,000,000. There was also heavy damage to orchards and forest trees due to breaking of ice-laden limbs. Damage of this kind probably amounted to half a million dollars. In some localities the icy conditions did not disappear until the 11th. It was one of the worst ice storms of record in this State.
>
> Climatological Data:
> New Jersey Section

# Cold Waves

The term *cold wave* describes a rapid drop in temperature within a twenty-four-hour period. A cold wave warning means substantially increased protection needed for agricultural, industrial, commercial, or social activities. The amount of the temperature drop and the minimum temperature required to justify cold wave warnings vary in different sections of the United States. As might be expected, there are different criteria for North Jersey and South Jersey because of the different degree of continentality in their basic climates. There are seasonal differences in the requirements, too. The high-winter period runs from December 16 to February 15. The prewinter period of November 15 to December 15 has the same figures as the late-winter period from February 16 to March 15. There are also limits for the spring-summer-fall period from March 16 to November 15.

Our winter cold waves are born in the interior of Canada. The vast region from central Quebec across Hudson Bay to the tundras of the Northwest Territories becomes locked in snow and ice in late autumn, and this almost uniform expanse serves as a surface to radiate heat to outer space during the long winter nights. The air in the lower layers of the atmosphere becomes colder and colder as it loses heat by night and gains little heat during the day from the low-hanging sun close to the southern horizon. The surface air, becoming denser and denser, causes barometric pressure to build, resulting in the creation of a large anticyclone whose core contains a central dome of very frigid air. Growing colder and colder through nocturnal radiation, these high-pressure areas remain in their northern source region for several days until the movement of a low-pressure system across the United States sets the cold airmass in motion southward.

New Jersey experiences its severest outbreaks of arctic cold when coastal lows move northeast along the Atlantic seaboard and deepen off New England. The intense circulation around these draws the Canadian airstreams southward across the Great Lakes and directly into the Middle Atlantic region. Since we are only about fourteen hundred miles from the center of the source region around Hudson Bay, an airstream traveling at 40 miles per hour would require only about thirty-six hours to reach us. If the ground is snow covered along the route, little modification of its original frigidity takes place. Our coldest temperatures are usually reached on the second night after the arrival of the cold air, following a night with clear skies, little wind, and intense radiation.

A Rutgers University study has shown that the extreme northwest corner of the state can expect a temperature as low as 0°F almost every year, and the entire northwest quarter about once every two years. In the northern section the combined effects of latitude, topography, and elevation create favorable radiational cooling conditions at night, with low temperatures resulting. A secondary zone of low minimum temperatures is found in the Pine Barrens, where the flat terrain and strong radiational quality of the sandy soil result in low readings. The central part of Burlington County can expect a zero reading once every two years. The central and south coast are the least susceptible to zero temperatures, with an expectancy of less than once every ten years. Urban complexes such as Newark and

### Cold Wave Standards

| | Location | |
|---|---|---|
| Dates | North | South |
| 11/16–12/15 | Drop of 20° to minimum of 15°F | Drop of 20° to minimum of 20°F |
| 12/16–2/15 | Drop of 20° to minimum of 10°F | Drop of 20° to minimum of 15°F |
| 2/16–3/15 | Drop of 20° to minimum of 15°F | Drop of 20° to minimum of 20°F |
| 3/16–11/15 | Drop of 20° to minimum of 25°F | Drop of 20° to minimum of 28°F |

Trenton can expect a zero reading only once or twice in ten years as a result of the heat island effect resulting from the retention of heat by buildings and pavements and the reduction of nocturnal radiation by the polluted atmosphere.

## Colonial Cold

Was it colder in colonial times than now, and did thermometers drop to greater extremes? Since there are no thermometer records for New Jersey until the time of the War of Independence, there is no quantitative answer to this question. The settlements of the seventeenth and eighteenth centuries took place, however, in the period known to paleoclimatologists as the Little Ice Age, so named in contrast to many centuries of warmer conditions that had followed the melting of the ice sheet. Glaciers advanced in Europe, and the northern limit of the grain-growing region in the North Atlantic basin retreated southward. We have no concrete evidence of climate conditions in New Jersey during the years of early settlement.

There are references in colonial literature to the cold winters of 1697–1698 and 1740–1741, which were reputed to have been the severest in the pre-Revolutionary period. The main evidence relates to the length of time that rivers and lakes remained frozen and to questionable estimates of snow depths depending on memory. Peter Kalm, a Swedish traveler visiting Philadelphia in the 1750s, heard many references to the severity of these winters. He echoed the prevailing belief that the climate at that time was becoming milder, that winters were not as cold as they used to be, and that the seasons were changing.

The reputations of all previous severe winters and the belief in climate change were erased by the realities of the Hard Winter of 1780 that coincided with one of the darkest periods of the War of Independence, when Washington's troops were housed in log cabins at Morristown. A thermometer at the British headquarters in New York City was reported to have dropped to −16°F (−27°C). If correct, this would be just about equal to the coldest ever registered in the modern period by an official thermometer in New York City: −15°F (−26°C) at the Central Park Observatory on February 9, 1934. The core of the Hard Winter occurred in January, which appears to hold the title of the coldest calendar month in the region's history. David Rittenhouse's thermometer in downtown Philadelphia registered an above-freezing reading on only one day of that month, and tradition has it that the eaves of houses dripped on only one day that month, as well. The Delaware River at Philadelphia froze on December 21, 1779, and did not open for large ships until March 4—a period of seventy-five days. The waters around Manhattan Island were frozen for five weeks, preventing ships from arriving with supplies.

## The Cold Week of January 1835

The coldest extended period during the first half of the nineteenth century occurred during the Cold Week of early January 1835. The editor of the *Sussex Register* (January 12, 1835) took notice:

> The late severe cold weather is the theme of remark in all directions. Wherever we have heard from, the thermometer is generally represented to have sunk below zero—varying one to ten, and even to 32 degrees below. It is believed there may have been for a day or two, within the memory of man, full as cold weather—yet such uninterrupted severity for five or six days—and beneath a sky, too, undimmed during the whole time by a single cloud—exceeds the experience of our most venerable citizens.

Temperatures around the state on the morning of January 5, 1835, were reported in the press: Belleville −20°F (−29°C), Elizabeth −18°F (−28°C), Newark −13°F (−25°C), Philadelphia −6°F (−21°C). A significant figure was reached on just over the border at Goshen in Orange County, New York, where the academy thermometer registered −32°F (−36°C); Goshen is only about 13 miles (21 km) from Sussex County and conditions there are representative of many locations in the highlands of North Jersey.

## A Zero Day in January 1859

On only one day in the history of thermometer records in North Jersey has the mercury remained below zero all through the daylight period. On the maximum- and minimum-registering thermometer of William Whitehead at Newark, the temperature sank to −12.75°F (−24.9°C) on the morning of January 10, 1859, and rose only to −0.5°F (−17.5°C). The temperature began tumbling on the eighth and reached its nadir on the morning of the tenth; the following day was also extremely cold.

At Erasmus Hall in Brooklyn, it was the coldest day since the record keeping started in 1826. January 10 averaged −5.1°F (−20.6°C). At Philadelphia's Central High School, Professor Kirkpatrick had a maximum of only 4°F (−15.6°C) at his afternoon observation.

The editor of the *Sussex Register* (January 15, 1859) took notice of the cold in his vicinity:

> The coldest snap that has been endured in this quarter for 25 years, commenced on Monday and lasted until

nearly noon on Tuesday. At sunrise on Monday morning the thermometer stood at 12 degrees below zero, and did not through the day rise more than 6 or 7 degrees. In the evening the mercury fell to 10 below, and sunk gradually until 7 A.M. on Tuesday, when it reached 15 below—the severest cold ever remembered at Newton.

## The Arctic Week of February 1899

"The cold wave of February 9th to 11th will go on record as the most severe during this century, certainly during the present generation. We have examined the records covering a period of fifty years, and they show nothing to compare with it." This is how the state climatologist described this memorable period.

The month at New Brunswick opened with minimums in the single figures on the first two days. Then came a brief warm spell with the thermometer climbing to 44°F (7°C) on the fourth—this was to be the last above-freezing reading for ten days. The arrival of a cold front on February 5 dropped minimums to the low 20s each night until the eighth, when the mercury began to plummet with the arrival of an arctic airstream of extreme frigidity and staying power. The wintry situation was compounded by a snowfall ranging from 6 to 12 inches (15 to 30 cm) over the state on the seventh and eighth, with northwest gales creating huge drifts.

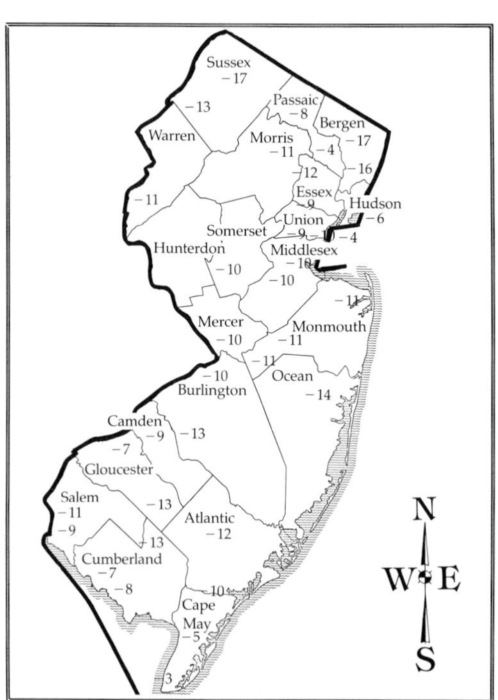


*The most severe cold wave of the nineteenth-century, February 10–11, 1899*

At New Brunswick the temperature continued its descent to a low of −4°F (−20°C) late on the ninth and reached the nadir of −10°F (−23°C) on the morning of the tenth. A third frigid morning followed, with a reading of −9°F (−23°C). Then came a mighty snowstorm that lasted three days and produced the greatest snow depths state-wide in meteorological history.

Daily Maximum and Minimum Readings at New Brunswick: February 9–16, 1899

| | Temperature | | | |
|---|---|---|---|---|
| | Fahrenheit | | Celsius | |
| Date | Maximum | Minimum | Maximum | Minimum |
| February 9 | 17 | −4 | −8 | −20 |
| February 10 | 9 | −10 | −13 | −23 |
| February 11 | 14 | −9 | −10 | −23 |
| February 12 | 11 | 3 | −12 | −16 |
| February 13 | 11 | 5 | −12 | −15 |
| February 14 | 25 | 5 | −4 | −15 |
| February 15 | 33 | −3 | 1 | −19 |
| February 16 | 35 | 6 | 2 | −14 |

February, wearing two masks, presented its warm face after the sixteenth. The first fifteen days of the month averaged 17.3°F (−8.2°C); the last thirteen days averaged 37.3°F (2.9°C). The thermometer soared to 56°F (13°C) on the twenty-second.

For the state as a whole, the month of February 1899 produced a mean of 25.8°F (−3.4°C), 5.3°F (2.9°C) degrees below the contemporary normal for 1887–1899, but even so it was warmer than February 1895 by 2.2°F (1.2°C). The lowest reading in New Jersey during February 1899 was −17°F (−27°C) at Sussex (then known as Deckertown) near the New York border and close to the present ski resorts of Vernon Valley and McAfee. Every station throughout New Jersey registered below zero on at least one morning, the highest station minimum for the month being −3°F (−19°C) at Cape May City.

# New Jersey's Coldest Morning: January 5, 1904

The thermometer of the observer of the New Jersey Weather Service at River Vale on the upper Hackensack River in northern Bergen County plunged to −34°F (−37°C) on the morning of January 5, 1904. That established the all-time minimum for New Jersey during the pe-

*The coldest day on record, January 5, 1904*

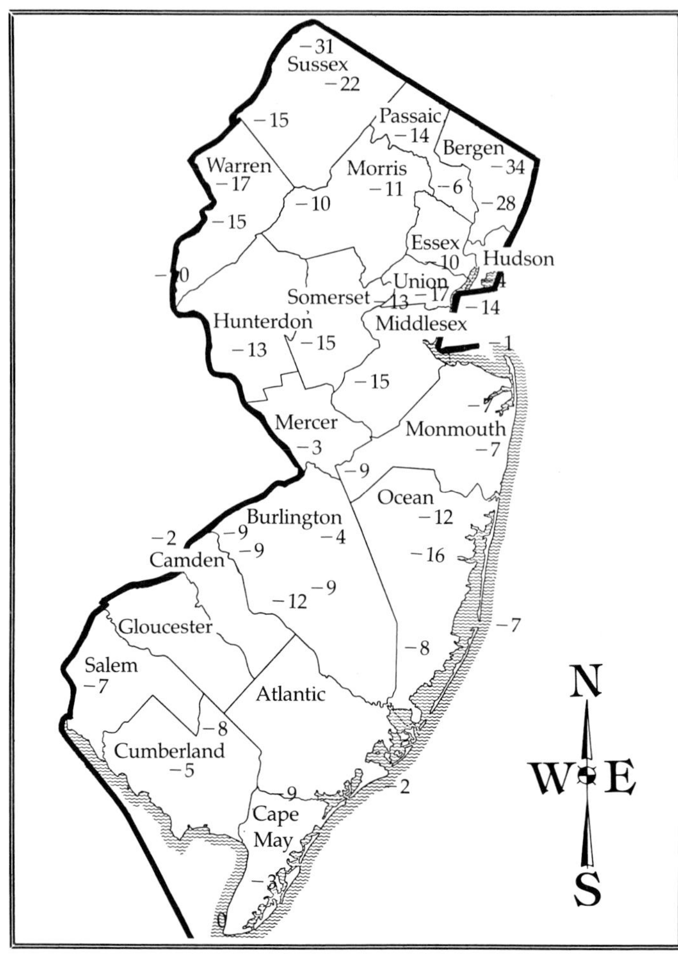


riod of record from 1885 to the present. This low reading was backed up by a mark of −28°F (−33°C) at nearby Englewood and −31°F (−35°C) at Layton in Sussex County. These are "cold hollow" locations in valleys surrounded by higher terrain that favor drainage of cold air from the hills to lower elevations. Radiation conditions must have been at optimum levels that night, since city locations were gen-

**Coldest Morning Temperature: 1904**

| Location | | January 4 | | January 5 | | January 6 | |
|---|---|---|---|---|---|---|---|
| | | Maximum | Minimum | Maximum | Minimum | Maximum | Minimum |
| River Vale | F | 15 | −22 | 15 | −34 | 20 | −27 |
| | C | −9 | −30 | −9 | −37 | −7 | −33 |
| Layton | F | 6 | −14 | 9 | −31 | 20 | −23 |
| | C | −14 | −26 | −13 | −35 | −7 | −31 |
| New York City | F | 11 | −1 | 13 | −4 | 23 | 2 |
| | C | −12 | −18 | −10 | −20 | −5 | −17 |
| Philadelphia | F | 14 | 3 | 14 | −2 | 25 | 9 |
| | C | −10 | −16 | −10 | −19 | −4 | −13 |

erally well above their previous minimums. The only other low reading—of −22°F (−30°C)—came from the town of Sussex. Over the entire state thermometers went below 0°F (−18°C) at all locations except at Cape May City, where the minimum was exactly 0°F. In the central part of the state the lowest official reading was −17°F (−27°C) at Elizabeth; farther south Toms River had the same reading.

It is interesting to note the urban heat island effect in New York City of −4°F (−20°C) and Philadelphia of −2°F (−19°C) in comparison to the rural localities.

# The War Winter of 1917–1918

The cold season of 1917–1918 was the only winter included in the twenty-month duration of United States participation in World War I. Its severity was emphasized by the civilian fuel crisis that developed and the sufferings of many soldiers housed in flimsy barracks.

During December the temperature fluctuated from warm to cold several times until the day after Christmas, when it started down-

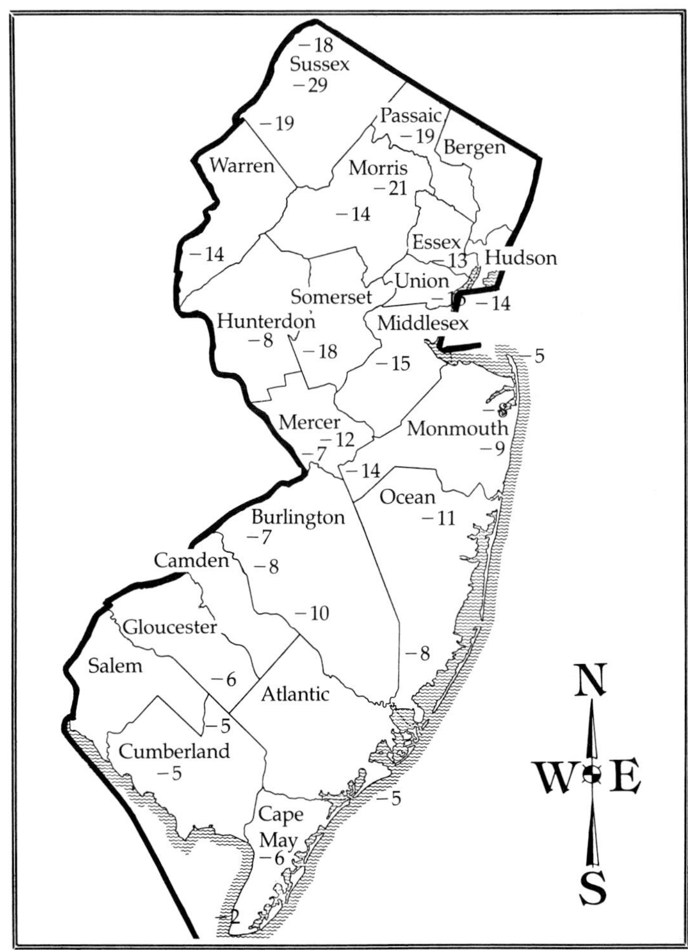


*Cold wave, December 30,1917*

ward. With the arrival of a true arctic front on December 28, the mercury at New Brunswick tumbled all day, reaching 1°F (−17°C) on the morning of the twenty-ninth. The longest series of near- and below-zero readings in the state's meteorological history followed. Minimums at New Brunswick on subsequent mornings were: −15°F (−26°C), −12°F (−24°C), −7°F (−22°C), −2°F (−19°C), 3°F (−16°C), and −3°F (−19°C). The highest afternoon reading during this period was 13°F (−11°C) until January 4, when it rose as high as 18°F (−8°C).

The seven days from December 29 to January 4 averaged only 4.1°F (−16°C). The three days from December 30 to January 1 had a mean of −3.3°F (−19.6°C), certainly the coldest trio of days to usher in a New Year in recent history. The coldest single day at New Brunswick came on December 30, when the mean was −10°F (−23°C).

The lowest reading reported throughout the state during the cold period was −29°F (−34°C) at Culvers Lake in Sussex County on the last day of December. The state average for the month, 24.8°F (−4°C), 8.2°F (4.6°C) degrees below the December normal, made for the coldest December in the record books, before or since.

## The Coldest Month: February 1934

Cold wave after cold wave continuing down to the very end of the month swept over New Jersey during February 1934, resulting in the lowest state average for any full month on record. The state figure, deduced from the observations of thirty-six stations, was 18.6°F (−7.4°C), or 12.1°F (6.7°C) below normal and 1.8°F (1.0°C) below the former record-cold month, January 1918.

There were only three days when daily means at any place in the state rose above normal. On the coldest morning, February 9, the minimums reached at various stations ranged from −9°F (−23°C) to −26°F (−32°C). The lowest reading was observed at Canoe Brook in western Essex County near the Morris County border; this also established a new New Jersey low for February. The highest temperature during the month was 54°F (12°C) at Boonton in Morris County on the twenty-second; this was the only day when temperatures rose above normal everywhere in the state.

New Brunswick records indicate that the coldest days, with means 12°F (6.7°C) below normal, came on February 3, 4, 6, 8–10, 14, 17, 20, and 24–28. This demonstrated the effect of the successive surges of cold air sweeping the state, as well as the final five-day period that assured the record.

# Extreme Temperatures in South Jersey: January 1942

The minimum temperatures of −22°F (−30°C) at Belleplain in Cape May County and −23°F (−31°C) at Pleasantville in Atlantic County on January 11, 1942, are the lowest of record for extreme South Jersey. (Farther into the interior, Indian Mills in Burlington County registered −25°F (−32°C) on the record-cold day of February 9, 1934; this reading is lower than many North Jersey stations have ever attained.) Other low readings on January 11, 1942, throughout the south were: −12°F (−24°C) at Tuckerton and Clayton, −13°F (−25°C) at Hammonton, −16°F (−27°C) at Indian Mills, and −20°F (−29°C) at Chatsworth. The interior of the south is low and flat, with all the stations less than 100 feet (30 m) above sea level. Urban temperatures were much higher than rural: Philadelphia's lowest on this morning was 11°F (−12°C) and New York's 7°F (−14°C).

# Fifteen Cold Days in 1961

Neither January nor February 1961 set any record for monthly cold, but the fifteen days from January 20 to February 4 saw the mercury stay below freezing throughout the state with the exception of one day at three stations on the southeast coast. This long northerly domination of the weather map was sandwiched between two memorable snowstorms that marked that severe winter. The snow-covered terrain ensured excellent radiation conditions each night. Layton in Sussex County registered −29°F (−34°C) on January 22, only 3°F (1.7°C) from its all-time record low. There was a press report of a reading of −38°F (−39°C) on a privately owned thermometer at nearby Lake Owassa. The range on the thermometer at New Brunswick was from 28°F (−2°C) down to −6°F (−21°C).

# Two Cold Januarys

## 1970

January 1970 was the coldest first month since January 1918 in the north and since 1940 in the south. The departures from normal were: in the north, −9.4°F (5.2°C); in the south, −8.2°F (4.6°C); and along the coast −7.4°F (4.1°C). The state-wide average came to 23.3°F (−4.8°C), 8.7°F (4.8°C) below normal.

At New Brunswick, a representative central location, there were ice days with the mercury remaining below freezing all day on January

2–3, 5–6, 8–13, 15–16, and 20–25. The minimum at New Brunswick was −1°F (−18°C) on the ninth. The last six days turned quite warm, with maximums above freezing every day; a high of 50°F (10°C) was marked on the thirtieth.

There was little precipitation. The greatest amount of snow for the month was reported at Long Branch, with 12.5 inches (32 cm). Snow cover persisted throughout the month from Trenton and Highstown north and northeast, but the almost continual flow of continental air from the west and northwest inhibited precipitation during the first twenty-five days of the month.

## 1977

Bitter weather prevailed in January 1977 across much of the nation. In a zone from western Pennsylvania to central Iowa the mercury did not rise above the freezing mark throughout the month, the first such instance in the National Weather Service's 106 years of record in the region. Chicago's mean of 10.1°F (−12°C) was colder by 1.8°F (1°C) than any other month in its meteorological history.

At New Brunswick the cold period was ushered in on December 28, 1976, when the mercury went below freezing, remaining there until January 3, 1977. Throughout January there were only three days on which the thermometer did not drop below 20°F (−7°C); the highest minimum for the month was 23°F (−5°C). The mercury remained below freezing on January 12–20, 22–24, and 30–31. The coldest period came from the seventeenth to the twentieth, with minimums of −5°F (−21°C), −3°F (−19°C), and 0°F (−18°C). The final three days produced minimums of −1°F (−18°C), 0°F (−18°C), and 7°F (−14°C). On the coldest day of the month at New Brunswick, the eighteenth, the mean was 2.5°F (−16°C), with a maximum of 8°F (−13°C) and a minimum of −3°F (−19°C).

The state average for forty-four stations was 20.2°F (−6.6°C), 0.1°F below that of January 1918.

The maximum reading in January 1977 was 52°F (11°C) at the Atlantic City Marina on the tenth, the only reading in the state to top 50°F that month. Flemington's maximum was only 38°F (3°C). The minimum reading for the entire state during January fell to a moderate −15°F (−26°C), illustrating the period's relatively small range between highs and lows.

## February 1978

The mercury dropped below freezing at New Brunswick on January 28, 1978, and stayed below until February 7. Temperatures were consistently low throughout the month. There were only three nights when minimums rose above 20°F (−7°C): February 14, 25, and 26. After the seventh the maximums usually held in the low to middle 30sF (1–3°C). The month's high at New Brunswick was 43°F (6°C) on the twenty-sixth. Snow remained on the ground, assisting the nocturnal radiation process, throughout the month in central and northern sections.

The departure from normal by sections were as follows: in the north −8.7°F (4.8°C), in the south −9.4°F (5.2°C), and along the coast −8.2°F (−4.6°C). The state average, based on forty-one stations, was 23.2°F (−5°C), slightly below February 1895 and 1905, but 4.6°F (2.6°C) above the all-time coldest February in 1934. The lowest reading in the state was −12°F (−24°C) at Newton on the ninth and again on the twentieth. The month's maximum in the state was 49°F (9°C) at Belleplain in Cape May County; this was 5°F (2.8°C) below the maximum in the coldest month in 1934, yet 3°F (1.7°C) short of the very low maximum in February 1901.

# February 1934 and February 1979

A comparison between the daily cumulative coldness of February 1934 and February 1979 is interesting. In 1934 at Trenton February started out very cold and reached its nadir between the eighth and

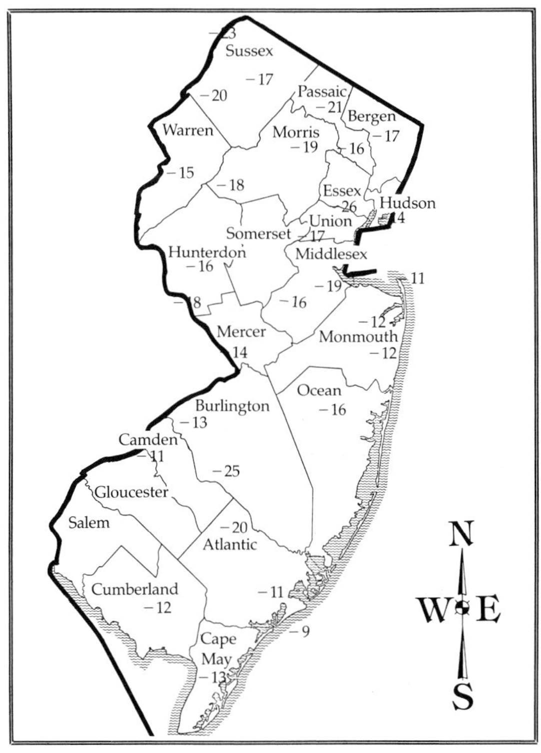


*The coldest day of the coldest month on record, February 9, 1934*

tenth, when these days averaged 25.5°F (14°C) below normal. It continued cold for the rest of the month, with only one day, the twenty-second, averaging above normal and then only by 1.8°F (1°C). The mean for the entire month was 18.5°F (−7.5°C), a departure from normal of −12.2°F (−6.8°C).

February 1979 began with moderate cold; not until the tenth did severe cold, with means about 20°F (11°C) below normal, start. From the ninth through the eighteenth, the daily mean averaged 22°F (12°C) below normal. On the fifteenth the accumulated departure from normal exceeded that on February 15, 1934. This situation continued through February 24, when February 1979 entered a slightly above-normal period. February 1934 was thus assured of its position as the coldest month—it had ended with a severe cold wave.

February 1934 averaged 2.5°F (1.4°C) colder than February 1979 at Trenton; it had been a close race until near the finish. The monthly extremes in 1934 were a 42°F (6°C) maximum and −14°F (−26°C) minimum, compared with extremes in 1979 of 54°F (12°C) and −1°F (−18°C). Nevertheless, the ten days in February 1979 from the ninth through the eighteenth were the coldest such period in central New Jersey records.

## Severity of Winters in Central New Jersey

A Rutgers University study developed a winter severity index whereby all winters from 1897 to 1980 were classified.* The records of the College Farm station on the grounds of Cook College in New Brunswick were used except for 1910 through 1914, when records for nearby locations were substituted. The index combines four elements: mean seasonal temperature departures (December, January, and February) from 1941–1970 normals, seasonal snowfall totals, number of days with minimum temperature 0°F (−18°C) or below, and number of days with maximum temperature 32°F (0°C) or below. Each winter was assigned a *severity index number*.

The four parameters were weighed to give a final index value ranging from 0 to 100. Seasonal snowfall and temperature departure from normal were considered the most important factors.

Five-year running means were constructed to show the trend of relative severity. A series of mild winters culminated in low indexes

*Michael D. Rubinfeld and Mark D. Shulman, "A Winter Severity Index for Central New Jersey," (Paper of the Journal Series, New Jersey Agricultural Experiment Station, Cook College, Rutgers University).

### Coldest Winter Months: 1885–1982*

| Year | December | Year | January | Year | February | Season | |
|---|---|---|---|---|---|---|---|
| 1917 | 24.8 | 1918 | 20.3 | 1934 | 18.6 | 1917–1918 | 24.7 |
| 1910 | 26.5 | 1893 | 21.6 | 1979 | 21.8 | 1903–1904 | 25.5 |
| 1904 | 27.0 | 1912 | 22.3 | 1978 | 23.2 | 1904–1905 | 25.8 |
| 1960 | 27.3 | 1940 | 22.4 | 1905 | 23.4 | 1919–1920 | 26.8 |
| 1958 | 27.5 | 1982 | 22.7 | 1895 | 23.6 | 1935–1936 | 26.8 |
| 1963 | 28.0 | 1904 | 23.2 | 1907 | 23.6 | 1976–1977 | 27.1 |
| 1926 | 28.4 | 1981 | 23.2 | 1885 | 23.9 | 1892–1893 | 27.4 |
| 1903 | 28.6 | 1970 | 23.3 | 1936 | 24.4 | 1977–1978 | 27.8 |
| 1976 | 28.7 | 1920 | 23.6 | 1904 | 24.8 | 1933–1934 | 28.0 |
| 1919 | 28.8 | 1948 | 24.1 | 1901 | 25.4 | 1947–1948 | 28.1 |

SOURCE: *Climatological Data, New Jersey* (Asheville, N.C.: National Climatic Center).
NOTE: From coldest to least cold, top to bottom.
*Monthly averages are derived by weighting each division by the number of reporting stations in that division.

### Warmest Winter Months: 1885–1982*

| Year | December | Year | January | Year | February | Season | |
|---|---|---|---|---|---|---|---|
| 1889 | 41.5 | 1932 | 42.4 | 1890 | 39.9 | 1889–1890 | 40.9 |
| 1891 | 40.9 | 1890 | 41.3 | 1954 | 38.7 | 1931–1932 | 39.3 |
| 1923 | 40.8 | 1950 | 40.7 | 1976 | 38.3 | 1936–1937 | 37.3 |
| 1956 | 39.7 | 1937 | 40.3 | 1891 | 38.0 | 1948–1949 | 37.2 |
| 1931 | 39.6 | 1913 | 39.5 | 1949 | 38.0 | 1956–1957 | 37.1 |
| 1971 | 39.6 | 1933 | 38.5 | 1957 | 38.0 | 1952–1953 | 36.6 |
| 1911 | 38.4 | 1949 | 38.0 | 1909 | 37.8 | 1949–1950 | 36.5 |
| 1953 | 38.3 | 1947 | 36.7 | 1925 | 37.3 | 1932–1933 | 36.0 |
| 1957 | 38.1 | 1906 | 36.5 | 1953 | 37.3 | 1912–1913 | 35.7 |
| 1972 | 38.0 | 1889 | 36.2 | 1939 | 36.3 | 1974–1975 | 35.6 |
| | | | | 1981 | 36.3 | | |

SOURCE: *Climatological Data, New Jersey* (Asheville, N.C.: National Climatic Center).
NOTE: From warmest to least warm, top to bottom.
*Monthly averages are derived by weighting each division by the number of reporting stations in that division.

for 1932–1933, 1954–1955, and 1974–1975. Series of severe winters were apparent in the early years of the century, with the index running above 60 from 1903 to 1912. The index dropped below 60 in 1921 and did not reach that figure again until 1964. Small rises into the 50s occurred in the mid-1920s, late 1930s, and late 1940s. The middle 1950s were the mildest of the century; the index remained above 50 from 1961 through 1973.

The severest individual winters were 1904–1905 and 1960–1961, with indexes of 91.5 and 89.8. The least severe were 1931–1932 with a value of only 1.4 and 1936–1937 with 12.8.

The greatest seasonal snowfall was 64.0 inches (163 cm) in 1906–1907; the second snowiest winter was that of 1960–1961, with 58.9 inches (150 cm). The winter of 1977–1978 had 57.3 inches (146 cm).

The season with the greatest number of days with the minimum temperature at 0°F (−18°C) or below was 1933–1934, with eight such days. The greatest number of ice days with the maximum at 32°F (0°C), or below was forty-two in 1976–1977. The next winter, 1977–1978, was a close second with forty-one such days.

The difference in departures of individual winters ranged from −8.0°F (4.4°C) in 1905 to +6.4°F (3.6°C) in 1932, a difference of 14.4°F (8°C) in winter means at New Brunswick.

# Heat Waves

Heat waves are part of a New Jersey summer. If a heat wave is defined as two or more consecutive days with the maximum rising to 90°F (32°C) or above, every summer month normally has one or more such periods. Some summer months have produced as many as twenty-two hot days. New York City experienced ten consecutive days with 90°F or more in August 1896, and Philadelphia endured twelve such consecutive days in June–July 1901.

Not all sections of the state suffer equally from heat waves, since the diverse topography and distance from the ocean create unequal heating effects throughout the region. The coastal strip from Cape May to Sandy Hook often enjoys a cooling sea breeze on a summer afternoon while the interior sections broil. Also, nighttime cooling in the hills of the north often brings the temperature down to comfortable sleeping levels, while the urban sites in the Hudson and Delaware valleys endure enervating heat and humidity.

The Bermuda high is the chief instrument in setting the stage for a heat wave in the northeastern United States. Though called a semipermanent area of high pressure, it does migrate north and south with the seasons and waxes and wanes in strength according to the different atmospheric circulation patterns prevailing over the hemisphere.

In summer the Bermuda high moves north in mid-ocean, with its east-west lateral axis lying between 32°N and 38°N. Its western periphery often reaches west to the coasts of the Carolinas and Virginia. This introduces anticyclonic conditions to the eastern part of the United States and shunts the summer storm track far to the north into Canada. At the same time the anticyclonic flow introduces a flow of tropical air of varying moisture content into the northeastern United States.

*High temperatures in July 1978 caused this stretch of track to buckle, derailing a North Coast Line passenger car in Spring Lake Heights near Asbury Park. (Asbury Park Press photo/Bob Bielk)*

Two main types of heat waves are experienced in New Jersey. When the western arm of the Bermuda high remains on the coastal plain, the air flow reaching the Garden State comes from the south and southwest, carrying moist tropical air from the Gulf of Mexico which creates enervating conditions with high temperature-humidity indexes. But if the Bermuda high extends a strong arm westward as far as Tennessee and Kentucky, the air flow reaching New Jersey will have a west or even northwest trajectory and the air will be from the dry expanses of the American Southwest or the Great Plains. It arrives here as a very hot but dry airstream.

## Battle of Monmouth Day

The most celebrated hot day in New Jersey history occurred on Battle of Monmouth Day, June 28, 1778. This military action took place near Monmouth Court House, now Freehold. Extreme heat dogged the British as they moved from the Delaware across the sandy plain of central Jersey to the waters of New York Bay near Sandy Hook. Though no contemporary thermometer records have been found for a New Jersey location, an instrument at the British headquarters in New York City is reported to have registered 96°F (36°C); readings

*Molly Pitcher was the wife of a gunner who fought at the Battle of Monmouth Bay on June 28, 1778. She is best remembered for bringing water to the thirsty soldiers. When her husband was killed, she took his place at the gun. (Currier & Ives, courtesy of the Library of Congress)*

close to 100°F (38°C) could have prevailed on the battlefield. The image of Molly Pitcher, first bringing water to the soldiers, then taking her husband's place in battle, has survived the centuries.

## August 1896

This was the "warmest ever" in the records of most stations reporting to the New Jersey Weather Service. The heat spell from August 4 to 13 still stands in New York City records as the longest number of consecutive days with 90°F (32°C) or more. The Newark record kept by Frederic Ricord exceeds this, reaching 90°F on every day from the second to the thirteenth. The mean at Newark for the first fifteen days of August 1896 was 81.3°F (27.4°C). At Toms River the thermometer reached 100°F (38°C) or more on four days of the month, hitting 105°F (41°C) on both the sixth and the ninth. After the sixteenth, the weather turned much cooler; very light frost was reported on the last two days of August in North Jersey.

## June–July 1901

The 1901 summer solstice introduced a memorable New Jersey heat wave. For the next sixteen days at Bridgeton temperatures reached 90°F or more every day, continuing through July 7. There were eight consecutive days with 100°F (38°C) or more from June 29 through

July 6, with the maximum of 104°F (40°C) on July 2. At Indian Mills in Burlington County, the thermometer rose to 105°F (41°C) on July 1 and to 107°F (42°C) on July 2. Somerville and Salem hit 107°F on the second.

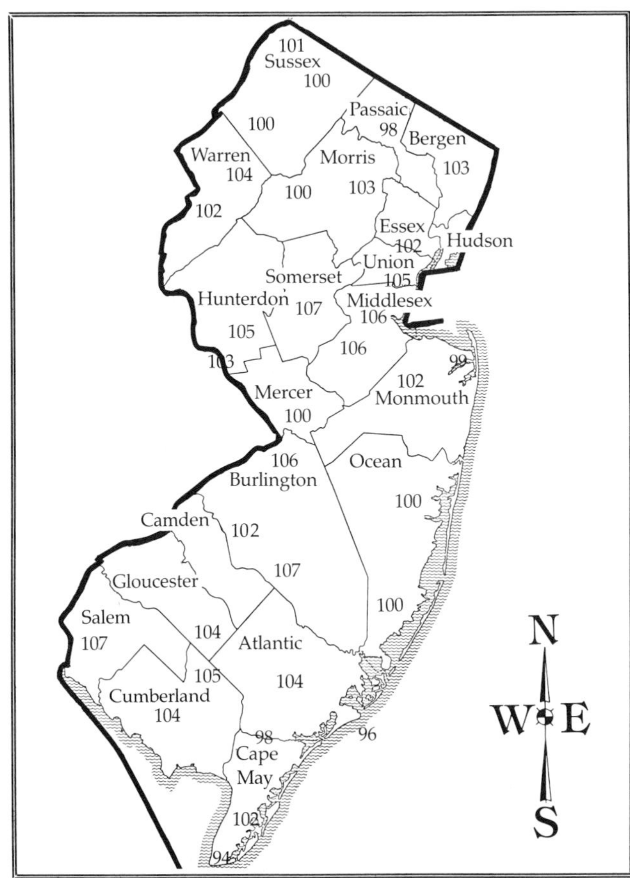


*Heat wave, July 1–2, 1901*

# July 1911

"Hot as the Fourth of July" is an old-time weather saying with great truth. Probably the hottest early-July spell came in 1911 when records for all-time maximum temperatures were set in several northeastern states. At Bridgeton in Cumberland County, the thermometer mounted to 90°F (32°C) or more on every day except two from July 1 to July 13. On four occasions it reached 100°F (38°C) or more. The peak came on the tenth and eleventh, with 102°F (39°C). Inland Somerville attained 100°F (38°C) on six days, but on the coast, Atlantic City had only one hot day, the eleventh, with 96°F (36°C).

In the Central Park records at New York City, July 6, 1911, with 98°F (37°C), and the eleventh, with 97°F (36°C), still stand as the hottest ever on those dates. The mean for July 2–6, 1911, 86.8°F (30.4°C), is the second hottest five-day period in New York City records.

# August 1918

The weather during August in the World War I summer was remarkable for its heat and humidity. The highest temperatures known in New Jersey until that time occurred on August 7, when the thermometer rose well above 100°F (38°C) in practically every portion of the state. Two stations, Flemington and Somerville, reported 108°F (42°C), a state record. Only Belvidere and Charlotteburg in the northern interior and Long Branch and Sandy Hook on the north coast failed to reach 100°F (38°C). Atlantic City had a maximum of 104°F (40°C).

On August 7 New York and Philadelphia had minimums of 82°F (28°C). The mean on the seventh at Philadelphia was 94°F (34°C) and at New York 92°F (33°C). On the same day the minimum at Layton in Sussex County dropped to 68°F (20°C), or 14°F (7.8°C) degrees lower than at Philadelphia and New York.

# The Early Heat Wave of June 1925

Few summers in New Jersey experience such an extreme heat wave as came well before the solstice in early June 1925. The month's mean temperature of 73.6°F (23.1°C) exceeded by 1°F (0.6°C) the previous hottest June mean, which occurred in 1923. This was also slightly higher than the normal for July, the first time that a June had been hotter than the July normal.

Indian Mills in Burlington County had the following readings from June 1 to 10: 93, 99, 100, 99, 102, 101, 101, 90, 89, and 92°F. The state maximum during this period was 103°F (39°C) at Belvidere on the fifth. Paterson, Elizabeth, and Belvidere, as well as Indian Mills, had three consecutive days with 100°F (38°C) or more. Burlington saw six consecutive days with maximums from 100°F to 102°F.

The heat wave was accompanied by an absence of rain until June 9, when some relieving showers fell in the northern counties, but not in the South. The drought was very damaging to strawberries and greatly shortened the growth of garden truck, grass, and pasturage. The combination of heat and dryness in June 1925 broke all previous records.

# New Jersey's Hottest Day

Although July 1936 averaged less than 1°F (0.6°C) above normal, an all-time record-breaking heat wave occurred from the eighth to the twelfth. The peak came on the ninth and tenth, when thermometers mounted to 100°F (38°C) and beyond at every reporting station in New Jersey except Atlantic City, where cooling sea breezes kept the maximum down to a mere 94°F (34°C). The existing maximum records were exceeded at about two-thirds of the stations.

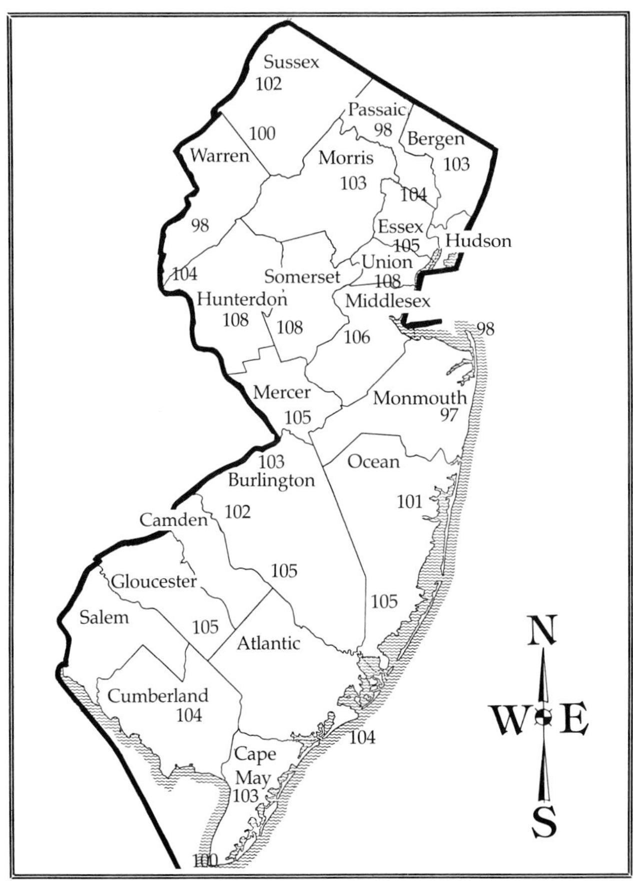


*Heat wave,*
*August 7, 1918*

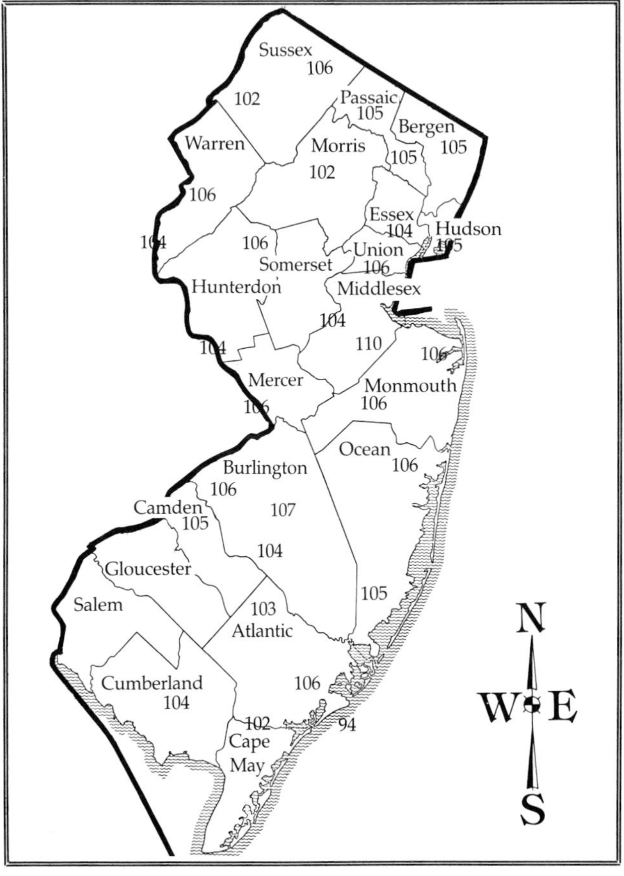


*An all-time record-breaking heat wave,*
*July 9–10, 1936*

The highest temperature ever measured on an official thermometer in a standard exposure, 110°F (43°C), was reached on July 10, 1936, at Runyon, which is in a sandy soil area in northeast Middlesex County just inland from New York Bay. Next highest in the state that day was Pemberton's 107°F (42°C). A number of stations reached 106°F. The daily maximums at Runyon during the heat wave were: 109°F on the ninth, 110°F on the tenth, and 105°F on the eleventh.

# The Record Hot Summer of 1955

The summer of 1955 brought delight to weather-record watchers. It produced the hottest month and also the wettest month in the period of official New Jersey records from 1885 to 1955.

July 1955 was the hottest and driest July of record, and August 1955 was the hottest and wettest August of record. Furthermore, July was the hottest month of any name and August the wettest in the seventy years of record.

July exceeded the long-term normal by 5.1°F (2.8°C), and the total precipitation of 1.13 inches (29 mm) was only 25 percent of the normal figure and 0.23 inch (6 mm) less than the next driest July. August exceeded the month's normal by 4.6°F (2.6°C) and the previous hottest August by 0.4°F (0.2°C). The state-wide precipitation average of 11.85 inches (301 mm) was 246 percent of the normal, over an inch greater than the previous wettest August, and 0.43 inch (11 mm) over

### Hottest Summer Months: 1885–1982*

| Year | June | Year | July | Year | August | Year | Summer |
|---|---|---|---|---|---|---|---|
| 1943 | 74.2 | 1955 | 79.2 | 1955 | 76.7 | 1949 | 74.9 |
| 1967 | 73.8 | 1949 | 78.0 | 1900 | 76.3 | 1955 | 74.5 |
| 1925 | 73.6 | 1901 | 77.3 | 1938 | 75.4 | 1973 | 74.0 |
| 1934 | 72.6 | 1952 | 77.0 | 1939 | 75.3 | 1911 | 74.0 |
| 1923 | 72.5 | 1931 | 76.6 | 1937 | 75.2 | 1900 | 73.9 |
| 1892 | 72.4 | 1921 | 76.5 | 1959 | 75.0 | 1943 | 73.9 |
| 1899 | 72.3 | 1911 | 76.0 | 1973 | 75.0 | 1952 | 73.8 |
| 1949 | 72.1 | 1935 | 76.0 | 1898 | 74.8 | 1901 | 73.7 |
| 1973 | 72.1 | 1966 | 76.0 | 1947 | 74.7 | 1937 | 73.4 |
| 1952 | 71.8 | 1900 | 75.9 | 1949 | 74.7 | 1898 | 73.4 |
| 1976 | 71.8 | | | | | 1959 | 73.4 |
| | | | | | | 1966 | 73.4 |

SOURCE: *Climatological Data, New Jersey* (Asheville, N.C.: National Climatic Center).
NOTE: From hottest to least hot, top to bottom.
*Monthly averages are derived by weighting each division by the number of reporting stations in that division.

Coolest Summer Months: 1885–1982*

| Year | June | Year | July | Year | August | Year | Summer |
|---|---|---|---|---|---|---|---|
| 1911 | 63.9 | 1891 | 70.1 | 1927 | 67.1 | 1927 | 68.4 |
| 1903 | 64.0 | 1895 | 70.9 | 1903 | 68.4 | 1903 | 68.6 |
| 1907 | 64.7 | 1914 | 71.5 | 1946 | 69.2 | 1902 | 69.5 |
| 1916 | 64.7 | 1962 | 71.5 | 1940 | 69.4 | 1907 | 69.6 |
| 1927 | 65.4 | 1909 | 71.6 | 1886 | 69.5 | 1886 | 69.9 |
| 1902 | 65.5 | 1924 | 71.6 | 1889 | 69.6 | 1924 | 70.1 |
| 1958 | 65.9 | 1920 | 71.7 | 1929 | 69.8 | 1946 | 70.2 |
| 1897 | 66.1 | 1923 | 71.9 | 1934 | 69.8 | 1915 | 70.2 |
| 1972 | 66.1 | 1956 | 71.9 | 1921 | 69.8 | 1897 | 70.4 |
| 1918 | 66.3 | 1978 | 71.9 | 1919 | 69.9 | 1904 | 70.6 |

SOURCE: *Climatological Data, New Jersey* (Asheville, N.C.: National Climatic Center).
NOTE: From coolest to least cool, top to bottom.
*Monthly averages are derived by weighting each division by the number of reporting stations in that division.

the previous wettest month of any name, July 1897. The excessive rainfall in August 1955 resulted from the deluges attending the passages of ex-hurricanes Connie and Diane over the state.

# Thunderstorms

Along with small rain showers, thunderstorms constitute New Jersey's major source of precipitation during the growing season. Without them, home gardens and commercial farms alike would need constant irrigation rather than sporadic watering. A thunderstorm's arrival often announces the beginning of the end of an extended heat wave and the introduction of a spell of cool, dry weather.

The fundamental requirement for the development of a thunderstorm is the ascent of warm air to higher levels. The atmosphere is said to be unstable if a layer of warm air, once given an upward impetus, continues to rise. It behaves like a hot-air balloon that finds itself in a colder environment whose greater pressure forces the warm air upward. This is the process of *convection.*

Conditions favorable for convective activity arise from several circumstances. Daytime heating over flat land may result in rising thermal currents whose continued ascent is stimulated by the already unstable condition of the atmosphere. Air overlying rough or mountain terrain may receive unequal heating that ultimately causes vertical movement. Airstreams passing over gradually rising ground or a mountain range may be lifted orographically to an unstable layer and continue their ascent to higher levels.

The frontal zone of a storm system may supply the lifting mechanism. An airstream accompanying a warm front may overrun cooler air at the surface and be forced aloft until it becomes unstable and continues upward. The convergence of airstreams of different temperature and humidity content along a cold front or a squall line can supply rapid lift that soon results in cumulo-nimbus development and thunderstorm formation.

An unstable atmosphere encourages the continuation of convection. Eventually, the rising thermal current cools sufficiently to reach its dew point, or condensation level; then the water vapor in the rising current passes from its invisible gaseous state into visible liquid droplets, which we perceive as cloud. In most cases this is the end result of the process—a cumulus cloud floating in the lower layer of the atmosphere. But if the vertical thermal currents have sufficient energy, the ascending air column will continue to rise, expanding laterally and upward, to become a swelling cumulus cloud with turrets reaching to higher elevations. A chimney effect of rising hot air forms the central core of the cloud. Then other forces come into play.

A developing cumulus cloud feeds on another source of internal energy. Upon the formation of visible cloud, the change of moisture from vapor to water droplets releases latent heat; this adds to the total heat energy available, thereby increasing the upward momentum of the cloud's vertical development. The rate of supply of new energy is directly related to the amount of water vapor being converted into liquid droplets or solid ice particles. If the upward flow of moisture is cut off, the cloud will cease to grow and will soon dissipate. If the supply is continued, the created rain, hail, or snow will acquire size and weight; when a sufficient mass has been attained to overcome the ascending currents in the central chimney, the water or ice particles will fall downward, some tossed outside the cloud and some descending around the central core.

The full-growth stage of the thunderstorm is reached when the main updraft is joined by one or more downdrafts created by the falling precipitation. The descending currents are fed and strengthened, as was the updraft, by the addition of entrained air and by evaporational cooling. Lightning accompanies the formation and descent of the precipitation, indicating a close relationship between the creation of electricity and the formation and splitting of ice crystals and raindrops. At maturity the thunderstorm cloud may measure several miles across in all directions at its base and may tower to altitudes of 40,000 to 60,000 feet (12,200 to 18,300 m). Some reach to the base of the stratosphere, where their vertical development halts. The swift winds in the upper atmosphere tear away the cloud top and carry its shreds downwind many miles ahead of the advancing cumulo-nimbus, producing the familiar anvil shape of the mature cumulonimbus cloud. The storm is now at its most violent phase. Lightning and thunder are incessant aloft; melting snow, hail, and rain cascade downward; violent vertical currents prevail, and a tornado funnel may lower toward the surface of the earth.

The storm cell soon passes its most violent stage and starts to break up. The cold downdrafts, upon reaching the surface, eventually strangle the warm updrafts that initiated the storm's development. With the rising air cut off, the cell is deprived of its source of sustenance. Precipitation gradually slackens off and the violent downdrafts subside. The top of the thunderstorm cloud begins to disintegrate by spreading out laterally and moving downwind. Soon a more stable equilibrium with the surrounding atmosphere is attained.

Thunderstorm occurrence at all stations in New Jersey reaches maximum frequency during the summer months, when surface heating of the earth is at a maximum. July has the most days, with both local convection and frontal activity contributing. Trenton reports an average of thirty-three days with thunderstorms in a year; Atlantic City has an average of twenty-six such days and Newark twenty-five. Probably for New Jersey as a whole, a figure of thirty per year would be approximate, with greater frequency in the western than in the eastern part of the state.

The number of thunderstorms per season varies greatly with the prevailing weather-map situation. An anticyclonic season featuring extended dry and hot periods inhibits thunderstorm development, while much cyclonic activity and frequent frontal passages lead to higher numbers.

The hours of maximum occurrence are late afternoon and early evening, when the effects of local heating are at a maximum. Thunderstorms forming over the Pennsylvania mountains in the afternoon are carried eastward and do not strike New Jersey until evening. Frontal passage thunderstorms can occur at any time of day or night, as the experience of awakening in the middle of the night to the twin spectacles of loud claps of thunder and sharp flashes of lightning demonstrates dramatically.

The blinding flash that illuminates the sky in and near a thunderstorm is simply a gigantic electric spark between regions of oppositely charged particles. It is produced by the polarity or separation of charges within a growing storm cloud. Negatively charged electrons accumulate near the base of the cloud. Because the earth's surface below the cloud is induced to be positively charged by the negatively charged cloud base, a potential gradient of about one thousand volts per meter is created between the cloud and the ground. When this potential becomes large enough, an electrical discharge in the form of leaders between ground and cloud and cloud and ground takes place. With this exchange electrons flow from cloud to ground and reduce the voltage differential. Lightning discharges may also take place between different parts of a single cloud, and may leap from cloud to cloud as well.

The sound emitted by rapidly expanding gases along the channel of a lightning discharge is thunder. Much of the energy of a lightning discharge is expended in heating the atmospheric gases in and immediately around the luminous channel. In a few microseconds, it rises to a local temperature of about 10,000°C, with the result that violent pressure waves are sent out, followed by a succession of rarefactions and compressions induced by the inherent elasticity of the air. These sound waves are heard as thunder. Thunder is seldom audible at points more than about 15 miles (24 km) from the lightning discharge, with 25 miles (40 km) being approximately the upper limit and 10 miles (16 km) a fairly typical range of audibility. At such distances, thunder has a characteristic rumbling sound of very low pitch. When heard at long distances, the pitch is low because of strong absorption and scattering of the high-frequency components of the original sound waves. The rumbling results chiefly from the varying arrival times of the sound waves emitted by the sinuous portions of the lightning channel, which are located at various distances from the observer, and, secondarily, from echoing and from the multiplicity of the strokes of a composite flash.

The sighting of a lightning flash is almost simultaneous with its occurrence. Since it takes about five seconds for sound to travel one mile, one can get an approximate distance in miles by counting the number of seconds between the flash and the arrival of the thunder and dividing by five.

## Hailstorms

Precipitation in the form of spheres or irregular conglomerates of ice makes a spectacular storm feature during the warmer part of the year. Hail originates in a convective cumulo-nimbus cloud which develops in the strong updrafts attending frontal uplift or an airmass thunderstorm. The most prolific hailstorms result from the formation of supercells in a thunderstorm whose enormous updrafts permit large hailstones to grow by accretion over periods of many minutes.

Most hailstorms cover only limited areas, with a scattering of stones falling, but a fully developed storm may loose vast quantities of icy matter over a considerable territory. Hail often falls in rectangular strips from 0.5 to 2.0 miles (0.8 to 3.2 km) wide and from 5 to 10 miles (8 to 16 km) or more in length as the developing storm moves downwind. These are known as *hailstreaks;* the ground can turn white and be covered to measurable depth by the icy accumulation. Total destruction to crops may result, and injury and even death may occur when animals are caught in the open by the bombardment from the sky. Human deaths as a result of hail within the United States are very rare.

Hailstones exhibit a great variety of shapes and structures. A stone may range in size from that of a pea to that of a grapefruit, or from less than 0.25 inch to more than 5.0 inches (0.6 to 12.7 cm) in diameter. Hailstones may be spherical, conical, or quite irregular in shape. Spherical stones, the most common form, exhibit a layered interior structure, sometimes resembling an onion, with layers composed of clear ice alternating with layers of rime ice that looks white because it contains many tiny air bubbles.

Hailstones grow by accretion around a small ice core in the presence of supercooled water droplets in a cloud. These freeze upon impact with the ice pellet. The growing hailstones must remain aloft long enough to acquire sufficient size to withstand complete melting in their descent through warmer air as they approach the ground. They continue to grow in size as long as the strong updrafts in the cloud can support their weight. Often hailstones are tossed out of the chimneylike updraft into descending currents, or until the supporting updraft weakens; the stone then starts its descent to earth as a potentially dangerous missile.

When hailstones are carried up and down in vertical currents several times, they melt a little in each descent and acquire a new sheathing of ice during their ascent. Stones with varying textures and appearances are thus produced. Some develop protruding lobes resembling feet, probably resulting from a spinning action in their descent. Sometimes several hailstones congeal together, forming irregular chunks of ice which often smash into pieces upon impact with the earth. As is the case with their frozen relatives, snowflakes, hailstones can have a vast variety of shapes, structures, and appearances.

Though New Jersey does not experience the massive hailstorms that occasionally strike the Great Plains to the lee of the Rocky Mountains, a great variety of types of hailstorms have hit the state. The following accounts are taken from contemporary records and illustrate some of the characteristics of local hailstorms.

# Fatal Hailstorm Near New Brunswick: June 1742

From New Brunswick we hear, that on Tuesday last they had a strong gust of wind, accompanied by some rain and hail of an amazing bigness; we are informed that in one house it struck 28 holes through the roof, the damage to the grain is so great that some who had already brought their last crop to the market, countermand the same, lest they should want bread. At Amwell a boy was killed by the hail, and a man and his wife were much hurt thereby.

New-York Journal,
*June 14, 1742*

# Hailstorm of May 24, 1758

To the author of the *New American Magazine,*
(Woodbridge), May 25, 1758

Mr. Americanus,
Being at Burlington yesterday, I was a spectator of one of the most extraordinary storms of hail and rain as perhaps has been seen in America; at least some very old men said they never had seen one like it.

At first there came a little rain but was soon followed by some large stones of hail, which, with the rain, encreased for the space of 8 or 10 minutes; when appeared to me a most amazing prospect—It seemed as if the whole body of the clouds were falling, half rain and half hail: The street appeared as another Delaware, full of floating ice, and the air seem'd a cataract.—I tho't in the midst of it, of Noah's flood, and my ideas made the storm its neat resemblance. The thickest of it continued about 15 or 20 minutes more, and then abated gradually,—After it was over the ground looked as if there had been a snow, and in some places the hail had drifted 6 inches thick, some of which remained on the ground till night, notwithstanding it continued warm after the storm.

—As soon as the gust was over, I took a walk to see how the fields, &c. had fared, and found a scene of desolation; the rye, flax, and oats, were cut to pieces; the peas, beans, and garden truck, where the storm fell thickest, intirely ruined; the trees appeared as if the caterpillars had been stripping them of their verdure; cherries, apples, peaches and leaves, almost covered the ground in places; in short, it afforded the prospect of a most astonishing sudden change,

Yours, &c. L.H.

New American Magazine
*(Woodbridge),*
*May 5, 1758*

# Sussex County Hailstorm: July 16, 1853

The hailstones, which ranged in bulk from the size of peas and hickory nuts to the dimensions of hens' eggs, fell thick and fast, and were assisted in the work of destruction by the fierce tornado which whirled them through the air. Fences were blown down, trees uprooted, the growing crops of corn cut back, wheat &c were cut to pieces and swept away like chaff. Hundreds of acres of corn and oats utterly destroyed. A considerable quantity of grain in shock was scattered and destroyed; and one farmer, Robert Lewis of Pleasant Valley had the product of nearly 20 acres exposed. . . . His two teams, stung by the hail storm, took fright and ran away, breaking the wagons and injuring severely but not fatally who was driving—the horses were unhurt. The window glass of every house within the area of the storm was, for the most part, demolished, many of the roofs damaged, and other injuries inflicted. Poultry, birds, rabbits, &c were killed by the pitiless pelting of the hail; and strange and incredible as it may seem, we learn that two cows, exposed to the storm, fell victims to the icy volleys which they encountered.

Never since the settlement of Sussex County has so extensive a calamity befallen her citizens. Violent hail storms have occasionally damaged her crops, but never so irremediably. By this visitation a large scope of fertile land was stripped as completely as if a hostile army had passed over it, pulling up by the roots the corn, oats, &c, and trampling the waving fields of grass into the earth. Saturday, the 16th of July, 1853, will be long remembered, as the most disastrous epoch in our history.

Sussex Register
*(Newton), July 24, 1853*

# Cross-Central Jersey Hailstorm: June 23, 1906

On the 23d a noteworthy hailstorm occurred over the central portion of New Jersey. The storm, as far as can be known, entered the State from southeastern Pennsylvania, over the western part of Mercer County and moved in a northeasterly direction to Jersey City and Sandy Hook, on the east, touching the interior of Somerset and Union counties on the north, and the northern part of Ocean County (Lakewood) on the south. At Imlaystown the storm was destructive over a large area; at Somerville the fall of hail lasted for about one hour; at Plainfield the stones measured the size of a walnut. At Perth Amboy the storm was unusually heavy and destructive; greenhouses and skylights were wrecked, window-glass on the northerly side of nearly every building in the city was broken, trees were stripped of their foliage and horses were stampeded. The hail-stones averaged from 1.5 inches to 2.5 inches in diameter, and in shape were, as a rule, almost perfectly spherical. Sixteen of the stones, gathered at random, weighed 2 pounds, and placed in contact in a row measured 32 inches in length.

Climatological Report:
New Jersey Section,
*June 1906*

# Camden-Burlington-Ocean Counties Hailstorm: May 29, 1925

Another hailstorm crossed the State from Gloucester county, across Camden and Burlington to Ocean county on the 29th. In Gloucester county some of the hail was as large as hen eggs and smaller to the eastward down to the size of rice grains at the shore. In Burlington county hail for an hour accumulated and the accumulations remained on the ground in sheltered places for three days.

Climatological Data:
New Jersey Section

# Hunterdon-Warren Counties Hailstorm: June 10, 1956

On the 10th from 6:00 to 9:00 P.M., in Hunterdon and Warren counties, a thunderstorm with accompanying hail, wind and lightning caused an estimated $250,000 damage to crops and other property. The principal damage was due to hail although some was caused by wind and lightning. Extensive damage to crops, houses, trees, shrubbery, greenhouses, and automobiles was reported in the storm area reaching from Belvidere to Clinton and Flemington. Hailstones varying in size from moth balls to golf balls were sighted, and in some places, piled 4 to 5 inches high.

Climatological Data:
New Jersey Section

# Point Pleasant Beach Hailstorm: November 4, 1970

An autumn storm which combined hail, high winds, heavy rain, and thunder and lightning, moved across the coastal area of the State during the afternoon and evening. Hail piled two and a half feet deep at Point Pleasant Beach in northern Ocean County. Some damage to late fall crops was caused by the hail. Windows were broken in some homes. Minor flooding was caused by the heavy rains, with the flooding of basements. Lightning strikes caused some damage to some homes in Atlantic County. High winds blew away porches and roofs from some homes.

Storm Data,
*November 1970*

# Mercer County Hailstorm: November 17, 1977

A severe thunderstorm moved eastward from Pennsylvania on November 17 into New Jersey near Titusville. The storm continued eastward across the state, reaching Jamesburg at 5:00 P.M. Trenton State College had extensive trim damage, broken windows, walnut-size hail, and some roof damage. Mercer County Airport reported gusts to 73 miles per hour. Two minor injuries on campus were caused by flying debris. Hail covered the ground at Princeton in some places six inches deep. At Monmouth Junction 0.75-inch diameter hail was reported, and smaller hail at Jamesburg.

Storm Data,
*November 1977*

# Floods

The steady pelting of endless raindrops, the surge of brooks and small streams, the rise and overflow of rivers, and finally the inundation of the flood plain—all occur while the residents of river valleys and lowlands stand helplessly by. A flood represents an inexorable hydrologic force. When the crests have passed and the waters receded, great problems of recovery and rehabilitation face both individuals and the public. Federal and state agencies are diverted from routine activities and are pressed into disaster relief. Yet the devastation of a flood can live on and blight a community for many months to come.

Over the years, floods have caused more death and destruction in New Jersey than any other meteorological force—hurricanes, tornadoes, or blizzards. Floods strike mainly at the industrial valleys of the state and their surrounding residential areas. In recent years the tempo of destruction has been accelerating, as the concentration of people and wealth along flood plains, in what is now the most densely populated state in the country, increase.

Floods can occur in New Jersey under a wide variety of meteorological and hydrological conditions. Heavy rainstorms resulting from cyclonic storms can strike at any time of the year and send rivers into high flood from excessive runoff, as occurred in October 1786, November 1810, January 1839, June 1862, February 1896, and November 1950. Heavy rainstorms plus snowmelt have created some of the highest waters, such as arose in January 1841, February–March 1902, and March 1936. Excessive rainfall in late summer resulting from the passage of tropical storms has also raised high crests, for example in July–August 1850, September 1882, August 1933, September 1938, August 1955, and August 1971. Ice-jam floods come almost every spring on some part of a New Jersey river, but most are harmless and temporary, unlike the massive backups of waters that occurred in February 1822, February 1857, and January 1904. Local cloudburst floods have inundated areas that seldom experience flooding, such as suburban Essex and Union counties in July 1889 or urban Bergen County in May 1968. Lately flash floods have become almost an annual occurrence in parts of Passaic and Bergen counties where housing and commercial developments have infringed on the flood plain. Furthermore, flood situations can be greatly aggravated by a burst dam that adds several feet to the crest. Successive rainstorms can trigger unusual twin crests, the first contributing to the second, as took place in the "one-two" floods of March 1936.

Generally, damaging floods of wide extent occur only in the northern half of the state, where the Delaware, Raritan, and Passaic rivers drain over 90 percent of the area of the northern counties. Each river has its own peculiarities in flooding characteristics. Hydrologists of the United States Geological Survey, with the cooperation of the New Jersey Division of Water Policy and Supply, Department of Conservation and Economic Development, have produced detailed studies of each river, and all the floods of the twentieth century have been analyzed.

## The Passaic Valley

The watershed of the upper Passaic River covers much of what was glacial Lake Passaic soon after the melting of the ice sheet about ten thousand years ago. Thomas H. Gordon, an early geographer of the state, wrote in 1834: "This stream is endowed with a very singular character. Rising in and flowing through a mountainous country, it is the most crooked, sluggish, and longest in the State." It flows through a diverse terrain, descending from rural highland country, meandering across the Great Swamp area and other extensive mead-

### Ten Greatest Floods at Great Falls, Paterson*

| Date | Peak discharge |
|---|---|
| November 1810 | 27,000 |
| July 1865 | 22,500 |
| December 1878 | 16,590 |
| September 1882 | 18,260 |
| February 1896 | 17,220 |
| March 1902 | 22,500 |
| October 1903 | 34,000 |
| March 1936 | 19,400 |
| July 1945 | 19,500 |
| May 1968 | 13,200 |

*Peak discharge measured in cubic feet per second.

*River and Bank streets in Paterson during the 1903 flood. An aerial life car can be seen in the center of the photograph. (Collection of the New Jersey Historical Society)*

ows, tumbling down two substantial falls, and emerging onto a large plain that has an enormous concentration of industrial, commercial, and residential development. It drains much of an eleven-county area of northern New Jersey and a small portion of southeastern New York.

The main tributaries of the Passaic—the Rockaway, Pompton, and Saddle rivers—flow southward to a confluence. The Rockaway and Pompton join above Little Falls and Great Falls, and their flood contributions flow into the great meadow area that stretches from Chatham to Fairfield. This serves as a large catch basin to impound the flood waters temporarily until it fills; then the excess overflows and rushes down the descents, over Little Falls into a gorge until it cascades over Great Falls and reaches the tidal plain. A flood through the gorge and over the falls presents an awesome spectacle. The Saddle River joins the main stream at Garfield on the plain below Passaic and Paterson.

## The Great Flood of 1903

The greatest rainstorm in the history of the New York metropolitan and northern New Jersey areas sent streams into the highest flood of record in October 1903. The storm system responsible was apparently the remnant of a tropical storm that followed a sinuous course through the Bermuda Triangle between the Bahamas and Bermuda from October 5 to 10, when it disappeared from the weather maps at about 37°N, 160 to 180 miles (257 to 290 km) off the Virginia Capes.

Rain fell over northeast New Jersey on October 7 but did not become general until the morning of the eighth. Judging from the hourly amounts at Newark and New York City, showery conditions prevailed until about noon, when steady downpours started and soon increased still further. Over an inch (25 mm) fell at Newark in the hours between 4:00 and 5:00 and 6:00 and 7:00 P.M. Heavy downpours continued through the night, next morning, and until 3:25 P.M. on the ninth, with only three hours not recording more than 0.20 inch (5 mm). In New York City the heaviest rains fell on the morning of the ninth, as much as 1.38 inches (35 mm) being measured between 8:00 and 9:00 A.M.

In the Passaic valley at Paterson the storm totaled 15.04 inches (382 mm) and at Little Falls 14.13 inches (359 mm). For the valley as a whole, the average was 11.74 inches (298 mm). All the tributary streams and rivers of the area—the Pompton, Ramapo, Wanaque, Pequannock, Rockaway, and Saddle—were soon swollen torrents pouring their discharges into the main stream. The peak flow at the Great Falls at Paterson topped 34,000 cubic feet per second, 126 percent of the next greatest, the estimated flow in November 1810.

The greatest destruction took place along the Ramapo River, the largest of the Passaic's upland branches. The violent flow within its confined banks caused almost complete destruction wherever the waters reached. Nearly all dams failed, and every bridge with one exception was carried away. Some small clusters of dwellings were completely swept away. The heaviest damage resulted at Pompton Lake, where a small dam impounding the waters at the Ludlum Steel and Iron Company failed, emptying the entire body of water, which covered 196 acres (79 ha). In all, about one hundred houses were inundated at Pompton Plains, and great damage resulted to roads and culverts. Key bridges over the Wanaque and Pequannock rivers were carried away.

The flow through the constricted channel at Little Falls and then on to Great Falls was attended by huge damage. The flooded district of Paterson extended over 196 acres and involved the closing of 10.3 miles (16.6 km) of streets. Along roads close to the river the height of the water reached 12 feet (3.7 m), sufficient to inundate the first floors of most buildings. Within the limits of Paterson, all bridges except two were carried downstream. Damage to real property was placed at $2.7 million.

Below Paterson in Passaic and Clifton losses were large, although the property was not as valuable as higher up the river. Newark suffered a loss of $753,199. Total damage was placed at not less than $7 million in 1903 values.

# The Raritan Valley

The Raritan River drains a large portion of central New Jersey, extending into northern Morris County on the north, western Hunterdon County on the west, and western Monmouth County on the south. The North Branch and South Branch meet west of Somerville at Raritan to form the main stream. The principal tributary from the south, the Millstone River, joins between Manville and Bound Brook and often is a critical contributor to high-flood situations. Until reaching Raritan the two main branches flow through generally rural hill-and-valley country, but downstream from there it is highly industrialized and commercialized, with targets of heavy potential damage almost every mile, in addition to many urban residential-shopping communities along a wide flood plain between Somerville and New Brunswick.

The Raritan is subject to different hydrologic responses than the Delaware and Passaic rivers. The largest flood in its basin during the nineteenth century occurred in a warm rain and snowmelt situation in February 1896, while the other rivers were experiencing less damaging rises. The Hurricane Flood of September 1938 struck savagely in the Raritan basin, but only moderate rises occurred on the Delaware and Passaic. Tropical storm Doria sent the middle Raritan into its highest flood of record on August 28, 1971, because its watershed lay astride the rather narrow zone of excessive rain.

During the nineteenth century, the greatest floods occurred in November 1810, July 1865, September 1882, and February 1896. In the twentieth century, the highest stages at the Manville station near Bound Brook took place on October 10, 1903; February 2, 1915; July 23, 1938; September 22, 1938; March 15, 1940; August 9, 1942; August 13 and 19, 1955; October 15, 1955; and August 28, 1971.

## The Great Flood of February 1896

In early February 1896 three conditions were present to make for high floods in central New Jersey. The ground was frozen, there was a considerable amount of snow on the ground, and a sudden, warm rain of great intensity set in. On February 6 there was generally from 6 to 8 inches (15 to 22 cm) of snow lying over the Raritan watershed. It grew suddenly warm and began to rain in the forenoon, the temperature reaching a maximum of about 52°F (11°C) in the highlands and 55°F (13°C) in the central plain. The rainfall amounted to about 3.7 inches (94 mm) in twenty-four hours. Just before noon on the sixth, the snow began to melt and went off with great rapidity, adding an average of about 0.6 inch (15 mm), so the total 4.3-inch (109 mm) depth of water over the entire watershed resulted from the combined rainfall and melting snow.

At the Delaware and Raritan Canal dam below Bound Brook, the river began to rise at 8:00 A.M. on the sixth and during the afternoon continued to do so very rapidly. It reached a height of 15.2 feet

*The largest flood in the Raritan River basin in the nineteenth century occurred in February 1896. This scene shows Berkeley Hotel and Voorhees Hall in Bound Brook during that flood. (Collection of the New Jersey Historical Society)*

(4.6 m) above the crest of the dam. The peak of the flood came about midnight, and by 8:00 A.M. on the seventh the river had fallen about 2 feet (0.6 m). At the mouth of the Millstone about 5:00 P.M. on the sixth the crest was reported to have increased by 10 inches (25 cm) in as many minutes.

Much damage occurred in the Millstone–Bound Brook area. The highway bridge at Finderne was carried away, as was the Philadelphia and Reading Railroad bridge, and the banks of the railroad were washed out. The tracks of the Central Railroad of New Jersey and of the Lehigh Valley line were under water for some distance, and traffic was seriously impeded on the Central and Reading tracks. The water was also deep in the lower streets of Bound Brook, and a fire caused by the flood reaching some stored lime added to the damage.

At Raritan, the flood of 1896 was 15.5 inches (0.4 m) higher than in the great flood of 1865, and at Neshanic it was 2.21 feet (0.7 m) higher.

# The Delaware Valley

Legend has it that there once was a farmer in southern Schoharie County in New York State who claimed that the water from the roof on the west side of his house drained into the watershed of the Susquehanna River, from the east side into the Delaware River, and from the north side into the Hudson drainage basin, all eventually entering the Atlantic Ocean but by three different routes.

The two branches of the Delaware River rise about six miles apart, close to the border of Delaware and Schoharie counties near Stamford, New York. They flow roughly parallel in a southwesterly direction for about sixty miles before joining at Hancock, where the main stream of the Delaware begins. The united waters then flow southeast between New York and Pennsylvania to Port Jervis, New York, at the junction of those states with New Jersey. Here the river trends southwest again, with New Jersey on the eastern shore and Pennsylvania on the western. The drainage area above Port Jervis is about 3,076 square miles (7,967 km) of rural territory, while below that point it flows for 220.8 miles (355 km) to the mouth of the river, mostly through a highly industrialized and largely urban region.

In New Jersey about half of Sussex, Hunterdon, and Mercer counties, a western strip of Monmouth, about half of Burlington and Gloucester counties, and most of Salem County drain into the Dela-

## Elevations of Major Floods on the Delaware River (in Feet above Mean Sea Level)

| Miles above Trenton gauge | Location | January 1841 | October 1903 | March 1936 | August 1955 |
|---|---|---|---|---|---|
| −34.0 | Philadelphia, Pennsylvania—Race Street | | 7.5 | | 8 |
| −16.2 | Burlington, New Jersey—Water works | | 9.7 | | 9.8 |
| −15.0 | Bristol, Pennsylvania—Mill Street | | 10.1 | | 9.6 |
| −11.9 | Florence, New Jersey—Municipal Building | | 13.6 | | 13.3 |
| −6.2 | Bordentown, New Jersey—Mouth Crosswick Creek | | 17.5 | | 15.9 |
| −1.0 | Trenton, New Jersey—Freeway bridge | | | | 22.6 |
| 0 | Trenton, New Jersey—U. S. G. S. gauge | | 28.5 | 24.4 | 28.6 |
| 3.5 | Yardley, Pennsylvania—Highway bridge | | 39.1 | 35.8 | 41.4 |
| 7.4 | Washington Crossing, New Jersey—Highway bridge | | | 47.4 | 53.9 |
| 14.3 | Lambertville, New Jersey—Highway bridge | 66.5 | 70.1 | 67.1 | 73.4 |
| 17.5 | Stockton, New Jersey—Highway bridge | | 81.7 | 79.7 | 84.5 |
| 29.4 | Frenchtown, New Jersey—Highway bridge | | 124.2 | | 127.7 |
| 33.1 | Milford, New Jersey—Highway bridge | 132.5 | 135.6 | 133.0 | 140.1 |
| 40.0 | Riegelsville, New Jersey—U. S. G. S. gauge | | 161.0 | 157.6 | 164.0 |
| 48.6 | Phillipsburg, New Jersey—Railroad bridge | 187.1 | 191.2 | | 198.8 |
| 48.9 | Easton, Pennsylvania—U. S. W. B. gauge | | 193.5 | 188.1 | 198.9 |
| 62.8 | Belvidere, New Jersey—U. S. G. S. gauge | | 255.1 | 251.5 | 256.6 |
| 72.5 | Portland, Pennsylvania—Highway bridge | | 296.1 | | 298.9 |
| 103.1 | Dingmans Ferry, Pennsylvania—Highway bridge | | 384.4 | 379.6 | 383.4 |
| 111.8 | Montague, New Jersey—U. S. G. S. gauge | | 405.4 | 400.1 | 405.1 |
| 120.0 | Port Jervis, New York—U. S. G. S. gauge | | 438.6 | 432.9 | 439.3 |
| 145.0 | Barryville, New York—U. S. G. S. gauge | | | | 626.6 |

SOURCE: D. M. Thomas, *Floods in New Jersey: Magnitude and Frequency* (Trenton: Department of Conservation and Economic Development, Division of Water Policy and Supply, 1964).

Comparative Stages of Twentieth-Century Floods in the Delaware Valley (in feet)

| Location | October 1903 | March 1936 | August 1955 | Other |
|---|---|---|---|---|
| Port Jervis, New York | 23.1 | | 23.91 | 25.5 (March 1904 ice jam) |
| Montague, Sussex County | 35.5 | | 35.5 | |
| Belvidere, Warren County | 28.6 | 25.0 | 30.21 | |
| Riegelsville, Warren County | 35.9 | 32.45 | 38.85 | |
| Milford, Hunterdon County | 35.8 | 32.57 | 40.25 | |
| Frenchtown, Hunterdon County | 24.3 | 21.93 | 27.79 | |
| Stockton, Hunterdon County | 81.7 | 79.7 | 84.45 | |
| Lambertville, Hunterdon County | 70.0 | 67.0 | 73.27 | |
| Washington Crossing, Mercer County | 51.9 | 47.30 | 53.77 | |
| Trenton, Mercer County | 20.7 | 16.66 | 20.83 | 22.8 (March 1904 ice jam) |

SOURCE: D. M. Thomas, *Floods in New Jersey: Magnitude and Frequency* (Trenton: Department of Conservation and Economic Development, Division of Water Policy and Supply, 1964).

NOTE: Gauge heights are not comparable between stations since each has its own height criteria.

ware River. Cumberland and Cape May counties belong to the drainage area of Delaware Bay.

At Trenton, where the falls line of the Piedmont is met and the tidewater of the coastal plain begins, the upland drainage basin amounts to 6,796 square miles (17,602 km). Trenton lies just one hundred miles (161 km) upriver from the opening of Delaware Bay between Cape May and Cape Henlopen.

## Historic Floods of the Delaware River

Soon after the settlement of the portion of the Delaware valley in the vicinity of Delaware Falls (Trenton), two high floods (in 1687 and 1692) were mentioned in a letter written by Phineas Pemberton, dated February 27, 1692. He related that the water reached the upper stories of the houses on the lowlands, or about 12 feet (3.7 m) above the usual high-water mark at the falls. The Indians had warned the first settlers of the danger of flooding at that location but had been ignored.

The magnitude of the 1692 flood was attested to by a recent statement in a United States Geological Survey report: "The flood of Feb. 27, 1692, may have been as great or greater than that of August 1955."

A valuable account of historic floods on the middle Delaware along the Hunterdon County river frontage appears in the family Bible of George Wyker of Upper Tinicum Township, Bucks County, Pennsylvania. The account was copied and read before the Bucks County Historical Society in 1927 as part of a paper on "Floods and Freshets in the Delaware and Lehigh Rivers." Here is part of it.

> Earliest Flood—On the 4th of June, 1734, was the greatest flood in the Delaware since the country was settled (even to this day, 1846), for it covered all the banks from one to five feet deep, and the people had to flee to the hills for safety.
>
> On the 23d of May, 1736, occurred another flood within about foot as high as the one mentioned above, which caused the settlers to sell out and buy lands away from the river. My grandfather, Henry DeKillian, saw both of these floods.
>
> On the 8th of May, 1781, there was a very high flood in the river. It ran nearly all over Marshall's Island, and they caught shad on Marshall's grain field. This fresh I seen myself. G.W.
>
> On March 16th and 17th, 1784, was the greatest ice fresh ever known in the Delaware, and there has been none since now at this day, 1846, which did so much damage to the shores.
>
> On the 7th day of October, 1786, happened what was called the "Pumpkin fresh," it being the highest flood since 1734 and 1736. G. Wyker.
>
> I have also accounts of many other freshets in the Delaware, which I have recorded, but the flood of the 8th and 9th of January, 1841, exceeded them all, except those of 1734 and 1736, in height of water by 3 or 4 feet. G. Wyker.
>
> On the 15th day of March, 1846, quite a high flood in the river, but not by 2 or 3 feet as high as that of 1841. The above I have written on the 8th day of April, 1846, being now in my 80th year. George Wyker.
>
> (Copied from another page of the same Bible):
>
> On Friday and Saturday, the 8th and 9th of January, 1841. the river Delaware was higher than it had been for 107 years before, for in 1734 it covered what is now called the Erwinna flats or lowlands from one to five feet deep and the inhabitants had to flee to the hills; but this fresh

was not by three feet as high, so that the families could stay in their houses, but the fresh carried away four bridges on the Delaware and five on the Lehigh, besides doing a great deal of damage to property of every description; and on the Lehigh it carried away several houses, with all their furniture, and several lives were lost.

*George Wyker*

## The Great March Floods of 1936

One of the greatest flood periods in the history of the northeastern United States occurred in the middle of March 1936. It was a typical spring-flood situation: the deep snow cover on the interior hills and valleys was already beginning to soften and melt when two warm rainstorms brought large amounts of precipitation to swell the water volume in the ground, leading to a massive runoff toward the sea.

The season had followed a pattern typical of a moderately severe winter until February 25, 1936, with temperatures running low and stream flow at a minimum. Then came an uneven rise in the thermometer with little precipitation falling throughout the Delaware basin. The thaw came and went intermittently until March 10 in the upstream areas of New York and Pennsylvania but established itself more steadily in the southern part of the valley below Easton and Phillipsburg. It was not of sufficient intensity, however, to remove all the snow cover or draw all the frost out of the ground in the middle stretches.

Snow cover over the watershed on March 10, expressed in inches of water content, ranged from 5.00 to 8.00 inches (130 to 203 mm) over the headwaters in New York and Pennsylvania down to bare ground below Trenton and Morrisville. The surface layer of the ground remained almost completely saturated, and only a few inches down the earth continued frozen, resulting in complete and rapid runoff of the rains to come.

Precipitation in northern New Jersey during the first storm period (March 11–12) ranged from 2.00 inches to over 3.00 inches (51–76 mm). Charlotteburg in Passaic County reported 3.52 inches (89 mm) for the two days, and Culvers Lake in northwestern Sussex County had 3.30 inches (84 mm). Port Jervis, New York, measured 2.15 inches (55 mm) and Mount Pocono in northeastern Pennsylvania had 1.56 inches (40 mm). The rainfall maps showed the greatest concentration of intensity in the eastern portion of the watershed. The amounts were not exceptional for a March storm, but they were concentrated over the runoff area. When added to the potential snowmelt water, the runoff potential became large.

During the first storm the runoff attributable to snowmelt varied with temperature and snow cover conditions; it amounted to about 2.4 inches (61 mm) in upstream areas, about 2.75 inches (70 mm) in the middle portion, and about 1.50 inches (38 mm) farther downstream. The first crest reached all points along the New Jersey riverbank on March 13 and removed the ice jams in the rivers with resulting damage of $200,000.

The second storm lasted longer, some rain falling over the area every day from March 17 to the twenty-second, but the main concentration on March 18–19 resulted in the peak crests. Mount Pocono measured 2.60 inches (66 mm) on both the eighteenth and the nineteenth—5.20 inches (132 mm) in forty-eight hours—and a storm total of 7.20 inches (183 mm) for four days. Stroudsburg, close to the Delaware in Pennsylvania, measured 6.92 inches (176 mm) on March 18–19. Amounts were also substantial in neighboring New York State: Jeffersonville had 4.58 inches (116 mm) and Port Jervis 4.75 inches (121 mm). These amounts were matched in northern New Jersey: Layton in Sussex County recorded 4.07 inches (103 mm), Charlotteburg in Passaic County 4.52 inches (115 mm).

The first storm's crest had a significant influence on the height of the second crest. At Riegelsville near the border of Warren and Hunterdon counties, hydrologists attributed an addition in river height of 2.55 feet (0.8 m) to the first crest. At Trenton, the addition was judged to be 1.25 feet (0.4 m).

The main crest reached Riegelsville on March 19 between 8:00 and 10:00 A.M. and the Calhoun Street Bridge at Trenton about 4:00 P.M.

The highway bridges at Columbia and Riegelsville were closed for several days, and the roads along the Delaware were washed out in a number of places. The town of Lumberville was isolated by flood waters for many hours. At Trenton, two hundred people were made homeless, and at Camden some of the principal streets were flooded as the Cooper River backed up when high tide coincided with the river's high-flood level. Along the Passaic River two streets in downtown Paterson were flooded and Route 23 near Pompton was closed by high water. No loss of life was directly attributable to the flood in New Jersey.

## The Hurricane Floods of August 1955

Ex-hurricane Connie bypassed New Jersey on August 13, 1955, by taking a route that curved northwest from Chesapeake Bay over central Pennsylvania to eastern Lake Erie. As far as wind was concerned, the storm was not particularly damaging in the Garden State. The most significant feature proved to be the tropical downpours from the eleventh to the fourteenth. Amounts in the Delaware valley from Trenton north averaged over 7.00 inches (178 mm). Some of the largest measurements were: Phillipsburg 7.28 inches (185 mm), Lambertville 7.80 inches (198 mm), Long Valley 8.55 inches (217 mm), and Clinton 9.16 inches (233 mm).

Moderate flood conditions resulted along the main stem of the Delaware, but no station reached its maximum stage for the month except on Assunpink Creek, which flows westward through Trenton and empties into the Delaware close to the War Memorial Building. The Trenton gauge located near the creek caught 6.20 inches (1.57 mm) on August 11–13, adding to a previous fall of 4.22 inches (107 mm) on August 7–8. The Assunpink rose to a crest 2.02 feet (0.6 m) above the stage that would come during ex-hurricane Diane's rainfall period a week hence. The maximum stage during the ex-hurricane Connie runoff on the main stem of the Delaware at Trenton reached 5.61 feet (1.7 m) above flood level at 10:00 A.M. on the thirteenth, and the river remained high for several days.

Most of the flooding in New Jersey occurred north and west of a line from Trenton to Staten Island. The three major river systems—the Passaic, Raritan, and Delaware—experienced record or near-record flood levels. Though damage was extensive over this region, it was widely distributed and not concentrated in any particular area except along the main stem of the middle Delaware, where it was the greatest and the most damaging flood of record.

Industrial installations along the Delaware north of Trenton suffered very heavy losses as a result of the speed with which the flood rose. Warnings to downstream areas helped lessen losses to factories and commercial enterprises in the Trenton area. Damage to public property, such as roads and bridges, was great, and communications were severed.

The bridges across the Delaware underwent a battering such as they had not experienced since the mid-nineteenth century. Only the recently built crossings at Montague, Sussex County, and at Trenton were passable during the height of the flood—all others were either inaccessible as a result of high water or had missing spans.

Four bridges between New Jersey and Pennsylvania were either completely destroyed or so damaged as to need replacements: the crossings between Columbia and Portland, Phillipsburg and Easton, Byram and Point Pleasant, and West Trenton and Yardley. The old covered bridge between Columbia and Portland near the Delaware Water Gap, which was started in 1831 and completed in 1869, had withstood all the intervening floods until the water surge in August 1955 collapsed the structure when it was about three-quarters submerged. Very little of the Byram–Point Pleasant bridge remained after the flood. The Phillipsburg-Easton bridge, which was an eyebar sus-

*The "world's fastest car wash," the sign said, and indeed it was for this Easton car wash service when the Delaware River flood was at its 43-foot peak in August 1955. (From* The Express, *Easton, Pennsylvania)*

pension type, presented an unusual picture when the center of the main span collapsed, leaving shorter suspended sections cantilevered out from the supporting towers on each side.

The center of ex-hurricane Diane, crossing the central part of the state during the early morning hours of August 19, reached the coast just south of Asbury Park about 5:00 A.M. Again wind speeds were not damaging, but Diane brought north from the tropics an enormous quantity of moisture and triggered vast amounts of precipitation over the adjacent highlands of New Jersey, Pennsylvania, and New York.

Rainfall totals in New Jersey were very high to the north of the storm track, especially in Sussex and Passaic counties: Sussex 8.10 inches (206 mm), Canistear Reservoir 7.69 inches (195 mm), and Layton 7.54 inches (192 mm).

Streams rose extremely rapidly. The Delaware River at Montague, Sussex County, swelled from a low between the two hurricane periods of 6.14 feet (1.9 m) at 6:00 A.M. on August 18 to 16 feet (4.9 m) by midnight and to 35.15 feet (10.7 m) at 9:00 A.M. on the nineteenth. The Delaware at Trenton rose from a low stage of 2.44 feet (0.7 m) at midnight on the seventeenth to 20.83 feet (6.3 m) at 6:00 A.M. on the twentieth.

Peak discharges increased from 233,000 cubic feet per second at Port Jervis, New York, to 329,000 cubic feet per second at Trenton. At Riegelsville in Warren County the Delaware reached a peak of 340,000 cubic feet per second, 1.2 times the previous highest peak in fifty-three years, and the stage was 3.0 feet (0.9 m) higher.

The river crested at Port Jervis, New York, at 5:30 A.M., August 19, at Belvidere at 8:00 P.M., August 19, and at Trenton at 6:30 A.M., August 20. The distance from Port Jervis to Trenton is 120 miles (193 km), so the average travel time of the crest was 4.8 miles per hour (7.7 km/h).

Tributaries of the Delaware in New Jersey also had notable floods. The peak of Paulins Kill at Blairstown in Warren County, for instance, reached 8,750 cubic feet per second, nearly twice the previous maximum in thirty-five years of record. At Flat Brookville in Sussex County it reached a peak of 9,560 cubic feet per second, 2.6 times the previous record.

## Recent Floods in New Jersey

Since the drought years from 1961 to 1966, New Jersey has experienced a series of heavy rainstorms which have created successive flood situations; several have resulted in the state being declared a disaster area. The first flood of the series occurred in late May 1968 when the Passaic River rose in some communities to the highest levels since October 1903; several counties were declared eligible for Federal relief. In 1969, a succession of overflows affected New Jersey on June 14–16, July 27–30, August 4, August 15, and September 15; these caused local flooding, but nothing on a major scale.

In late August 1971, tropical storm Doria bisected the state from south to north in the wake of a very heavy warm-front rain. Its additional downpours created high-water conditions everywhere, and the central Raritan rose to its highest crest of record.

Ex-hurricane Agnes's tropical deluges in June 1972 followed closely on the showers that had attended three cold-front passages. Flooding took place in parts of Passaic and Morris counties, and the continued rains in the south resulted in very heavy losses to truck farms and orchards. Moderate to heavy rains on November 8, 1972, caused numerous evacuations of residents in the northeastern counties, and on the fourteenth additional urban flooding occurred in the southern counties. November 1972 ranked as a record or near-record month for precipitation.

A storm system moving from Pennsylvania produced the most devastating urban flood in recent central New Jersey history on August 2, 1973. Hardest hit were Plainfield, Bound Brook, Cranford, and surrounding communities. A total of 7.30 inches (185 mm) fell between 7:30 A.M. and noon across a relatively narrow belt of Union, Somerset, and northern Middlesex counties. In some places the water rose as high as 15 feet (4.6 m). Railroad service was curtailed, power was shut off, and telephone lines were down. Six persons were killed as a direct result of the flooding.

A severe coastal storm on November 8–9, 1973, dropped over 5.00 inches (127 mm) of rain on northeastern sections, resulting in high water. Again the Bound Brook and Cranford areas were hard hit and residents had to be evacuated.

Mid-July 1975 brought double disasters to New Jersey. On the thirteenth to the sixteenth, a series of thunderstorms dropped from 5.00 to 8.00 inches (127 to 203 mm) of rain over the northern counties, resulting in widespread flash flooding. There were five drownings, and damage to crops and property loss were estimated at $40 million. Parts of the state were declared disaster areas. On July 21 the worst flood since August 1955 swept through Mercer County, rendering a thousand people temporarily homeless. Assunpink Creek in Trenton reached a record crest and stopped all rail traffic between New York

*On July 21, 1975 the worst flood in twenty years hit Mercer County. The flood waters of Assunpink Creek, which normally flow in a channel alongside the Trenton Conrail Station, rose to platform level.* (Trenton Times *staff photo)*

and Philadelphia. Damage was assessed at $25 million, and Mercer County was declared a disaster area. Following a four-day period of rain in late September, additional flash flooding took place over the northern half of the state.

In early November 1977, a tropical storm that merged with a weak cyclonic system off the New Jersey coast produced strong winds, high tides, and excessive rainfall. Over the northeastern counties about 2.00 inches (51 mm) fell on the seventh; this mounted to over 8.00 inches (203 mm) on the eighth, when the tropical moisture arrived. Bergen, Passaic, Essex, Hudson, and Monmouth counties reported heavy floods with water damage totalling about $100 million. Lodi on the Saddle River near Hackensack suffered a devastating inundation, the worst in its long flood history.

# A Rural Flood: January 26, 1839

> The storm of Saturday, the 26th ult. swept over a vast extent of country, and occasioned the destruction of an immense amount of property. From every quarter of the compass, we hear nothing but details of ruin and devastation. Our own country too, has suffered severely. Our favorable position, in the mountains, which generally exempts us from the disasters to which the lowlands are subject, did not avail us this time. The streams fairly leaped full-grown from their sources, swelling at every bound, and sweeping away every obstruction to their turbulent course. Meadows of vast extent were submerged, the public highways in many places rendered impassable, and bridges, mill dams, &c. demolished. On the Wallkill, at Sparta, the forge dam of Lewis Sherman & Co. was destroyed, as was also the mill dam of J. E. Edsall, Esq. of Hamburg, on the same stream. The new stone bridge in the village of Vernon was nearly destroyed, and the dam and saw mill, a short distance above, torn away. On the Paulinskill, the Baleville Bridge, the small bridge at Pleasant Valley, the Lower Cassidy bridge, the Emmons' bridge, and the bridge at Theophilus Hunt's, were all demolished, and their fragments carried off by the impetuous torrent. At Stanhope, the banks of the Canal were much injured, and the canal aqueduct, over a small stream, about a mile below, was undermined, and nearly destroyed. On the Flatbrook two bridges are washed away, one at Fuller's Mill, and the other near the mouth of the brook.
>
> Sussex Register
> *(Newton),*
> *February 4, 1839*

# A Suburban Flood: July 30–31, 1889

The fierce downpour on the 30th and 31st did considerable damage, especially in the vicinity of Plainfield and the Oranges. At Plainfield three dams gave way and the entire town was flooded. Several large ice houses were destroyed and some of the finest residences were damaged. All the Oranges were flooded and many houses were damaged or destroyed. Fritz's dam was swept away, and the waters almost completely wrecked Epples Park. The tracks of the Erie Railroad were badly undermined and all traffic was stopped. In East Orange many elegant residences were in an open sea, fences, roads, and all landmarks having disappeared. The low meadows along the Passaic River and in its branches were flooded, destroying thousands of acres of hay. This crop estimated at $5.00 per acre, which shows a loss of from $60,000 to $65,000. The rainfall at South Orange, 18.58 inches, is phenomenal, and the wonder is that the damage was not greater than it was. Five stations report a total for the month exceeding 14.00 inches, three exceeding 12.00, and ten 10.00. The excess (above the average at all stations) is from 0.34 inch on the Atlantic coast to 14.26 inches at South Orange.

Monthly Weather Review
*(Washington, D.C.),*
*July 1889*

# Drought

Dry spells occur sporadically in various seasons, but the term *drought* is reserved for periods of moisture deficiency that are relatively extensive in both time and space. During dry periods the loss of moisture from the surface of the earth is large and may be damaging to plant life. Meteorologists use the term *evapotranspiration* to describe the loss of moisture from the surface of the earth combined with that from the leaves of plants directly to the atmosphere. Almost every growing season witnesses a dry spell of sufficient severity to check plant growth at least temporarily. A period of abnormal moisture deficiency of sufficient length may cause a serious hydrologic imbalance that results in crop damage, water supply shortage, and economic disruption.

Drought Severity Index

| Index number | Description |
|---|---|
| 4 or more | Extremely wet |
| 3 to 4 | Very wet |
| 2 to 3 | Moderately wet |
| 1 to 2 | Slightly wet |
| .5 to 1 | Incipient wet spell |
| .5 to −.5 | Near normal |
| −.5 to −1 | Incipient drought |
| −1 to −2 | Mild drought |
| −2 to −3 | Moderate drought |
| −3 to −4 | Severe drought |
| −4 or more | Extreme drought |

Drought of varying intensity is an almost annual occurrence in New Jersey. Fortunately, the high summer months of July and August are normally the wettest of the year as a result of the greater availability of atmospheric moisture and the frequency of thunderstorms. A Rutgers University study has shown that the period from September 19 to October 17 is usually the driest of the year; fortunately, this is after the growing season of most crops. The driest months in New Jersey history, state-wide, were: June 1949, 0.23 inch (6 mm); September 1941, 0.28 inch (7 mm); October 1963, 0.34 inch (9 mm); and October 1924, 0.41 inch (10 mm).

In recent years a rather sophisticated indication of drought severity has been developed which takes account of antecedent weather and computes an index based on the difference between the actual rainfall and the computed amount of rainfall that would have sustained the evaporation, runoff, and moisture storage characteristics of the area. The Drought Severity Index remains at or near zero in any climate as long as temperature and precipitation conditions are near normal. Extended periods of anomalous weather produce an index ranging from +4 or above during periods which were much wetter than normal to −4 or below during exceptionally dry periods. In addition, a modification geared to agricultural drought, ignoring the moisture required to maintain stream flow and moisture storage, is issued weekly during the season as a crop moisture index to indicate current moisture-supply conditions.

# Early Droughts

Droughts have occurred periodically over the years since the region was first settled, and doubtless long before that, as well.

## 1762

Two excerpts from the Letter Book of John Watts of New York City describe conditions during the severe drought period of 1761 and 1762 that was general over the Middle Colonies and New England:

> New York City, June 20, 1762
> Provisions of all kinds continue amazingly scarce & dear with us, was it not for the assistance of Ireland we should really be distressed for several articles . . . a succession of two years Drouth has rendered it difficult to support in the usual manner.
>
> New York City, August 23, 1762
> All necessarys for Life both for Man and Beast are astonishingly dear & scarce, owing in a great Measure to the most severe Drouth that ever was known in this part of the World. How food will be provided for Cattle during a long dreadful Winter, God alone knows.

## Newark, August 1894

A later drought made an equally strong impression:

> What was detestable in the month was its refusal to make up for the deliquency of June and July in paying their share of the water debt due from summer to the fields and gardens, the streams and forests. To these creditors June went off indebted to the amount of 2.27 inches. July ran away owing 2.62 inches, and August, which in full payment of summer's debt, should have given 6.75 inches, stole away after leaving the beggerly amount of 1.47 inches. It looks like a case of robbery and murder. Our gardens are in ruins, our fields are withered, our streams are dried up, and our forests are putting on their autumn clothing. With its waterfall of only 4.62 inches we have just passed through the driest and most cheerless summer of the last half century. The mean temperature of the summer just ended was 72.7 degrees, which is just one degree above the mean of the last 51 summers. The waterfall, as already stated, was 4.62 inches, while the average summer waterfall is 13.13 inches.

*Frederick W. Ricord, in the* Annual Report of the New Jersey Weather Service, *July 1894*

# Twentieth-Century Droughts

There have been three periods of severe drought in the state in the twentieth century: July 1929 to September 1932; June 1953 to July 1955; and August 1961 to September 1966. Droughty conditions have occurred at other times, but none lasted more than thirteen months.

## July 1929–September 1932

A drought began in northern New Jersey in July 1929 and continued to September 1932, a period of thirty-nine months. Eight months in this period had severe drought and fifteen were rated moderate according to the Drought Severity Index. The maximum severity reached −3.91. The agricultural effects were most severe during the summer and fall of 1930. In southern New Jersey the duration was the same, with eleven months in the severe category and ten in the moderate. The maximum severity was −3.74. For the state as a whole, 77 percent of the normal amount of rain fell in 1930. Only June had more rain than normal. Extreme heat from the middle of July to the middle of August added to the effects of the drought. October 1932 brought the first break in the situation when precipitation amounted to 159 percent of normal. A deluge of 5.86 inches (149 mm) fell at Phillipsburg on October 6, and the month brought a high total of 9.64 inches (245 mm) at Charlotteburg.

## June 1953–July 1955

In the north the drought continued for twenty-six months, from June 1953 to July 1955, reaching a maximum index of −3.63. Two months during this period were in the severe category and thirteen were moderate. In the south drought conditions continued for twenty-four months, from August 1953 to July 1955. The maximum index was −4.70. Four months were extreme, one severe, and one moderate. Along the coast the drought continued for twenty-nine months, from September 1953 to January 1956. The maximum index was −3.19; one month was severe and nine moderate. The heavy rains of August 1955 did not affect the southern half of the state.

The average precipitation for the state in July 1955 was 1.13 inches (29 mm), 3.52 inches (89 mm) below the normal and 0.23 inch (6 mm) below the previous driest July in 1910. Monthly totals ranged from a scant 0.06 inch (1.5 mm) at the Princeton Water Works to 4.64 inches (118 mm) at the Bass River State Forest in Burlington County, the latter the result of a coastal storm that affected the rest of the state only slightly.

## The Great Drought of the Early 1960s

Drought conditions prevailed over most of New Jersey for a five-year period from August 1961 to September 1966. It was the longest and most severe such period in the state's history. The period of greatest impact came from July to October each year, when the demand for water was the greatest.

The basic atmospheric circulation pattern placed an upper-air trough of low pressure off the Atlantic coast and a high-pressure ridge over the central United States. This induced a flow of northwest winds from a dry continental source. Cold fronts moved southeast in this situation, but the southwest flow preceding them was usually brief and the flow of tropical air was cut off. With the absence of tropical air, summer thunderstorm activity was less frequent and intense than normal and rainfall totals much less than expected. Also, there was a distinct absence of the coastal storms or northeasters that annually supply a good part of the precipitation budget in both summer and winter. The placement of the trough offshore probably accounted for the storm track being well at sea for both coastal storms and the few tropical storms that strayed north during this five-year period.

Drought conditions began in August 1961 in coastal sections, in September in the north, and in October in the south. The subsequent months were all much drier than normal except December, which averaged out about normal. In 1962, the drought intensified gradually, reaching an index of −2.19 in July; then it decreased to a year-end figure of −1.25. In 1963, conditions became more severe, reaching an index of −4.05 in October, a very dry month. Good November rains reduced the figure to −2.07 in December. In 1964, average rains during the spring and early summer kept the index higher than −3.00 until July; thereafter drought conditions intensified to bring the index down to −4.55 in November. The droughty year closed with the index standing at −4.13 in December.

In 1965, the index improved to −3.48 in February, but thereafter reached the drought maximum of −5.09 in July. There was only a small improvement through November, but the December mark rose to −4.08, the best in many months.

During the first eight months of 1966 the severe drought situation continued over the entire state, but September brought relief to all sections. Northern New Jersey, which had experienced sixty-one months of drought, showed considerable improvement. Very heavy rainstorms on September 14 and 21 resulted in as much as 7.00 inches (178 mm) of precipitation in portions of Union, Essex, and Middlesex counties. It was the heaviest rainstorm in some sections since the great flood of October 1903.

**End of the Drought: 1966 (Monthly precipitation and departure from normal, in inches)**

| Month | Region | | | | | |
|---|---|---|---|---|---|---|
| | North | | South | | Coastal | |
| September | 7.24 | +3.18 | 8.32 | +4.53 | 6.92 | +3.25 |
| October | 4.21 | +0.79 | 5.17 | +1.82 | 3.86 | +0.56 |
| November | 3.80 | −0.08 | 2.13 | −1.61 | 1.81 | −1.78 |
| December | 3.91 | +0.35 | 3.94 | +0.68 | 4.00 | +0.66 |

The year of 1965 appears to have been the driest in New Jersey history since at least 1885. The amounts received ranged from only 19.85 inches (504 mm) at Canton in the southwest to 39.96 inches (1,014 mm) at Mahwah in the extreme northeast. The south averaged 65 percent of normal, the north 65 percent, and the coast 73 percent.

In contrast, the wettest year in New Jersey weather records appears to have been 1882, when the station at Paterson measured 85.99 inches (2,184 mm). Most of this was contributed by a very wet September total of 25.98 inches (660 mm), the greater share coming from a tropical storm that stalled offshore.

## The Summer Drought of 1980

During the summer of 1980, drought returned to the daily headlines for the first time since the autumn of 1966. A period of copious rainfall in March and April filled the reservoirs, but four of the five months from May through September showed serious rainfall deficits. At Newark the precipitation catch amounted to only 48 percent of normal for the five months.

There were scattered heavy thunderstorms across parts of the state during early July, but after the fifteenth anticyclonic conditions set in; it turned intensely hot and continued so for a month, then moderated somewhat. The higher temperatures stimulated greater water consumption and also encouraged evaporation of soil moisture. Combined with the lack of any replenishing rainfall, New Jersey moved into the drought category. By September 1, the Palmer Drought Index was −2, or moderate drought, and by October 1 was −4, or extreme drought. For the last three months at Newark, July brought only 69 percent of normal precipitation, August 21 percent, and September 59 percent. Other stations were little better off: Lakehurst had 57 percent and Atlantic City 70 percent of normal.

The northern counties, with their great concentration of population and heavy industry, suffered acute water shortages toward the end of

September. Hardest hit was the Hackensack Water Company, the chief supplier in Bergen County, whose reservoirs were down to 28 percent of capacity on September 27 and had only a sixty-day supply left.

On September 27, Governor Byrne issued an emergency order mandating water rationing for 114 North Jersey communities. The object was to reduce consumption by 25 percent. The rationing covered parts of seven counties, ranging from wealthy suburban areas of Bergen, Morris, and Somerset counties to the state's poverty-riddled urban and industrial centers in Essex, Hudson, Union, and Passaic counties. Some of the cities affected were Newark, Jersey City, Paterson, Bayonne, and Elizabeth.

Central and South Jersey communities were not affected by the order, since most obtained their water supply from ground wells or from river flow such as the Delaware River, not yet affected by the failure of precipitation.

After a dry September, near-normal precipitation in October and November helped to raise water levels in reservoirs, but a dry December and January prolonged drought conditions. Finally, a wet February with snowmelt brought near satisfactory levels. Soil moisture for agricultural purposes was close to one hundred percent at the beginning of the farm season in early April. Water restrictions were phased out by Governor Byrne between April 16 and May 18, 1981.

## The Driest Month: June 1949

Dry weather set in about May 25 and continued through June until July 5. Several stations reported no measurable rain at all. Nearly all stations had less than 0.50 inch (13 mm), and only two reported as much as 1.00 inch (25 mm) for the month.

The first half of June was practically rainless. Seven out of eighty-five stations reported light amounts up to 0.10 inch (2.5 mm) on June 4–5, and sixteen stations had up to 0.24 inch (6 mm) on the eleventh. The only general rains of the month occurred on June 17–19, when amounts ranged from a trace to 0.56 inch (14 mm). Some stations reported measurable rains on four consecutive days, but all were light. Showers fell on June 25–26 at about half the stations. They were heavy at Belvidere (0.92 inch, or 23 mm) and moderate at Glassboro (0.52 inch, or 13 mm). Aside from the heavy shower on the twenty-fifth, Belvidere received only 0.09 inch (2 mm) of additional rainfall during the entire month.

As a result of the extended dryness, crops suffered heavy damage. Hardest hit were early sweet corn and early commercial potatoes. Yields of both crops were estimated to be reduced by more

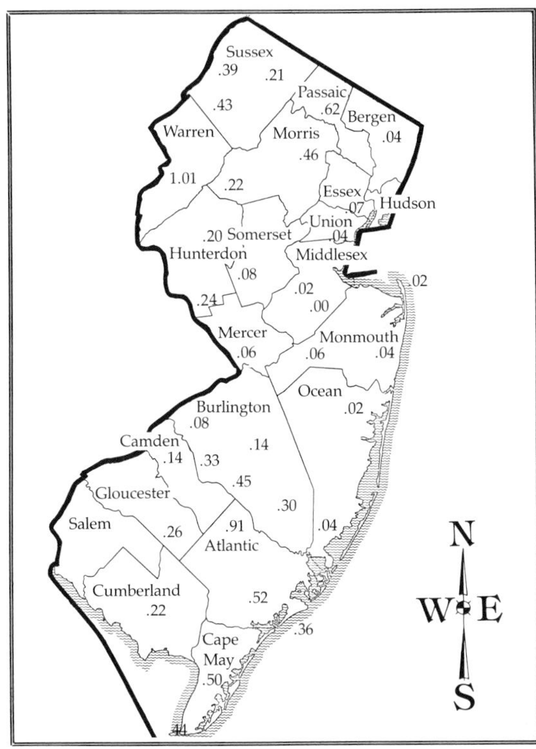


*The driest month on record, June 1949*

than 50 percent. Pastures were brown and dairy production greatly diminished.

The mean total precipitation of the state, computed from the observations of forty-six first-class stations, was 0.23 inch (6 mm), 3.60 inches (91 mm) below normal.

# Drought and Fires

Second only to the impact of drought on agriculture is drought's contribution to conditions conducive to forest fires. This applies particularly to the Pine Barrens, where drying conditions favor the combustion of forest fuels. Weather conditions leading to the start and spread of forest fires are: high atmospheric pressure with stable air; high winds from a land trajectory; low relative humidity; and antecedent drought conditions. Generally speaking, relative humidity of less than 40 percent, winds greater than 13 miles per hour (21 km/h), and precipitation of less than 0.01 inch (0.25 mm) add up to conditions leading to forest fires in the Pine Barrens. The presence of a low-level jet flow also helps spread the flames. The season of greatest fire threat runs from March through May, though extensive fires have occurred in the summer and autumn months. Fires have been reported in the Pine Barrens since Europeans first arrived. In 1755 one is said to have burned over an area of 30 miles (48 km).

## 1838

Probably the largest fire in the first half of the nineteenth century occurred in early September 1838. A report from Bordentown on September 5 stated:

> A space of 20 miles in length by 14 in breadth, through Burlington and Monmouth counties, and consisting chiefly of pine woods and cedar swamps, is now in a state of conflagration. The clouds of smoke are seen some twenty miles off, and at night the air is filled with a lurid blaze which dims the moon. The grass and woods are so packed from the drought that the flames spread with lightning-like rapidity, presenting at night a scene of unparalleled sublimity. A great many houses and thousands of cords of wood are destroyed; and it is feared a number of persons, hemmed in by the flames have perished.
>
> New York Herald,
> *September 7, 1838*

Weather conditions during late August and early September 1838 favored the development and spread of fires. The good records maintained at the Pennsylvania Hospital in downtown Philadelphia at the time give an accurate picture of the scene. After a very heavy rain of 2.13 inches (54 mm) on August 11, only 0.12 inch (3 mm) fell for the next thirty-one days through September 11. From September 3 to September 8, "not a cloud was to be seen," according to the notes of Dr. John Conrad, the observer at the hospital. Maximum temperatures were in the 80°F range (27°–32°C) from the fifth to the eighth. The fire threat ended in most emphatic form on September 11–12 when rains from an offshore hurricane dumped no less than 6.01 inches (153 mm) in twenty-four hours, including 4.19 inches (106 mm) in an eight-hour period. This was the heaviest one-day rain in the hospital records through 1871 and has been exceeded only once in the past 110 years of government records.

## 1885

The summer of 1885 witnessed the largest fires for many years. "Not since 1838 has the country been so dry and favorable for the spread of flames," reported a dispatch in the *Monthly Weather Review* of July 1885, from the scene of the fires, which were burning simultaneously in Burlington, Camden, and Atlantic counties. "Yesterday the towns of Atco, Jackson, Sloantown, Waterford, Pestletown, Winslow, Weekstown, Hammonton, Atsion, and a number of other small places in Camden and Burlington counties near the Camden and Atlantic railroad, were surrounded by brush and wood fire, and all the inhabitants were out fighting the flames. Large tracts of cedar timber and several dwellings have already been burned, and many of those fighting the flames have had narrow escapes." Severe thunderstorms swept the area on the afternoon of July 26, "checking to a great extent the extensive forest fires raging in the interior of the State," according to a dispatch from Atlantic City, where 1.10 inches (30 mm) were measured. It was estimated that 128,000 acres (51,800 ha) were burned.

July 1885 was a very hot, dry month, according to the Philadelphia records. During the first fourteen days, 1.46 inches (37 mm) of rain fell. June was also very dry, with a total of only 0.74 inch (19 mm). The effect of the dryness was greatly increased by very high temperatures and low relative humidities. Philadelphia endured its most prolonged heat wave from July 16 through July 26, when the thermometer topped 90°F (32°C) for eleven consecutive days, also a record. It reached 97°F (36°C) on two days during this spell. Both the heat and the dry spell were ended on July 25–26, when 0.80 inch (20 mm) fell in thunderstorms. These were apparently quite severe storms along the coast at Atlantic City.

## Twentieth-Century Fires

A "New Jersey Historical Fire Record" has been maintained since 1906 by the New Jersey Forest Fire Service. It lists the following years in which more than 100,000 acres (40,000 ha) burned throughout the state: 1915—150,258; 1922—106,086; 1923—137,743; 1930—267,547; and 1963—202,116. Both 1976 and 1977 had more than 2,000 individual fires, the most since 1941, but the acreage burned in these recent fires was much less than in the former extensive fires.

The fires on April 20–21, 1963, were described as "the worst in 40 years" and "the worst forest fire period in the State history." Seven deaths and a number of injuries, mainly to firefighters, resulted, and 186 homes and 197 outbuildings were consumed by the flames. The precipitation record at Chatsworth, "the capital of the Pine Barrens," showed that only 0.30 inch (8 mm) had fallen during the first twenty days of April in three small showers. Maximum temperatures on April 20 and 21 were 80°F and 75°F (27°C and 24°C).

The most recent outbreak of fires in the Pine Barrens occurred from March 30 through April 1, 1977. March had normal precipitation: Chatsworth measured 1.04 inches (26 mm) on the eighteenth and 1.67 inches (42 mm) on March 22–23. No more fell during the month, and a heat wave raised the Chatsworth thermometer above 80°F (27°C) on the last three days; the maximum reading was 85°F (29°C) on March 30. High winds played a role in the spread of the flames. Atlantic City recorded 44 miles per hour (71 km/h) on March 31. Forty blazes destroyed 14,000 acres (5,600 ha). One of the main fires was centered in the Wharton State Forest and burned on both sides of Route 206. One firefighter was killed in an auto accident. Five homes and six automobiles were destroyed.

On April 18 the fires broke out again. An eight-mile section of the Garden State Parkway had to be closed when flames spread on both sides between Lakewood and Bricktown. Seven hundred acres (280 ha) were involved.

# Air Pollution

Air pollution is not a new problem. It arises from both natural sources and from human activity. Volcanoes, forest fires, vegetation, and dust storms have always contributed impurities to the atmosphere, but the world-wide dispersion of their products results in a low average concentration in a particular locality. This is not so with pollutants of human origin, which have a tendency to concentrate near urban complexes and thus affect large numbers of people.

Urban pollution has been a problem since Roman times. In western Europe measures were taken in the late Middle Ages to control smoke emissions, and the Industrial Revolution of the nineteenth century greatly exacerbated the situation by adding other impurities to the atmosphere. This type of pollution came to be referred to as *classical smog*. The apt word *smog*, a combination of *smoke* and *fog*, was first used in 1905 to describe London's famous "pea-soup" fogs. American cities, too, experienced troublesome carbon-combustion problems when coal was the principal energy source of fuel and power. It was considered a nuisance and not a major problem, however.

Not until after World War II did the implications of air pollution for many aspects of modern life become clearly understood. In California's Los Angeles basin the recognition of *photochemical smog* and the identification of automotive exhaust as the principal contaminating agent came in the early 1950s. In 1948 the Donora disaster in western Pennsylvania, when anticyclonic conditions caused a smog blanket to rest over the Monongahela valley for three days, resulted in the death of twenty persons. It demonstrated the danger of chemical pollution in the atmosphere and served as a warning to other communities with similar geographical and industrial situations.

With the great increase in vehicular traffic and the proliferation of industrial plants, air pollution problems came to plague most urban concentrations. In 1963, the federal government recognized the nation-wide scope of the problem with a clean air act aimed at air pollution that "endangers the health or welfare of any persons." This was

*Smog covers the upper floors of buildings in downtown Newark. (Courtesy of Newark Public Library)*

strengthened with the enactment of important amendments, providing more federal direction in setting standards, speeding their implementation, and making provisions for their enforcement. Air-quality standards are enforced by the Environmental Protection Agency. In naming national air-quality control regions according to the severity of atmospheric pollution, the federal Environmental Protection Agency designated the New Jersey–New York–Connecticut Interstate area as Region 2 in priority and the metropolitan Philadelphia Interstate area as Region 3. The New Jersey Interstate area (southeast counties) and Northeast Pennsylvania Upper Delaware Valley Interstate area, by contrast, are numbers 150 and 151 respectively.

Current air-pollution problems arise from the varying quantities of potentially hazardous gases and particulates that are introduced into the atmosphere as a result of human activities. Pollutants are emitted from furnaces, factories, refineries, smelters, and in particular by automobile engines. In the process of burning fossil fuels, gases and smoke particles are vented; they spend a great deal of time reacting chemically with other substances and cause the formation of toxic compounds. The most widespread and potentially hazardous gaseous pollutants are carbon monoxide, sulfur dioxide, nitrogen oxides, and hydrocarbons.

The current state of the atmosphere is the key to whether an air-pollution situation will develop and become a serious threat to community well-being. Cyclonic storm conditions, characterized by rapid movement of air, frontal activity, and changes of airmass, cause an unstable condition of the lower atmosphere, that is, the temperature decreases with height and encourages convective currents to rise. But anticyclonic conditions, with light wind movement, subsiding air from aloft, and no change of airmass, tend to create stable conditions, that is, the temperature decreases very slowly or not at all and vertical currents are inhibited. The latter conditions eventually result in the formation of a temperature inversion in which a layer of warm air overlies cooler air at the surface. This prevents the normal venting upward of the pollutants in the lower atmosphere because they are trapped in a relatively thin layer of air at the surface. With more pollutants entering this layer constantly, a pollution situation develops and grows gradually worse as long as the inversion condition persists.

A Rutgers University study has demonstrated that the concentration of pollutants in the atmosphere exhibit seasonal, daily, and hourly variabilities resulting from changing meteorological conditions. Data from the monitoring sites of the state Department of Environmental Protection indicate the following seasonal trends: sulfur dioxide concentration is high during the winter and reaches a low level during the summer months due to the fact that it is largely derived from the use of fuel for space heating. Nitrogen oxide collectively exhibits a similar but less marked seasonal dependency; and nitric oxide specifically exhibits a strong relationship with season, but for nitrogen oxide there is no such indication. Oxidants, produced in the atmosphere as a result of photochemical reactions catalyzed by light energy, reach a peak in summer and decrease considerably during the winter when there is less sunlight. Carbon monoxide and hydrocarbons, being largely derived from motor vehicles, exhibit no seasonal relationship.

The daily variations in pollutant concentration are brought about largely by meteorological factors, particularly wind speed and direction. Pollutant levels in general are higher when the air is stable than when there is air movement capable of carrying the pollutants into the higher atmosphere where they are diluted many times. Wind direction is an important consideration in determining pollutant concentration with respect to a specific source.

The hourly variability differs according to the type of pollutant. For sulfur dioxide and nitrogen oxide the peak is at the mid-morning rush hours. Meteorological data indicate that during these hours wind speed tends to be low and barometric pressure slightly higher than in the late hours of the day. For oxidants and aldehydes the peak occurs shortly after noon, illustrating the dependency of these on sunlight for their initiation.

New Jersey experiences both classical and photochemical smog. The urban complexes of the Metropolitan Philadelphia Interstate and the New Jersey–New York Interstate regions were long plagued by an excess of smoke and particulates in the atmosphere from coal burning. The substitution of oil and gas in home heating and industrial processes greatly reduced this type of contamination as smoke-abatement programs went into effect. But very little was done about industrial contaminants, especially sulfur dioxide, which is converted to sulfuric acid when mixed with atmospheric water. It can harm the lungs, attack plants, injure wildlife, and eat away masonry. The sulfur-bearing particles in the atmosphere also serve as nuclei for the formation of raindrops and are ultimately carried to the ground as rain or snow. The problem of acid rain has been given increasing recognition of late; plants, animal life, and water sources far downwind from emission sources have been seriously polluted by it.

The great increase in automotive traffic after World War II added photochemical smog to the already serious problem. This type of pollution results from the incomplete combustion of automotive fuel, which produces nitric oxide; this reacts with other hydrocarbons under sunlight to produce ozone and other irritating chemical reactions. The main effect on humans is eye irritation and respiratory afflictions, with other long-range side effects. It also attacks crops and vegetation.

In recent years the "heat island" condition of the local atmosphere has become a recognized aspect of New Jersey's air-pollution situation. *Heat island* describes the thermal condition of an urban complex whose areas of large buildings and pavements tend to absorb more solar radiation in daytime than do rural areas, with their covering of foliage and grass. The urban heat is retained and concentrated close to the center of the city and released only gradually after sundown. If an excess of pollutants is present in the air over the city, radiational cooling is inhibited and the heat is trapped in the lower layers of the atmosphere. In rural areas under clear-sky conditions, the daytime intake of heat is radiated to outer space at night and surface temperatures drop considerably. Sizable temperature contrasts can develop between urban and rural areas, and sometimes a secondary circulation is set up, with warm air rising over the city and cool air flowing in from the suburbs at low levels. Radio and television weather reports feature these morning temperature contrasts, and commuters are familiar with the pall of pollution often observed over cities during an early morning approach. The increased heating from the rising sun usually eliminates these inequalities by late morning.

New York City and northeastern New Jersey have endured a number of air-pollution experiences in the recent past, notably in 1953, 1956, 1957, 1962, 1966, and 1970. During the 1970s there were no major episodes, an indication of the effectiveness of the new federal air-quality standards and their enforcement by the Division of Environmental Quality of the state's Department of Environmental Protection. In 1974, an official in the department estimated that the sulfur dioxide content of the air was only one-fifth what it had been before the regulations were enforced.

The first major episode, November 12–23, 1953, caused the deaths of at least 175 people in the New York City area from cardiac and respiratory distress. From November 29 to December 5, 1962, stagnant air conditions hovered over New York, Newark, and Philadelphia for five and a half days. Peak levels of sulfur dioxide in the atmosphere reached four times the normal dosage, with a high count on the afternoons of November 30 and December 1 and a secondary high on the afternoon of December 3 and morning of the fourth. A significant increase was noted in the occurrence of respiratory complaints in all New York City homes for the aged, but there was no significant increase in the death rate.

An episode during the Thanksgiving holidays from November 20 to November 25, 1966, resulted from the stagnation of a strong high-pressure area. The peak concentration of pollutants came from November 22 to November 24. The sulfur dioxide level on Thanksgiving Day, November 24, rose from 0.97 parts per million, well above the acceptable level. The carbon monoxide level rose from 8 parts per million on the twenty-second to 35 parts per million on the twenty-fourth. The levels of oxides of nitrogen and hydrocarbons also peaked at this time. There was an increase of twenty-four deaths per day over the normal death rate during the episode. A cold front moved through the region on the night of the twenty-fifth to break up the inversion and carry the polluted air over the Atlantic Ocean.

Despite improvement in air quality over the past decade, New Jersey remains susceptible to daily air pollution. Each year an estimated 250,000 tons of hydrocarbons are released into the air by 14,000 manufacturing companies, making the state's air among the dirtiest in the nation. New state regulations have been adopted, including a special section imposing stricter controls on eleven chemicals considered toxic and believed by many to contribute to New Jersey's high cancer death rate. There are about 15,000 such deaths in the state each year, about 120 percent of the national average.

CHAPTER 5

# Weather in New Jersey History

## The Weather of the War of Independence

New Jersey's central location provided avenues for both British and American armies to march and countermarch as preliminaries of several important battles fought on its soil during the War of American Independence. The campaigns for control of New York City in the summer and autumn of 1776 and for control of Philadelphia in the autumn of 1777 took place just beyond New Jersey's borders, with important consequences for the new state. Furthermore, for four out of the five winters from 1776–1777 to 1780–1781, Washington's army camped on New Jersey territory, keeping watch on the British at their winter quarters in New York City.

After disasters on Long Island and at White Plains and the fall of Fort Washington on upper Manhattan Island in the late summer and autumn of 1776, Washington's decimated and discouraged army retreated across the central plain of New Jersey, first to the Raritan and then to the west bank of the Delaware River. The weather until the middle of November had been excellent for campaigning, with Indian summer conditions prevailing for many days in a row. Then the circulation changed and unsettled conditions attended by the passage of cyclonic storms took over. Much cloudiness and rain marked the closing days of November.

With the Americans driven west of the Delaware, the British went into winter quarters. Three outposts were established at Trenton, Bordentown, and Mount Holly. With terms of enlistment expiring at the end of December, Washington determined to make a bold stroke to revive the morale of both the army and the country at large. The Hessian garrison at Trenton, numbering about fourteen hundred men, was selected as the target. A three-pronged attack across the Delaware was planned, with two forces to strike above and below Trenton and a third to cross downriver at Bristol, Pennsylvania, and move on Mount Holly.

# The First Battle of Trenton: 1776

The first cold wave of the winter descended on the Delaware River area on the night of December 18–19, dropping the thermometer at Philadelphia to 21°F (−6°C) and keeping the mercury below freezing all day. Ice developed in the Delaware River, but in the vicinity of Trenton it did not freeze all the way across. Alternate freezing and thawing followed until another cold period set in on the twenty-fourth and kept the temperature below freezing that day and on Christmas Day. No one has left a good description of the actual ice conditions on Christmas night, but from the testimony of those attempting to cross it seems there was shore ice extending out from each bank and large cakes of solid ice running in the center of the river.

On Christmas morning the Philadelphia area was enjoying anticyclonic conditions with a barometer at 30.50 inches and a light wind out of the north. Christopher Marshall's diary entry described Christmas as "a fine pleasant sunshine morning." The temperature again stood at 21°F (−6°C).

During the afternoon, a falling barometer, a shift of wind to the northeast, and increasing cloudiness heralded an approaching storm. A cyclonic disturbance, apparently located just off the Carolina coast, was spreading snow northward. It had started during daylight hours in Virginia (and eventually dropped over two feet of snow there). The precipitation reached Philadelphia before Marshall's evening observation at 10:00 P.M., and a newspaper account of the battle stated that snow began in the vicinity of Trenton before 11:00 P.M.

The storm in the Trenton area started as snow but soon changed to a mixture of snow and sleet. Trenton stood on the northern periphery of the vast storm system. The 32°F (0°C) isotherm dividing freezing from above-freezing temperatures ran right through central New Jersey, as it often does in this type of storm at this time of year, causing a mixture of frozen and liquid precipitation. Mixed snow and sleet fell in the Trenton area and northward; to the south it was a combination of sleet and rain, and then all rain. The Philadelphia barometer fell almost an inch in the twenty-four hours following Christmas afternoon; the twenty-sixth there was described as "a very stormy day with much rain and hail & snow. Cleared about 5 P.M."

Of the three American forces attempting to cross the Delaware on Christmas night, only Washington above Trenton was able to get his men and artillery across; the landings just below Trenton and at Bristol were frustrated by shore ice and large cakes running in the middle of the river. Washington was fortunate in securing a number of the large boats employed to transport produce on the river, known lo-

*Washington and his men crossing the Delaware, December 25–26, 1776. Painting by Emanuel Leutze. (Courtesy of the National Archives)*

cally as Durham boats. These were handled by experienced sailors from Marblehead, Massachusetts.

Though the snow and sleet of the early morning caused delays in the treacherous crossing and in assembling the troops for the march on Trenton, it proved a distinct benefit to Washington in achieving surprise. The Hessians had been alerted by a false alarm the evening before and had sent out patrols on the Pennington Road well before daybreak. But finding nothing, and with the storm increasing in fury, they withdrew, leaving a checkpoint on the north edge of the town and planning no more patrols until daylight. It was during this interval that the Americans approached, overwhelmed the lightly held outpost, and rushed into the center of the town. A short fight resulted in the capture of the center of the town and about two-thirds of the defending force.

# The Battle of Princeton: 1777

After the Hessians' defeat at Trenton, Lieutenant General Cornwallis sought to retaliate by sending a force of eight thousand British regulars to the Delaware. Their progress from New Brunswick through Princeton was greatly impeded by a New Year's Day thaw with temperatures as high as 51°F (11°C) melting the snow cover and turning the roads into bottomless tracks. This was followed by an overnight rain. Nevertheless, the British sloshed forward on January 2, and met the enemy outposts in Maidenhead (now Lawrenceville). The Americans resisted briefly at several points but fell back during the afternoon to the south bank of Assunpink Creek, which runs through the southern part of Trenton. Here the Second Battle of Trenton took place. After a show of force in the late afternoon, Cornwallis decided to wait until next morning before launching a full-scale attack to "bag the fox," as he supposedly remarked.

A cool January 2 followed the overnight rainstorm. The wind held to the northwest all day, and the thermometer remained steady near 39°F (4°C). While his troops were withdrawing through Trenton, Washington's experienced weather-eye noticed these conditions and thought that "a providential change in the weather" might be in the making. He knew from experiences on his plantation in Virginia that a northwest wind all day in January was usually followed by an overnight freeze.

The American army was in a desperate position, with the ice-clogged river to the west, roads deep with mud to the south, and a superior force closing from the northeast. At a council of war among his generals, Washington urged a daring maneuver: anticipating an overnight freeze that would harden the roads and make them passable, he would lead his troops on an end run around the east flank of the British facing him across the narrow creek. A recently hewn out road (now Highways 535 and 533) ran east, then northeast to Princeton, where the Americans would be well in the rear of the British main army and across their line of communications with their base at New Brunswick and Perth Amboy.

The temperature tumbled soon after dark, as Washington had anticipated, and the mud solidified, so the army started to move soon after midnight on the eight-mile (13-km) trek to Princeton. Dawn of

*Washington leads a charge at the Battle of Princeton, helped by cold temperatures following an unseasonable and troublesome thaw, January 3, 1777. (Courtesy of the National Archives)*

January 3 found the rebels on the farmlands just southwest of the college town. Anticyclonic weather conditions prevailed: the temperature now was about 21°F (−6°C), and "the morning was bright, serene, and extremely cold, with a hoar frost which bespangled every object," according to Lieutenant Colonel James Wilkinson.

Even the fields were frozen solid, enabling Washington to deploy his troops in open country and beat off an attack by a sizable British rear guard. The town was carried after a forty-five minute firefight. Upon hearing the roar of the guns in their rear, the main British force was soon on the road back to Princeton in an attempt to catch Washington, but the Americans were quickly on the road again, heading north to the safety of the Watchung Mountains. Soon after noon the sun softened the frozen roads and muddy conditions prevailed, but for fifteen hours they had been solid, allowing Washington just enough time for his daring tactical move and enabling him to secure a more strategic location for the ensuing winter.

# The Battle of Monmouth: 1778

Upon taking command of the British forces in America in the spring of 1778, General Henry Clinton decided that the price of holding Philadelphia was not worthwhile, and he ordered its evacuation. Part of his forces went by ship down Delaware Bay, around Cape May, and along the New Jersey coast to New York Harbor; the bulk of the infantry were ferried across the Delaware River for a 75-mile (121-km) march across the sandy plains of central New Jersey to the southern shore of New York Bay near Sandy Hook. Philadelphia was completely evacuated on June 18, 1778. Hot and humid weather prevailed.

When definite intelligence of the direction of the British movement was received at Valley Forge, Washington sent his army in pursuit across central New Jersey on a course that would intercept the British before they reached the protection of the Monmouth Hills near the shores of New York Bay. The paths of the two armies converged on June 27, the Americans concentrating at Englishtown only three or four miles (5 or 6 km) from the British, who were strung out on the line of march near Monmouth Court House (now Freehold). An extended heat wave beginning on the twenty-second made the march of both armies doubly miserable. In the words of Private Joseph Martin, who was with the Americans: "It was uncommonly hot weather and we put up booths to protect us from the heat of the sun, which was almost unsufferable."

Broiling hot weather continued on the day of the battle, Sunday, June 28, 1778. Private Martin again described conditions on that important day:

> The sun shining full upon the field, the soil of which was sandy, the mouth of a heated oven seemed to me to be a trifle hotter than this ploughed field; it was almost impossible to breath. . . . The weather was almost too hot to live in, and the British troops in the orchard were forced by the heat to shelter themselves from it under trees. . . . I presume everyone has heard of the heat that day, but none can realize it that did not feel it. Fighting is hot work in cool weather, how much more so in such weather as it was on the twenty-eighth of June 1778.

In his summary after the battle, Washington attributed to the debilitating effect of the heat the failure of the American troops to pursue the enemy who withdrew from the field after a standoff fight:

> The extreme heat of the weather, the fatigue of the men from their march through a deep, sandy country, almost entirely destitute of water, and the distance the enemy had gained by marching in the night, made a pursuit impracticable. It would have answered no valuable purpose, and would have been fatal to numbers of our men—several of whom had died the previous day with heat.

How hot was it that day? Accounts state that the temperature ranged from 92°F to 97°F (33°C to 36°C); one even says it was 112°F (44°C). The most quoted figure is 96°F (36°C), and this appears in a summary of the battle in one of General Clinton's letters to his sister, dated July 6. This was probably the reading of the thermometer at the British headquarters in New York City, where Clinton was that day. The Philadelphia record, which would have been representative of the heat at Monmouth, ended in May 1778, leading to the surmise that the weather observer was a Tory and left the city when the British did.

The heat and thirst took quite a toll that day. A total of 112 British and German soldiers were killed in battle, and 62 died from the heat, according to the diary account of Major General Carl L. Baurmeister. No accurate count was made by the Americans, but historians have attributed the death of at least 37 missing Continental soldiers to the heat.

## The Hard Winter of 1780

There is only one winter on record when the waters of New York Bay and Delaware Bay have been frozen over and remained closed to navigation for weeks at a time. That season is the so-called Hard Winter of 1780. It occurred in a critical year of the War of Independence when General George Washington's poorly quartered, ill-clad, and undernourished troops were wintering at Morristown and keeping a watchful eye on the British Army, which was enjoying the relative comfort of New York City some twenty miles distant. George Washington kept a "Diary of the Weather" that provides much firsthand information about that winter.

There were three phases. First came a series of three exceptionally severe snowstorms, with much drifting, in late December 1779 and early January 1780. Washington took note of the third and final storm: "Jan. 6—Snow & sunshine alternately—cold with wind west and northwest & increasing—night very stormy—The snow in general is eighteen inches deep, is much drifted. Roads almost impassable. Jan. 7—Very boisterous, from west & northwest & sometimes snowing, which being very dry drifted exceedingly—Night intensely cold and freezing—Wind continuing fresh."

In western New Jersey the Somerset militia were called out to break a road from Hackettstown to Princeton. They later reported, "The whole face of the country lay buried from three to five feet deep; roads, fences, and frozen streams were obliterated, and as the storm had been accompanied by very high wind, in places the drifts were piled ten to twelve feet high." (Andrew Mellick, Jr., *The Story of an Old Farm, or Life in New Jersey in the Eighteenth Century* [Somerville, N.J., 1889], p. 514). Though no more snow fell during January, the deep cover remained practically undiminished until mid-February.

"Frigidissime" was the diary entry of David Schultze of Goshenhoppen near Philadelphia to describe the cold of January. In the center of Philadelphia, David Rittenhouse's thermometer went above freezing on only one day in the entire month, the thirtieth, and several diary keepers noted that the eaves of the roofs dripped on only one day during the month. No thermometer records for New Jersey have survived for this winter, but an instrument at the British headquarters on Manhattan Island is said to have read −16°F (−26°C), about equal to the lowest in the modern record for New York City.

By mid-January the cold had caused all the principal harbors from North Carolina to Maine to freeze over, putting a stop to navigation. Always an early freezer, the Delaware River at Philadelphia closed on December 21 and did not open again to navigation until March 4. It was at New York City that the freezing of the rivers and bays proved most critical. For six weeks after January 15, no supply ships could get through the Narrows from the Lower Bay to the Upper Bay; the British on Manhattan Island were cut off from their normal channel of supplies. Eventually the ice became solid enough to support the heaviest cannons, which were dragged over the ice to bolster the defenses of Staten Island. The British feared that the ice might provide a highway for a quick American attack on their base. Not until February 11 did the first break in the long siege of winter arrive, and not until the twenty-first could a small vessel sail through the Narrows and reach Manhattan Island.

The unusual meteorological conditions prevailing throughout the region excited great curiosity among the scientific gentlemen of Philadelphia, and the American Philosophical Society appointed a committee "to make and collect observations on the effects of the severe and long continued cold of last winter."

## The Battles at Springfield: 1780

A crucial turning point of the war was fought on June 23, 1780, at Springfield, a bridge site and crossroads settlement astride the highway leading from tidewater at Point Elizabeth to the hill country around Morristown. West of Springfield lay the Watchung Mountains and the strategic Hobart Gap, through which communications lines reached the Passaic River valley and western New Jersey.

On the night of June 6–7, 1780, British forces numbering about six thousand crossed from their forward bases on Staten Island. They hoped to strike a quick, telling blow at General Washington's army, whose strength was reported to have been decimated by desertions and whose morale was at a low ebb after the bitter winter and backward spring spent in the hungry hills about Morristown. The army, numbering about thirty-six hundred able-bodied men, was spread out over the interior of North Jersey, protecting supply lines and scouting enemy movements.

Two brief encounters made up the short campaign: one at Connecticut Farms (now Union) on the afternoon of June 7 and a second a little over two weeks later on June 23 at Springfield. Both villages were burned by the invaders. The key factor in turning prospective victory into a British defeat was the prompt rallying of the New Jersey militia to the defense of their homes and farms. British intelligence had reported that the local populace would favor an overthrow of the rebel government if the British would make a show of force in their state, but this was not the case. The New Jersey Continentals in the regular army, too, displayed unaccustomed energy and determination in defending their home territory. After a stalemate before Springfield, the British burned the village and began to withdraw while experiencing damaging harassing fire along the route as they had at Lexington and Concord.

There is little direct meteorological evidence as to what conditions were during the Springfield campaign. No continuous weather records for New York City or northern New Jersey have survived, and the detail of diary material is rather thin for the period. George Washington concluded his useful weather diary on June 3, 1780, just three days before the first engagement at Connecticut Farms. Lieutenant George Mathew with the elite British Guards took part in both engagements and left a vivid description of the severe thunderstorm that disrupted the British withdrawal on the night of June 7–8.

Of conditions on the battle day of June 7, Thomas Fleming writes in *The Forgotten Victory*, without quoting sources, "With the sun up the day promised to be hot and sultry . . . the air was redolent with sunlight . . . sultry June heat." The day of the battle was typical of early summer conditions for the Jersey coastal plain, with the thermometer rising to near 90°F (32°C) and the humidity at a high level. These conditions accompany a falling barometer and a southerly air flow, usually the harbingers of a cold front approaching from the west which will set off more violent weather.

During the late evening of June 7, while the British army was engaged in a difficult withdrawal from Connecticut Farms to Elizabethport, the cold front arrived and a thunderstorm broke. "It was the darkest night I can remember in my life," wrote Lieutenant Mathew, "with the most heavy rain, thunder, and lightning known in this country in many years. . . . It rained, I think, harder than I ever knew, and thundered and lightened so severely as to frighten the horses, and once or twice the whole army halted, being deprived of sight for a time."

Lieutenant Mathew continued: "Nothing more awful than this retreat can be imagined. The rain, with the terrible thunder and lightning, the darkness of the night, the houses at Connecticut Farms, which we had set fire to, in a blaze, the dead bodies which the light of the fire or the lightning showed you now and then on the road, and the dread of an enemy, completed the scene of horror."

If the severe weather inconvenienced the British withdrawal, in the American camp it caused frustration, since it militated against an immediate, organized counterattack on the retreating British columns. Washington, always offense-minded, wished to attack, but a conference of his senior officers decided against the venture. As Thomas Fleming has pointed out, eighteenth-century soldiers could not use their muskets in the rain; water dampened the powder in the priming pans and caused them to misfire.

About the weather on the day the British returned to the attack on Connecticut Farms, June 23, there is no firsthand evidence. Fleming writes that "it was another hot, sultry day." At a London court-martial in 1781, the following exchange was quoted to have taken place on the field of battle:

"A hot day, Colonel Gordon," said Colonel Lovelace, apparently oblivious to the bullets singing over their heads.

"Hot in more ways than one," said Colonel Gordon with forced joviality.

# Airship and Sea Disasters

## The *Shenandoah*'s Wild Ride

During the afternoon and early evening of January 16, 1924, winds were blowing at a steady 25 miles per hour (40 km/h) across the Naval Air Station at Lakehurst, New Jersey, where the U.S.S. *Shenandoah*, the first lighter-than-air craft of the zeppelin type to be built in the United States by the U.S. Navy, was undergoing initial trials with an experimental mooring mast. The weather had been favorable on previous days when two short flights were made with dockings to the mast, but conditions changed on the afternoon of the sixteenth as an active low-pressure system with cold and warm fronts approached from the southwest. After sundown the barometer fell rapidly, and at the 7:00 P.M. observation winds were roaring across the field at 52 miles per hour (84 km/h) and gusting to 57 miles (92 km/h) just before the warm front passed the station. A gust blew over the instrument shelter atop the Aerological Observatory, breaking the thermometers and psychrometers inside.

While on an inspection visit soon after 7:00 P.M. to the stern of the ship, where the large vertical fin had been giving trouble, Lieutenant Roland Mayer heard a wrenching noise when the stabilizer gave way before the buffeting of the wind. Its collapse caused a violent shock to pass through the frame, followed by a twisting motion of the whole ship. The torsion severed the bow plate, and fragments of this ruptured the forward gas cells.

The nose of the ship dipped toward the ground; ballast water was dropped to counteract the descent. Then the ship took off with the gale and swept within fifty feet of the tree tops of the Pine Barrens before some control was established and altitude gained. The engines were started, and the German consultant aboard, Captain Anton Heinen, was able to keep the nose of the ship into the wind now veering through south to southwest.

The anemometer atop the Whitehall Building at the lower end of Manhattan Island lost its cups while spinning at 54 miles per hour (87 km/h) around 8:00 P.M., when the *Shenandoah* was heading that way. Atlantic City, well south of the route, had a sustained wind of 62 miles per hour (100 km/h) close to the time of the frontal passage. Back at the airfield at Lakehurst, the observations indicated the arrival of the cold front between 9:00 and 10:00 P.M., when the wind had gone into the west-southwest and dropped to 22 miles per hour (35 km/h). The rain ended at 9:30 P.M., and breaks appeared in the clouds by 11:00 P.M.

*The damaged nose section of the U.S.S.* SHENANDOAH, *January 1924. (Cole Zepplin Collection, Special Collections, University of Oregon Library)*

The radio of the *Shenandoah* had been disassembled for repairs that day, but by 9:00 P.M. the operator had it back in working order and established contact with Mitchel Field, the Army Air Corps base on Long Island. He sent the message "All okay. *Shenandoah* will ride out the storm. We think we are over New Brunswick. Holding our own. Verify position and send us weather information."

Control had been gained and the wild ride backwards checked. The *Shenandoah* was not reported from the ground until she reached Westfield, Union County, about 8:30 P.M., flying at an altitude of about 400 feet (122 m). Shortly thereafter, the ship changed her course and took a more northerly direction. She was seen over Hillside between Elizabeth and Newark, heading in the direction of New York City. Great excitement spread over the metropolitan area when commercial radio stations commenced to broadcast news of the wild ride and feature reports of new sightings from the ground every few minutes. I well remember listening to WOR in Newark that night when the announcer made radio contact with the operator aboard the *Shenandoah* and gave the positions frequently.

After leaving the Newark area, the ship was sighted over the meadows near Jersey City and then southward over Bayonne and Staten Island, where it hovered over the waters of Newark Bay for a while. Then it was off to the southwest and was sighted about 11:15 P.M. over Rahway, now flying much higher in the direction of Lakehurst.

With the cold front well past the vicinity of the flight, the winds diminished considerably aloft and the *Shenandoah* was under full control. The wind was blowing at only 14 miles per hour (23 km/h) and only three-tenths scattered clouds covered the sky at 3:20 A.M., when the ship was secured and put into its hangar.

# The Loss of the *Akron*

When Commander Frank C. McCord of the U.S.S. *Akron* called a conference with his forecasters at 4:00 P.M. on April 3, 1933, at the Lakehurst Naval Air Station, the only unfavorable weather factor appeared to be a low ceiling of 300 feet over the field as the result of a light northeasterly flow bringing sea fog inland. An occluded front with little storm activity occurring ran through central Pennsylvania to a warm front located over Virginia. The skipper decided to take off on a training flight that was planned to lead to Newport, Rhode Island.

Leaving Lakehurst at 7:28 P.M., the *Akron* headed west away from the fog area along the coast. At 8:30 P.M., when she was cruising over Wilmington, Delaware, sharp flashes of lightning were seen to the south, so the course was changed to a heading east and then northeast over New Jersey again. A secondary low-pressure center had developed over Virginia late in the afternoon and was moving northeast over Maryland. Severe turbulence and thunderstorms broke out in advance of the small storm center, with thunder and lightning reported at Washington at 7:35 P.M., at Philadelphia at 9:49 P.M., and at Atlantic City at 10:14 P.M. The zone of turbulence was quite concentrated, with no thunderstorms reported westward at either Harrisburg or Reading, Pennsylvania.

When the *Akron* crossed the coastline heading seaward, the atmosphere was relatively stable, but by 11:00 P.M. intense lightning, both cloud-to-ground and cloud-to-cloud, enveloped the ship and severe turbulence was encountered, so the course was again reversed to westward. Upon returning to the coastline in the vicinity of Barnegat Light about midnight, the skipper reconsidered his position. Hoping to get seaward ahead of the advancing thunderstorm area and ride out the turbulence above the surface of the sea rather than over land with its obstructions, the skipper headed the *Akron* southeast. The wind at the surface was strong, about 40 knots (46 mi/h or 85 km/h) from the northeast, with rain, light fog reducing visibility, and heavy thunder.

At 12:15 A.M. off Long Beach Island on the central New Jersey shore, the *Akron* hit a descending current of air and lost altitude rapidly. Ballast was dropped, control regained, and the ship righted at an altitude of 1,600 feet (488 m). Three minutes later, caught in another downdraft, she began to sink again, this time at the extreme rate of 14 feet (4.3 m) per second. Engines were given full power, causing the nose of the 785-feet-long (239 m) ship to point upward at an angle of 20 to 25 degrees. Suddenly a shock was felt throughout the entire frame—the lower rudder and controls were torn away, apparently having struck the surface of the water while the ship was angling upward. The impact resulted in the progressive destruction of the frame.

Soon all of the *Akron* was down in the water and the sea was pouring into the control gondola. The accident occurred around 12:30 A.M. about 19 nautical miles (35 km) south-southeast of Barnegat Inlet. The wreckage floated for a while and was later found on the bottom of the ocean about 27 nautical miles (50 km) southeast of Barnegat and due east of Little Egg Inlet. Investigators speculated that if the *Akron* had had only 100 feet (30 m) greater altitude at the time of her descent, the crash might not have occurred.

Partly from lack of lifesaving equipment and partly from the coldness of the water, the loss of life was almost total. Of the seventy-six aboard, only three were rescued from the water, these by a German freighter which had been close enough to see the lights of the *Akron* disappear into the sea.

According to a reconstruction of the situation following a congressional inquiry into the disaster, the commander of the *Akron* was thought to have been aware that a low-pressure center of rather small dimensions was moving northeast from the Washington-Baltimore area. By heading out to sea originally he might have crossed the projected path of the advancing storm well ahead of it and found more stable conditions over the ocean in the warm sector to the east. But

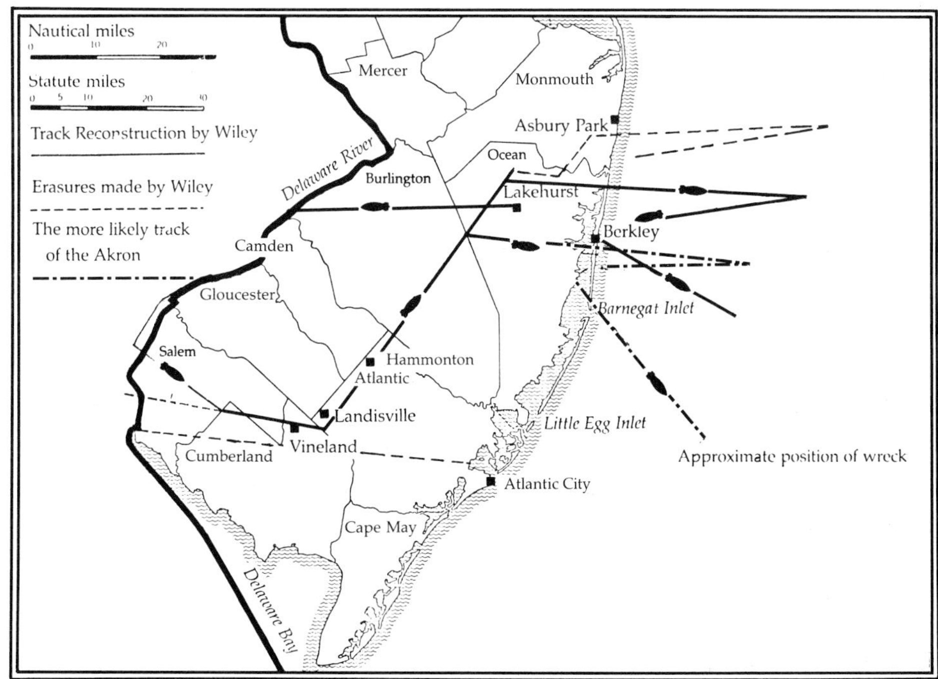


*Approximate track of the U.S.S.* AKRON, *April 3–4, 1933, as reconstructed by Lieutenant Commander H. V. Wiley. (From* The Airships Akron and Macon *by Richard K. Smith. Copyright © 1965, U.S. Naval Institute, Annapolis, Md.)*

when the weather became very turbulent around the ship and lightning played about, he assumed he was close to the center of the disturbance and reversed course to head west. Then, preferring to cruise over the sea rather than over land under the turbulent conditions existing, he changed course southeast, hoping to move into the rear of the storm. This apparently brought him on a collision course with the most turbulent sector of the storm center.

## The Loss of the *Hindenburg*

Captain Max Pruss was a veteran airship commander; he had made ten trips to the United States and eight to South America in the pride of the Nazi regime, the zeppelin *Hindenburg*. He described conditions on May 6, 1937, the day of his airship's disaster: "We had bad weather. About two o'clock we were over New York, made a few circles, and then went on to Lakehurst. Then we saw a big thunderstorm over New Jersey and knew we couldn't land and thought it better to go back to the sea. We went along the coast to Atlantic City and back, and we waited for the storm to blow over to the ocean."

The weather map on the morning of May 6 located a low-pressure center over eastern Lake Ontario with a cold front running southward through east-central Pennsylvania, then bowing to the southwest over central Virginia and southward to about Wilmington, North Carolina. The thunderstorms in the New Jersey area were caused by the passage of a line of instability accompanying the cold front late on the afternoon of the sixth.

On the ground at Lakehurst the weather was being watched carefully by all concerned with landing the *Hindenburg*. The following exchanges took place between the two parties:

At 5:12 P.M. Naval Air Lakehurst radioed: "Thunderstorm moving from west over station surface temperature 70 falling surface wind west sixteen knots gusts twenty one wind shifted from north at 1600 est pressure twenty nine sixty four rising."

At 5:35 P.M. Captain Pruss queried: "How is visibility from Lakehurst westward." The Naval Air Station replied: "Visibility westward eight miles unsettled recommend delay landing until further word from station. Advise your decision."

Captain Pruss answered: "We will wait report that landing conditions are better."

At 6:12 P.M. Lakehurst radioed: "Conditions now considered suitable for landing ground crew is ready period thunderstorm over station ceiling 2000 feet visibility five miles to westward surface temperature 60 surface wind west northwest eight knots gusts to 20 knots surface pressure 29.68."

*The* HINDENBURG *was destroyed by fire at Lakehurst Naval Air Station on May 6, 1937. (Collection of the New Jersey Historical Society)*

At 6:22 P.M. Lakehurst radioed: "Recommend landing now commanding officer."

At 6:44 P.M. Captain Pruss replied: "Course Lakehurst."

The local record of the weather observer at the Naval Air Station at Lakehurst reported the passage of a cold front at 5:05 P.M., EDT, attended by mild to moderate thunderstorms and a wind shift to northwest with gusts mounting to 21 knots. By the time the *Hindenburg* returned to the field at 7:18 P.M., EDT, conditions were described as seven-tenths clouds with light rain alternating with heavier showers. Winds were very light to calm, mostly southeast and south. Occasional lightning flashes were seen to the south and southwest toward the front. Skies were clearing rapidly to the west.

The *Hindenburg* dropped its landing lines at 7:21 P.M., EDT. Almost immediately flames roared through the hydrogen cells, and the frame of the ship settled to the ground. Thirty-six people died: twenty-two crew members, thirteen passengers, and one member of the ground crew.

Though the disaster has been subjected to formal government inquiry and reassessed periodically by private investigators, the cause of the fire has never been finally ascertained. Some believe that static electricity, a residual of the earlier thunderstorm activity, formed upon making contact with the ground and ignited leaking hydrogen. Others believe that an act of sabotage sent the swastika-emblazoned airship to its fiery ending. Captain Pruss, who survived, was a member of the Joint American-German Commission to investigate the disaster. He concluded, "It might have been sabotage; it might have been lightning. Nobody knows."

The local record sheet for May 6, 1937, at the Lakehurst Naval Air Station reads:

Thursday 6th: Overcast with intermediate types lowering to low St [stratus] and mild thunderstorms and thundershowers occurring about 0045 to 0100, with rain continuing until about 0330. Cold front passed about 1605, preceded by mild to moderate thunderstorms and thundershowers; wind shifted to NW with gusts to 21 kts., wind becoming fresh at times, then falling away to light variable. Heavy showers fell between 1700 and 1800. HINDENBURGH [sic] OVER FIELD ABOUT 1818, SURFACE TEMPERATURE 60, REL. HUM. 98%, BAROMETER 29.72 INCHES, INVERSION (1) 60, (2) 59, (3) 57; WEATHER 7 ST. CLOUDS WITH LIGHT RAIN IN BETWEEN HEAVY SHOWERS. LIGHT VARIABLE SURFACE WINDS, MOSTLY SE & S, CALM TO 1 KT. WITH NO GUSTS. TOWER WINDS W & WSW 5 TO 6 KTS. OCCASIONAL LIGHTNING FLASHES OBSERVED TO DISTANT S & SW; SKIES CLEARING RAPIDLY TO WESTWARD AND SKIES IN GENERAL CLEARED RAPIDLY AFTER SUNSET AND BECAME MOSTLY CLEAR BY MID-NIGHT. VARIABLE VISIBILITY FOR THE PERIOD, MOSTLY FAIR.

*F. A. L. Dartsch, Lieut.,*
*USN. Aerological Officer.*
*J. L. Kenworthy, Comdr.,*
*USN. Commanding*

*Note:* C. E. Rosendahl, Comdr., USN. *is typed in the "commanding" line, but* Kenworthy *is written over it in ink and with a rubber stamp.*

# Two Marine Tragedies: 1854

Many sailing ships foundered on New Jersey's storm-tossed shore in the days before steam power enabled threatened vessels to maneuver and stand offshore when approaching a coastline to leeward. No year was more tragic in New Jersey history than 1854, when two ships bearing German immigrants stranded, bilged, and broke up, with a combined loss of over five hundred people.

Just previous to this a lifesaving service had been instituted as the result of the work of Dr. William Newell of Allentown and Toms River. Having witnessed the loss of thirteen seamen near Manahawkin in 1839, he set to work devising a means of shooting a line to a stricken vessel and then removing the stranded passengers and crew by an open breeches buoy. Then Joseph Francis, a Toms River boatbuilder, designed a life car with a watertight lid that could be guided by the lifeline in bringing seamen ashore in safety. Newell was elected to Congress in 1846 and crusaded for the organization of a federal

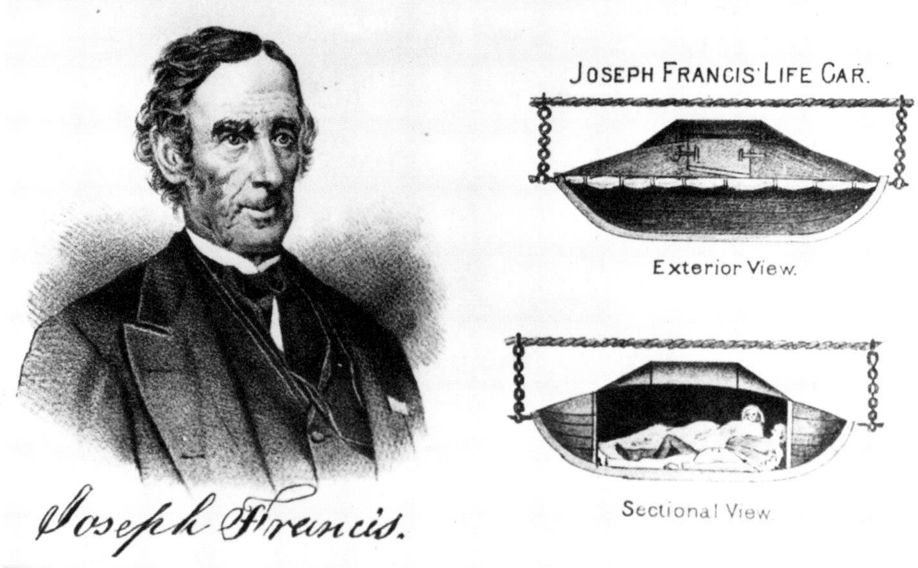


*Joseph Francis, a Toms River boatbuilder, invented an unsinkable lifeboat in 1838. It was first used along the New Jersey coast in several spectacular rescues. (Special Collections, Rutgers University)*

lifesaving organization which would employ the new lifeline and life car. Two years later $10,000 was appropriated, and eight lifeguard stations were established on the shore between Sandy Hook and Little Egg Harbor in 1849. Though originally staffed by volunteers, this was the beginning of the United States Lifesaving Service, now part of the Coast Guard. Shortly thereafter the lifesaving devices were responsible for saving 201 people when the immigrant ship *Ayrshire* from Newry, Northern Ireland, stranded on January 12, 1850, along the south side of Woodlands near Squan Beach. A coastal storm prevailed with very heavy rain on the eleventh, followed by fog the next day. The heavy seas caused the ship to break up. With the lifeline carrying two to four people at a time, it took one afternoon and the next morning to get all but one person safely ashore.

Not so lucky were the passengers and crew of two other immigrant ships, the *Powhatan* and the *New Era*, which stranded within seven months of each other in 1854.

## The *Powhatan*

The greatest Jersey-coast shipwreck tragedy in terms of lives lost occurred when the immigrant ship *Powhatan* became stranded on a sandbar off Long Beach Island on Easter Sunday, April 16, 1854, during a mighty coastal storm. More than 300 persons, perhaps as many as 340—all the passengers and crew—lost their lives in the high surf when the ship broke up only a hundred yards or so from the safety of the beach. A memorable northeast storm raged along the North Atlantic coast from the fourteenth to the seventeenth, and at least twenty other wrecks were reported from Sandy Hook to Cape May.

The story of the tragedy can best be told by a witness, a Captain Jennings, the wreck master of the newly established lifesaving service on the island:

> On Saturday the wind blew with great violence from the northeast. The sea ran very high all day, and I supposed that there would be many a wreck along the coast from Barnegat to Egg Harbor. On Sunday morning [16th] I observed a ship of about 900 tons thumping on the bar about one hundred yards from the shore. . . .
>
> The vessel then lay E.S.E. had shifted from the N.E. Her foremast was gone at this time. I suppose she lost it before she struck on the bar. About 5:00 P.M. on Sunday the ship keeled over to windward from the shore. The sea then, of course, made a clean breach over her, and passengers began to be washed over in great numbers. The sea running mountain high, and completely hiding the vessel from my view, I could no longer hold any communication with the captain. I never saw him since.
>
> The main and mizzen mast soon went by the board, and bodies appeared floating in the surf in great numbers. Some seventy-five bodies, mostly women, came on shore about a mile south of the wreck.
>
> About dark, the sea rose to a great height, and one large wave, fully a hundred feet high, struck the unfortunate vessel, and in one moment the hull was scattered into fragments which tossed wildly through the surf. The shrieks of the drowning creatures were melancholy indeed, but I could render them no aid, as the sea ran so high I could not get near the unfortunate people. In a few moments all disappeared beneath the surface of the water, except a few fragments of the wreck. Never did I see such a sight in my life. Never do I remember witnessing such a dreadful gale or such high running sea. In many places, it made complete breaches over the island, and carried, no doubt, many a poor fellow into the bay behind it.
>
> *Captain Jennings, in the*
> New York Times,
> *April 22, 1854*

There is no meteorological report from the immediate shore area, but William Whitehead's account (which appeared in the *Newark Daily Advertiser*, May 1, 1854) of this storm period at Newark gives a good idea of the general conditions prevailing:

> On the afternoon of the 14th—the wind being from the northeast—snow commenced falling at 4½ o'clock, and continued to do so, mingled with some sleet, until noon of the 15th—the quantity deposited being four inches; and in

> the evening, at 10, more rain falling, made up nearly an inch and three-eighths of water as the result of the storm; which had held up, however, only for a short time; for about 1 P.M., of Easter Sunday [16th], the snow commenced falling again, and continued, with little intermission, until the evening of the 17th—rain and sleet taking its place for a while about noon of that day. Although the snow melted to some extent as it fell, yet nine or ten inches on a level remained after the storm passed; but the fresh gale that prevailed most of the time, drifted the snow considerably. The maximum temperature of the 16th was 40½°; but the mercury fell to 28¼° the ensuing night: and on the 17th, did not rise above 36°. . . . Nowhere did the storm of 16th and 17th rage more violently than in this latitude and the loss of several vessels on the Jersey Coast—particularly the ship *Powhattan* [sic], with every soul on board, 340 in number—will render it ever memorable.

## The *New Era*

The immigrant ship *New Era* had been at sea for six weeks and five days after leaving Germany when the vessel struck a sandbar during stormy weather about 6:00 A.M. on Monday, November 13, 1854. The sandbar was off Great Pond (now Deal Lake), which forms the northern boundary of Asbury Park. The *New Era* was launched in April 1854, and was on the return from her maiden voyage. She had sailed with 426 people on board, including passengers, officers, and crew. The ship's company numbered 29, and there were 12 cooks for the passengers. Captain Thomas J. Henry declared, "Our passage from Bremen was very rough. During all my experience on the ocean, I do not know that I ever made a voyage when the weather for so long a time was more severe."

Captain Henry continued his statement and gave some of the details of the weather and the stranding:

> The last observation I took was on Friday last, when I was in 66 deg. lon., 41 deg. 50 min. lat. Since that time I was prevented from taking an observation on account of the thick and rainy weather. On Saturday judged the ship to be in 72 deg. 30 min lon, 40 deg. 25 min. lat. On Saturday night we had a strong wind from the eastward, which changed to the southeast at about midnight, and the wind began to blow and the rain to fall heavily. The lead was thrown every hour, and I supposed the ship to be on the coast of Long Island, and I carried a heavy press of sail to keep her off. At 5½ o'clock on Monday morning, on sounding, we found that we were in from thirteen to fifteen fathoms of water. At six o'clock, the weather being very thick

> and the sea rough, we struck. The first mate was on the deck some ten minutes before the vessel struck. I was in the cabin, about going on deck myself, when all at once I heard him ask the watch forward, "What it was that looked so light forward?" On hearing this, I immediately jumped on deck, and then, for the first time, heard them cry out "Breakers!" I at once order the wheel up, and in the same moment the ship struck. I at once caused the yards to be braced aback, to get her off, but we only thumped further on. She went head on, made two or three thumps, and swung broadside to, and I found that she was hopelessly aground. The sea at once commenced breaking over her side, breaking up everything upon the deck.

Rescue workers from Deal and Long Branch were soon on the scene and succeeded in getting a lifeline across the deck of the *New Era*. A lifesaving boat of conventional design was hauled to the ship with difficulty. It was partially filled with water, which Captain Henry and some of the crew attempted to bail out. While they were doing so, some passengers tried to jump into the small boat; Henry pulled away and finally reached the shore, though the boat capsized. The lifeline then broke; there was no replacement. Henry continued his statement: "At the time I got ashore the passengers were in the fore, main, and mizen rigging, and so remained through the night, as no earthly assistance could be offered to them from shore. The scene on board my ship was dreadful. I hope in heaven I may never behold a like again."

As soon as word of the wreck reached New York, a news yacht carrying reporters left for the scene. Elias Smith on the *Achilles* described the situation:

> About 3 o'clock we came in sight of her, lying broadside to the beach, heading to the southward, with her fore, main, and mizzen topsails still standing. On reaching her she proved to be level with the water and full, and the swell breaking in heavy surges across her decks. We had already passed many pieces of the wrecks. . . . As we approached the wreck so as to get a nearer view, a most harrowing spectacle met the eyes. The jibbon, rigging and top of the ship, fore and aft, were filled with human beings closely packed together, and clinging to each other and to the ropes, while the ship surged to and fro with each returning wave, which broke in wild spray far up the rigging and over the ship, drenching and suffocating the passengers, while the poor creatures filled the air with the most soul harrowing and pitiful outcries for assistance. On the beach were some two hundred persons, gathered in groups, apparently consulting as to how to act, while

> others sat leisurely upon the gunwhale of the boats, which the heavy surf rendered it certain destruction to launch.

Captain Henry described the night and next day: "The night was warm and pleasant, and the sea had fallen greatly—the wind having changed to the west southwest—else not a soul would have lived through the long night." On Tuesday morning the sea had so far lulled that wreckers were able to put off to the ship in surfboats in which the passengers who lived through Monday night were all safely landed. Two-hundred and forty of the 385 passengers lost their lives.

The nearest meteorological records that have survived are those at New York City and Newark, about thirty-five miles (56 km) away. The observations of Charles Goodell on Manhattan Island indicated that November 13 was a stormy day with rain at all observations. His temperature records varied from 50°F (10°C) to 57°F (14°C). Instead of cooling off overnight, it warmed up to 64°F (18°C) next morning at 7:00 A.M., and the day was listed as "pleasant." William Whitehead at Newark measured a storm total of 2.37 inches (60 mm) but made no mention of the wind. Dr. Conrad at Philadelphia also reported rain all day on the thirteenth, with a total of 1.73 inches (44 mm) and the wind out of the northwest at force 3 (winds were rated from 1 to 4 in strength; force 3 is a strong wind but not a gale).

## The *Morro Castle*

One of the most bizarre dramas of the seas was played out off the New Jersey coast on Friday and Saturday, September 7 and 8, 1934, while the winds of a tropical storm lashed the area. After a cruise to Havana, the S.S. *Morro Castle* was nearing New York harbor when two untold events occurred. The captain of the ship died under mysterious circumstances, and the ship caught fire. The death occurred at 7:45 P.M. on Friday, and the fire started about 2:45 A.M. on Saturday. The first event remained largely unknown to the passengers, but the second quickly involved all aboard.

The usual night-before-landing parties had been held and many of the 549 passengers were sleeping when the fire broke out in a lounge and quickly spread through the ship. Some of the passengers and crew who were lost never got out of their cabins; they died of smoke inhalation. The ship began to list from the water poured on the fire, and it drifted uncontrolled through the seas, which were whipped by 40-mile-per-hour (62-km/h) winds. The *Morro Castle*, still burning fiercely, came ashore at Asbury Park only a few hundred feet from the Convention Hall. The death toll was 134.

The tropical disturbance during which this occurred was first charted off the central Bahama Islands on September 5. It quickly developed hurricane force, as its lowest barometric pressure of 28.56 inches (96.7 kPa) indicated. The storm headed northwest, then north, passing near Cape Hatteras at 7:00 A.M. on the eighth. Already losing strength and becoming extratropical, the downgraded hurricane continued on a north-northeast track, passing about sixty miles (97 km) east of Atlantic City to make an eventual landfall on the central Long Island coast. The center was probably abreast of the disaster scene in late afternoon, close to the time that Sandy Hook, the nearest weather station, registered a north wind of 65 miles per hour (105 km/h) and a pressure of 29.54 inches (100.0 kPa). Torrential rains fell along the coast on the eighth, with Long Branch reporting 5.19 inches (132 mm).

## The *Mohawk*

Just five months after the *Morro Castle* disaster, another ship was involved in a wreck off the New Jersey coast. The *Mohawk* left her dock in New York City on the afternoon of January 24, 1935, carrying 164 passengers and crew. The ship halted for several hours in the Lower Bay to make repairs. While anchored she was passed by the Norwegian steamer *Talisman*, bound for South American ports.

Later, while overtaking the *Talisman* off the central New Jersey coast, the *Mohawk* suddenly swerved to the port and cut across the bow of the other ship. The *Mohawk* suffered a deep gash when the prow of *Talisman* knifed into her forward section. The crash occurred at 9:26 P.M., and forty minutes later the *Mohawk* sank in about 76 feet (23 m) of water about 6.0 miles (9.7 km) southeast of Sea Girt Light and about 6.5 miles (10.5 km) off Mantoloking.

Weather conditions were good according to all witnesses. New York had experienced a heavy snowstorm on January 22–23 but was now in a strong northwest flow of bitter cold air following the passage of the coastal storm northward. George Clancy, on watch in the bow of the *Mohawk*, described the scene: "Both vessels were headed south, *Talisman* clearly visible in the distance off our port quarter. The night was clear, the visibility was excellent, the sea calm and the cold was intense." A passenger testified that he had checked a thermometer about an hour before the crash and found the reading to be 7°F (−14°C). The severe cold greatly added to the suffering of those transferring from lifeboats to rescue ships, which soon were on the scene. Forty-five persons lost their lives either in the stricken vessel when it went down or in the icy waters.

The role of the weather in causing the accident was indirect, as the Steamship Inspection Service inquiry stated: "The board finds that the accident was due to the fact that the liquid in the telemotor pipes [of the steering mechanism] froze, thus rendering the telemotor gear useless." When the regular steering means was found to be defective, the *Mohawk*'s crew rigged a temporary wheel and steering system which required a verbal transmission of orders. A misinterpretation of a command to turn starboard put the ship on a collision course to port directly across the *Talisman*'s bow.

## The Collision of the *Eastwind* and the *Gulfstream*

The Coast Guard icebreaker *Eastwind* collided in fog with the Gulf Oil tanker *Gulfstream* on January 19, 1949, about sixty miles (97 km) southeast of Barnegat Light. The icebreaker was proceeding south from a New England port; the tanker was running north at 15 knots (28 km/h) out of Philadelphia. Both ships caught fire; it took seven hours to control the flames on the *Eastwind* under most difficult circumstances, since her magazines were in constant danger of exploding.

A fog bank was the cause of the accident. Watch officers on both ships testified that weather conditions were good when they went on duty at 4:00 A.M. The watch on the *Gulfstream* was quoted in the press as saying: "The sky was overcast with the moon behind it, but visibility was good, the sea slight." His counterpart on the *Eastwind* testified along the same lines: "The weather was very good, the visibility good, the sea slight. The stars were not out and I could see the outline of the moon behind a stratified layer of clouds."

A few minutes later the *Eastwind*'s watch reported that the weather was beginning to close in, and she soon ran into thick fog; visibility closed down. The Coast Guard ship's radar picked up the oncoming tanker, which had no radar, and changed course. "Suddenly he [the watch] spotted *Gulfstream*'s range light and heard her fog horn for the first time. The tanker, about 300 feet [91 m] off the starboard bow, loomed out of a fog pocket. At the same time visibility closed down to zero." The crash occurred at about 4:35 A.M.

Thirteen Guardsmen were killed in the accident and twenty-two injured. The *Eastwind* was towed back to port and saved.

## The Collision of the *Shalom* and the *Stolt Dagali*

The Norwegian tanker *Stolt Dagali*, weighing 19,150 tons, was cut in two by the Israeli liner *Shalom*, weighing 25,338 tons, shortly after 2:00 A.M. on Thanksgiving morning, November 26, 1964, off the North Jersey coast. The accident occurred about twenty-one miles

(34 km) south of Ambrose Light in heavy fog. According to the *New York Times*, the *Shalom* had been running south at full speed of 20.5 knots (38 km/h) "in clear weather, with considerable wind and heavy seas, when it suddenly ran into a wall of fog." The *Stolt Dagali* was proceeding north and had experienced fog for some time.

No United States agency conducted an inquiry, since the accident took place outside territorial waters and no American ship was involved, but many statements about weather conditions were made in testimony during subsequent litigation. Failure to reduce high speed through fog by the passenger liner and inexperience on both ships in interpreting radar images quickly played a large part in putting them on a collision course. There was disagreement as to how long the *Shalom* had been in the fog area before the crash occurred. Her speed had not been reduced. The ships were only four-tenths of a mile (six-tenths of a km) apart when the liner began to take evasive action.

The *Shalom*, cutting into the *Stolt Dagali*, opened a forty-foot (12 m) gash in its bow. The stern of the tanker sank soon after the crash while her forward three-quarters wallowed helplessly in rough seas. Nineteen crewmen were lost and twenty-four rescued. The *Shalom* was able to proceed back to New York without assistance.

## Commercial Airliners

Three major accidents involving commercial air carriers in New Jersey occurred within two months in a small area of Elizabeth, which lies athwart both the landing and takeoff paths of Newark Airport.

A C-46F aircraft, operated by Miami Airline of Florida, an irregular air carrier, crashed shortly after takeoff from Newark Airport on Sunday, December 16, 1951, about 3:09 P.M. All fifty-six occupants were killed, and the aircraft was destroyed by impact and fire. Seven people in nearby buildings were fatally injured. Newark weather was good, with a visibility of fifteen miles (25 km) and a variable west wind of 20 miles per hour (33 km/h).

The plane had proceeded 4.5 miles (8.5 km) west when it made an abrupt turn to the east over Stuyvesant Avenue in Union. While attempting to return to the airport, the aircraft stalled at an altitude of approximately 300 feet (90 m), banked sharply to its left, struck buildings, and crashed on the bank of the Elizabeth River close to the Westfield Avenue bridge.

The failure from fatigue of a cylinder's hold-down nuts caused the cylinder to separate from the crankcase and start a fire which spread rapidly and became uncontrollable, according to the Civil Aeronautics Board's investigation.

On January 22, 1952, at about 3:43 P.M., an American Airlines Convair 240 crashed in Elizabeth. All twenty passengers and three crew members were killed. The flight originated in Buffalo with scheduled stops at Rochester and Syracuse.

The aircraft crashed and burned near the intersection of Williamson and South streets in the South Elizabeth residential district. This position is about 2,000 feet (610 m) to the right or southeast of the glide path and 3.7 miles (6 km) from the touchdown point at Newark Airport.

The weather conditions at Newark at 3:40 P.M. were reported as "indefinite ceiling 400 feet [150 m], obscurement, visibility 0.75 mile [1.2 km], light rain and fog. Altimeter 29.97 inches [101.5 kPa]."

Weather conditions along the route from Buffalo to Newark included a strong flow of southerly winds causing advection of warmer air, which was riding over a cooler airmass near the surface. Winds were easterly at the surface, resulting in a wind shear and turbulence at the boundary of the two airmasses. There were no fronts along the route.

During the descent in the New York area, above-freezing temperatures were encountered at the 5,000-foot (1,600 m) level; any ice that may have been on the plane had probably melted by 4,000 feet (1,300 m). During this descent precipitation ranged from very light to moderate snow at 7,000 feet (2,200 m). It turned to drizzle with occasional moderate rain below 4,000 feet. By this time the boundary between the cooler surface air and the warmer air aloft had lowered to about 1,500 feet (457 m) in the Newark area. This wind-shear zone, extending from about 1,000 to 2,000 feet (305 to 610 m), was choppy and rather sharply turbulent, but had only small vertical currents. Meteorological conditions indicated no downdrafts near the surface; the cooler, denser air near the surface would tend to destroy descending currents. Also in this 1,000- to 2,000-foot zone the wind changed from about 210° at 50 miles per hour (81 km/h) to about 140° at 30 miles per hour (48 km/h). Below-ceiling minimums prevailed at LaGuardia, Idlewild (now Kennedy), and Teterboro airports.

Testimony of pilots who landed at or took off from Newark Airport near the time of the crash verify the reported ceiling and visibility. However, ground witnesses to the crash estimate that at the time of the impact the ceiling was about 100–150 feet with a light drizzle, a visibility of two to three city blocks, and little or no wind.

Conditions during approach and letdown were favorable for carburetor icing. Pilots who landed just before or after the accident did not experience any carburetor icing; all but one stated that they used carburetor heat during their approaches to avert icing.

The aircraft was headed in an easterly direction, below the overcast, in a near-level attitude, for a distance of approximately 1,300 feet (400 m), before it crashed.

The Civil Aeronautics Board's investigation concluded that there was not sufficient evidence to predicate a probable cause for the crash.

A Douglas DC-6 owned and operated by National Airlines crashed and burned after striking an Elizabeth apartment house after takeoff from Newark Airport on February 11, 1952. The crash occurred near the intersection of Scotland Road and Westminster Avenue at about 12:20 A.M.

Sixty-three persons were aboard the aircraft. Of these, twenty-nine died, together with four people in the apartment building.

The weather was satisfactory for Visual Flight Regulations (VFR) and had no bearing on the accident.

## The Most Costly Lightning Bolt

A bolt of lightning from an ordinary afternoon thunderstorm struck the grounds of the Naval Ammunition Depot at Lake Denmark, Rockaway Township, Morris County, about 5:15 P.M. on Saturday, July 10, 1926. Two vacationers were quoted the next day in the *New York Times*: "We were driving through the reservation near the gate. Everything was dead quiet and the storm seemed right on top of us. There was a tremendous clap of thunder, and right on top of it, so quick that we were completely stunned, there was a horribly terrific noise that shook the whole earth. A red ball of fire leaped to the sky and our windshield shattered and spilled in broken glass around us."

The bolt struck near one of the some two-hundred magazines on the 456-acre reservation, which served as a main supply base for the Atlantic Fleet. The exact circumstance leading to the ignition of the ammunition has never been determined. Witness reports appearing in the press were contradictory and did not establish how the stroke of lightning kindled the fire. The Naval Court of Inquiry merely stated that "lightning crashed within the ammunition depot at or near the southwest end thereof at about 5:15 P.M.," and "almost immediately thereafter black smoke was seen issuing from the northeast side of temporary magazine No. 8." The magazine was a small brick building with a tar-paper roof, terra-cotta gutters, and sheet-iron doors. It contained depth charges and cast TNT aerial bombs. Number 8 had a network of lightning conductors that were grounded at each end of the building. The court found that "the fire in the . . . magazine was caused by lightning, either from a heavy direct stroke or by induced currents, despite the fact that the building was equipped with lightning protection in accordance with the best practice of the day."

The first of a series of tremendous explosions took place about five minutes after the bolt struck. The explosions shook the country for miles around, tore houses from their foundations, hurled vehicles off the highways, and darkened the sky with barrages of smoke. For many hours big shells, depth bombs, cans of high explosives, and cases of powder continued to explode as fire or a stray shell reached one building after another. The scene for miles around was likened to a battlefield with shells landing and devastating the landscape. Some debris were found as far as twenty-two miles (35 km) from the scene. A reporter for the *New York Tribune* described the depot grounds the next day: "The entire area is charred and smoking. Not a blade of grass nor a green shrub remains. Trees are stripped of branches. The ground is pitted with craters. One of them is 100 feet long, 30 feet wide, and 50 feet deep."

It was feared that the U.S. Army's Picatinny Arsenal, which adjoined the depot, would blow up, too, but its buildings suffered only blast and concussion damage. The loss to the navy was placed at between $70 million and $93 million. Sixteen people were killed either on the depot grounds or in surrounding communities.

*Lightning caused this fire at the U.S. Naval Ammunitions Depot at Lake Denmark, July 12, 1926. The magazines burned for days. (U.S. Navy Photo)*

# Notable New Jersey Weather Events

GREAT DELAWARE FLOOD OF 1692. Spring flood at "Delaware Falls" drove early settlers of Trenton from homes, which were inundated to second story. Flood waters reputed to have been as high as any since experienced.

FIRST HARD WINTER OF EIGHTEENTH CENTURY (1740–1741). Delaware at Philadelphia remained frozen from December 19 to March 13. Cold and deep snows came in December, followed by thaw in early January, then a second winter in late January and February. Great suffering for want of food and fodder.

HAILSTORM AT BURLINGTON, MAY 25, 1758. Half rain, half hail filled streets with floating ice, creating a "scene of devastation" with crops destroyed and gardens ruined. Described in the *New American Magazine* published at Woodbridge.

TWO DEEP SNOWSTORMS OF THE 1760s. At Woodbury, March 17, 1760: "Snow in ye woods then level was one yard deep." At Philadelphia, March 28, 1765: "Greatest for many years, said to lie 2 or 2½ feet on a level."

HURRICANE OF SEPTEMBER 3, 1775. A storm center's inland track raised great southeast gales on Delaware Bay and caused the highest tide known on river. Extensive riverbank, shipping, and crop damage.

BATTLE OF TRENTON STORM, CHRISTMAS NIGHT 1776. Combined snow, sleet, and rain driven by northeast winds enabled Washington's army to achieve surprise and victory at First Battle of Trenton on morning of December 26, 1776.

SECOND HARD WINTER OF EIGHTEENTH CENTURY (1779–1780). Three violent snowstorms in late December and early January covered land with two to three feet of snow; then came month-long January freeze. New York Harbor was icebound for five weeks; Delaware River at Philadelphia closed for three months. Great suffering among American troops at Morristown.

HURRICANE OF AUGUST 19, 1788. Tropical storm of small dimensions but great wind force cut fifty-mile path northward from Cape May to Hudson River. Many trees downed. Philadelphia had 7.00 inches of rain. Repetition today would cause an enormous disaster.

HIGH FLOODS OF 1780s. No other such clustering of inundations as those of May 9, 1781; February 28, 1783; January 17, 1784; March 17, 1785; and October 4, 1786. All did extensive damage.

GREAT SNOWSTORM, JANUARY 27–28, 1805. Over 24 inches fell within forty-eight hours in Newark–New York area, the greatest since 1780 and a worthy rival to that of December 26–27, 1947. January 1805 probably was the snowiest month in Newark history.

HIGH WATER ON NEW JERSEY RIVERS, NOVEMBER 12–15, 1810. Flood stages that were not equaled at Paterson until 1903, on Delaware until 1841. At New Brunswick the scene was described as "awful and distressing."

YEAR WITHOUT A SUMMER, 1816. Cool period with frost on five consecutive nights, June 7–11. Droughty conditions in July–August combined with cool nights to prevent corn from maturing properly. Killing frosts on September 26–29 ended growing season. Corn in short supply, but no famine in New Jersey.

CAPE MAY HURRICANE, SEPTEMBER 3, 1821. Eye of vigorous hurricane passed northward over peninsula. Storm tide covered roads; ocean and bay waters met. Hotel unroofed. Path northward along present Garden State Parkway to Asbury Park, then over water to Rockaway Beach.

DESTRUCTIVE EASTERLY STORM, EASTER SUNDAY, MARCH 30, 1823. Hurricane-force winds raked entire state, doing great damage to trees and buildings. Snow fell to depth of 24 inches in Sussex County. Rain deluged central and southern sections. Very low barometer. Wind damage comparable to November 25, 1950.

HURRICANE OF JUNE 4–5, 1825. Full-fledged storm from Florida battered shipping, tore up trees, and caused structural damage. Worst early-season hurricane of record.

GREAT SNOWSTORM OF JANUARY 14–16, 1831. Snow from 18 to 30 inches covered state, greatest depths in south. Transportation immobilized for days.

NEW BRUNSWICK TORNADO, JUNE 19, 1835. Path of seventeen miles from Amwell in Somerset County east across Middlesex County, right through center of New Brunswick, then down Raritan River to New York Bay. Serious damage to 120 buildings; five persons killed.

SUDDEN THAW, JANUARY 1839. Deep cyclonic storm moving over Pennsylvania caused temperature rise from below zero to around 50°F in twenty-four hours on January 25–26. Heavy rains plus ice breakup brought flood conditions to all sections. Small streams in northern highlands suffered worst freshets known.

"BRIDGES FLOOD," JANUARY 1841. Heavy rains and ice breakup carried away all bridges except one between Phillipsburg and Trenton when the Delaware River rose to a record high. Four of six bridges between Paterson and Newark on Passaic River also swept away. Many buildings damaged along river banks.

"ARCTIC WEEK," JANUARY 1857. Cold storm on January 18–19, with zero temperatures, 12 inches of snow and northeast gales blocked all traffic. After brief warming, second cold wave dropped thermometers to record levels: −12°F at Newark, −17°F at Trenton, −32°F in Sussex and Warren counties.

LONG, SNOWY WINTER OF 1867–1868. New Jersey's snowiest and coldest winter. Snow cover and sleighing almost every day at Montclair from December 12 to end of March. Steady cold throughout: Newark's winter maximum 51°F. Departures from normal: December, −5.1°F; January, −3.1°F; February, −8.8°F; and March, none. Seasonal snowfall was a record 75 inches.

HURRICANE OF OCTOBER 23, 1878. Path over central Pennsylvania raised southeast gales of hurricane force, causing great damage to resort hotels at Cape May. All interior sections suffered structural, crop, and tree damage.

YELLOW DAY, SEPTEMBER 6, 1881. Smoke from Michigan forest fires filtered sun's rays, giving outdoor objects a weird, brassy hue.

CAMDEN-PHILADELPHIA TORNADO, AUGUST 3, 1885. Sweeping along Camden river front, a large tornado funnel wrecked steamer and many houses. Crossed river into northeast Philadelphia. Five killed; damage estimated at $500,000.

BLIZZARD OF '88, MARCH 12–14. Region's most famous snowstorm with all elements of a blizzard present: 20 inches of snow, temperature below 10°F, and strong gales. Snow blown into immense drifts, halting railroads and all travel. Entire state immobilized. Many shipwrecks on coast and in Delaware Bay. Several deaths from exhaustion and exposure.

"ARCTIC WEEK," FEBRUARY 1899. After about 8 inches of snow on February 7–8, temperature went below zero state-wide, except at Cape May; maximum readings generally below 10°F on eleventh; great blizzard on February 11–14 dropped 34 inches at Cape May; thermometer went above freezing on sixteenth for first time since fourth.

TROPICAL STORM, SEPTEMBER 1903. Ex-hurricane moving from southeast made a direct landfall on south New Jersey coast on September 16. Atlantic City measured 50-mile-per-hour winds; up to 6.00 inches of rain fell. Extensive damage at shore to beach and buildings, and to structures and trees across southern and central counties.

RAINSTORM AND FLOOD, OCTOBER 1903. Paterson area deluged by 11.45 inches on October 9, with storm total of 15.51 inches, October 9–11; caused greatest flood known in Passaic valley. Upper Delaware and Raritan rivers reached high crests but not equal to 1896. Enormous damage throughout state unequaled until 1955.

RECORD COLD, JANUARY 1904. Lowest thermometer reading of modern times on morning of January 5: −34°F at River Vale, Bergen County; −30°F at Layton, Sussex County; −28°F at Englewood, Bergen County. Other readings: −4°F at New York City; −3°F at Trenton; 0°F at Cape May.

CHRISTMAS NIGHT SNOWSTORM, 1909. Rapidly deepening low-pressure center near Cape May produced 21 inches of snow in Camden-Philadelphia area, greatest of all time there. Wilmington had 22.1 inches, Moorestown 21.6 inches, all falling within twenty-four hours on December 25–26.

EASTER WEEKEND SNOWSTORM, APRIL 1915. Up to 21 inches fell across central section on Saturday, April 3, as intense coastal storm moved north from Cape Hatteras. Clayton in southernmost Gloucester County reported 21.2 inches, center-city Philadelphia 19.4 inches, and Haddonfield 18 inches. Easter services cancelled and vacationers isolated at resorts.

SEVEREST WINTER IN MODERN TIMES, 1917–1918. December through February averaged 6.3°F below normal. Severe turn of the year with seven-day cold wave, temperature −29°F in the north. Snowfall averaged 11.4 inches in December and 18.9 inches in January. Severe fuel shortages during war winter.

GREAT SLEET STORM, FEBRUARY 4–7, 1920. Mixed snow and ice pellets fell to a depth of 17 inches in New York City and northern New Jersey; compacted into a solid mass defying removal. Roads extremely dangerous and traffic slowed until end of month.

HURRICANE, AUGUST 1933. Severe tropical storm crossing Chesapeake Bay from southeast gave South Jersey a severe lashing. Atlantic City had winds of 65 miles per hour from east and 10.95 inches of rain. Extensive local flood damage in southern counties.

TWIN FLOODS, MARCH 1936. Heavy rainstorms on 11–12 and 18–19, plus attendant snowmelt caused double crests on middle and upper Delaware River, with highest flood levels ever known. Raritan and Passaic rivers at highest since 1903.

BIG SNOW, DECEMBER 1947. Surprise heavy snowfall piled up to depths of 30 inches in Monmouth and Bergen counties, all within twenty-four hours on December 26–27. Traffic immobilized for days; situation compounded by damaging ice storm on New Year's Eve.

GREAT APPALACHIAN STORM, NOVEMBER 25, 1950. Rapidly deepening storm center moving north through Pennsylvania created hurricane-force winds from east and southeast in warm sector; Newark had gust at 108 miles per hour. Heavy deluges caused state-wide floods; numerous blackouts.

FLOODS, AUGUST 1955. Twin tropical storms raised state rivers. Connie's rains of 7–10 inches on August 12–13 saturated soil with minor flooding; Diane's contribution of 4–7 inches on 18–19 raised high floods. Trenton river front inundated. Loss of life small in New Jersey, but heavy across river in Pennsylvania.

HOTTEST HIGH SUMMER OF RECORD, 1955. July averaged 5.1°F and August 4.6°F above normal state-wide. July maximum hit 104°F and August 105°F.

HURRICANE DONNA, SEPTEMBER 12, 1960. Last major hurricane before David in 1979 passed about 80 miles east of Atlantic City; made landfall on central Long Island. Winds hit 72 miles per hour. Extensive damage to boats, docks, boardwalks, and beach cottages. Minor overflows on streams. Nine deaths.

THE TRIPLE SNOWSTORMS, 1960–1961. Prewinter storm on December 11–12 brought 20 inches to north; Kennedy inaugural storm on January 19–20 piled up from 16 to 26 inches across north; third big snow on February 3–4, with maximum of 27 inches. Newark's seasonal total of 73.5 inches was greatest of recent record.

*Main Street in Beach Haven after a violent storm forced hundreds of people from their homes along the shore, March 6–7, 1962. (Weatherwise, Princeton, New Jersey)*

GREAT ATLANTIC COASTAL STORM, MARCH 6–8, 1962. Long-fetch gales raised mountainous waves on top of storm tide; five successive extreme high tides resulted. Long Beach Island submerged, with enormous damage. Atlantic City and Cape May areas suffered extensive destruction and beach erosion.

NORTHEASTERN DROUGHT OF THE EARLY AND MID-1960s. Dry conditions began in autumn of 1961, reached serious proportions in October 1963, with water shortages. Reservoirs at record low levels in summer of 1965. Not until October 1966 did precipitation from coastal storms return; reservoirs were restored to normal by spring of 1967.

TROPICAL STORM DORIA, AUGUST 27–28, 1971. Movement of tropical storm across state caused general flooding, $138.5 million damages. Little Falls in Essex County measured 10.29 inches. Storm-generated tornado struck Cape May.

EX-HURRICANE DAVID, SEPTEMBER 6, 1979. David, downgraded to a tropical storm, moved north through Pennsylvania; New Jersey was subject to southeast gales, 54-mile-per-hour winds at Trenton; extensive tree and wire destruction.

SERIES OF COLD MONTHS, 1970s. Each winter from 1975–1976 through 1978–1979 experienced at least one severely cold month. New Brunswick departures from normal in degrees Fahrenheit for coldest months each winter were: January 1976, −5.2 degrees; January 1977, −11.6 degrees; February 1978, −9.2 degrees; February 1979, −11.6 degrees. Coldest full winter was 1977–1978 with average monthly departure of −5.1 degrees. Lowest minimum throughout state during four winters was −18°F at Sussex in February 1979: all-time record minimum was −34°F at River Vale in Bergen County in January 1904.

COLDEST CHRISTMAS, 1980. Temperatures plummeted throughout state on December 25, 1980. Newark Airport reported drop from 15°F just after midnight to 0°F at 10:00 A.M.; rose to 6°F by 4:00 P.M.; accompanying northeast gale produced bitter wind chill; departure from normal in degrees Fahrenheit, −24 degrees. Other minimum readings: New Brunswick, −1°F; Trenton, 2°F; Atlantic City, 9°F.

"COLD SUNDAY OF 1982." Temperature at Newark Airport dropped from 21°F at 10:00 P.M. to a morning reading of −4°F on January 17, later to −7°F, for coldest daylight period of modern record. Trenton reached minimum of −9°F, Atlantic City, −6°F. Strong northwest gales all day caused excessive wind chill temperatures.

*The bridges across the Delaware were battered by the flooding in August 1955. This one is the Delaware-Phillipsburg Bridge. (From* The Express, *Easton, Pennsylvania)*

CHAPTER 6

# Weather Information Sources

## Radio and Television

The National Oceanic and Atmospheric Administration (NOAA) maintains a nationwide network of radio stations that provide continuous weather, marine, and river information. The transmissions are on VHF-FM (very high frequency-frequency modulation) channels. Reception is usually satisfactory over a forty-mile radius from the transmitting station. Local radio and television stations can record and rebroadcast the material even though landlines might be severed. The transmissions, known as NOAA-VHF Radio, are continuous round the clock. Three high-band frequencies are employed throughout the United States: 162.40, 162.475, and 162.55 megahertz (MHz). Stations on the same frequency are spaced far enough apart to avoid interference. Many commercial AM-FM receivers contain a switch for weather-band reception.

The taped messages are repeated every four to six minutes and routinely revised about every three to four hours. They are amended as needed to match changing weather conditions. Information is provided for the general public, motorists, campers, sportsmen, boaters, and others who need detailed weather information. The emphasis is on public safety. When dangerous weather threatens, routine transmissions are interrupted and emergency warnings are broadcast.

As an added refinement, the National Weather Service can activate specially designed radio receivers by means of a tone signal. The signal is transmitted for about ten seconds before announcements of hazardous conditions. The tone signal alerts schools, hospitals, churches, and other places of assembly, public utility units, emergency forces, news media, and others to be ready for critically important weather messages. The broadcast stations in the New Jersey area are: New York City—KWO35, 162.55 MHz; Philadelphia—KH128, 162.475 MHz; Atlantic City—KHB38, 162.40 MHz; Allentown, Pa.—162.40 MHz.

## Airways Weather Reports

The Federal Aviation Administration (FAA) maintains a network of radio broadcast stations for the quick dissemination of current weather conditions at airports throughout the country. These voice broadcasts are continuous, though only forecasts are given from 11:00 P.M. to 5:00 A.M. The transmitter in New Jersey is located at the Teterboro Airport and the service is known as Newark-Elmira Radio, since the messages are transmitted simultaneously from the Newark area and from the Elmira, New York, area. The broadcasts are on 379 kilocycles (kHz); a receiver with a longwave band is required. Amateur multiwave receivers usually include this band. The broadcasts can be received over most of northern and central New Jersey.

The reporting stations are Newark, Islip, Teterboro, LaGuardia, White Plains, Albany, Watertown, Buffalo, Elmira, Rochester, Syracuse, Atlantic City, Washington, Boston, Wilkes Barre–Scranton, Bradford, Erie, Williamsport, Harrisburg, Philadelphia, Pittsburgh, Philipsburg, Burlington, and Cleveland, with hourly updates.

The broadcasts contain a brief synopsis of the weather map, flight precautions, route forecasts, and airport weather at the last hour, including sky condition, ceiling, visibility, obstructions to vision, temperature, dew point, wind direction and speed, and altimeter setting. In good flying weather some of the above are omitted. From 11:00 P.M. to 5:00 A.M. airport weather reports are not transmitted, only the synopsis and forecasts.

The National Weather Service and the Federal Aviation Administration, along with other aviation institutions, cooperate in producing A.M. Weather over the facilities of the Public Broadcasting Service. Both national and regional weather situations are discussed. The program is intended to inform pilots about the prospects for flying but includes much information of general interest to the public. The program is aired Monday through Friday over New Jersey Public Television Channels 23, 50, 52, and 57 at 7:45 A.M. and over Channel 12 in the Philadelphia-Wilmington area at 8:45 A.M. Since the programs are designed partly for use in schools, some of the channels do not broadcast during the summer vacation weeks.

# Multiple-Access Recorded Telephone Announcement System

This system provides the public with direct access to current weather information, forecasts, and warnings on demand via telephone. The weather information consists of local observations and forecasts recorded by the National Weather Service or the telephone company. More than a thousand calls can be handled simultaneously. New Jersey numbers are:
Northern New Jersey (201) 936–1212
Southern New Jersey (609) 936–1212

# Evacuation Maps

Detailed storm-evacuation maps have been prepared by the National Oceanic and Atmospheric Administration for low-lying areas vulnerable to flooding by hurricane-generated storm surges. These maps show portions that would be inundated by various levels of storm surge and the best routes for evacuation inland. They can be ordered from:

Distribution Division (C44)
National Ocean Survey
Riverdale, M.D. 20840

# Government Publications

LOCAL CLIMATOLOGICAL DATA. Contains daily temperature and hourly precipitation observations. Issued monthly. $3.50 per year per station. Send order and payment to National Climatic Center, Federal Building, Asheville, N.C. 28801. Published for Atlantic City, Central Park–New York City, Newark, Philadelphia, and Trenton.

CLIMATOLOGICAL DATA: NEW JERSEY. Contains daily temperature and precipitation observations for about forty New Jersey localities. Issued monthly with an annual summary. $5.10 per year. Make checks payable to Department of Commerce, NOAA, and send payments and orders to National Climatic Center, Federal Building, Asheville, N.C. 28801.

DAILY WEATHER MAPS—WEEKLY SERIES. Contains weather map of middle latitudes of North America for Monday through Sunday. Issued once a week. Annual subscription $30.00. Send payment and order to Public Documents Department, U.S. Government Printing Office, Washington, D.C. 20402.

STORM DATA. Contains details of severe local storms in each state. Issued monthly. $12.60 per year. Send payment and order to National Climatic Center, Federal Building, Asheville, N.C. 28801.

WEEKLY WEATHER AND CROP BULLETIN. Contains national coverage of temperature and precipitation data for past week and brief discussion of effect of weather on crop development in each state; also in certain foreign countries. Includes temperature and precipitation charts. Published weekly on Tuesdays. Annual subscription $25.00. Make check payable to Department of Commerce, NOAA, and order from NOAA/USDA Joint Agricultural Weather Facility, USDA South Building, Room 3526, Washington, D.C. 20250.

NEW JERSEY WEEKLY DIGEST. CROPS-MARKETS-WEATHER. Contains rainfall, temperature, growing degree data, and soil moisture conditions. Also discussion of crop conditions during past week and summary of fruit and vegetable arrivals. Published weekly on Tuesdays from April through October. Subscription free upon request to U.S. Department of Agriculture, Box 1888, Trenton, N.J. 08625.

# Commercial Publications

WEATHERWISE. THE MAGAZINE ABOUT WEATHER. A bimonthly publication containing articles on the progress of the science of meteorology and descriptions of outstanding weather events, past and current. Each issue presents a discussion of the last two months' main weather features. Annual subscriptions $15.00 to individuals, $22.00 to institutions. Send payment and order to: Weatherwise, Heldref Publications, 4000 Albemarle St., NW, Washington, D.C. 20016.

# Appendices
# Bibliography

*A view of Windmill Island near the Camden shore of the Delaware, 1754. Philadelphia is in the background. (Courtesy of the Historical Society of Pennsylvania)*

APPENDIX A

# Weather as an Energy Source

## Wind Energy

Windmills were once a familiar part of the New Jersey scene. They were heavily used to grind grain and pump water. Two of the most prominent mills were along busy waterways on either side of the state. In the early nineteenth century, long before the arrival of the Statue of Liberty from France, the most visible feature on the New Jersey skyline from New York Harbor was Isaac Edge's windmill on Paulus Hook in Jersey City. For many years its whirling sails, in addition to grinding grain for local residents, lent a picturesque appearance to the original Dutch settlement. Its cloth sails were torn by hurricane gales on September 3, 1821. The Jersey City windmill gave way to progress in 1839 when the land was needed for the passage of a railroad; it was dismantled and shipped to Southold on eastern Long Island where it was reassembled and used for many years.

Another familiar sight in the early nineteenth century lent its name to Windmill Island in the Delaware River off Cooper's Point, Camden. Cooper's Point was attached to the mainland at low tide by a sandspit which could be crossed by farmers' wagons carrying grain for grinding. Windmill Island was first cut through to expedite the direct passage of ferries on the Camden-Philadelphia run and later entirely eliminated by dredging for harbor improvements.

South Jersey was a favorite site for small windmills on farms in the nineteenth century, since winds from the ocean and bay supplement the normal continental flow from the west. The shoreline of Long Beach Island once possessed attractive landmarks in the presence of two large windmills engaged in pumping water for the railroad and local hotel. Newspaper accounts reported that the severe tropical storm of September 16, 1903, took a heavy toll of windmills; most were not replaced. The coming of electricity rendered them temporarily obsolete.

During the 1960s several research projects for the efficient production of wind power were undertaken in New Jersey engineering colleges. The urgency of the subject was heightened by the energy crisis of the mid-1970s. Small wind generators were soon at work privately, and plans for the commercial production of power were studied. The most grandiose project for producing power in New Jersey was the brainchild of Professor William E. Heronemus, then a lecturer at the

University of Massachusetts, whose proposals were introduced into a state legislature hearing on wind power in March 1974. He envisioned placing 360 steel towers along a 150-mile stretch of the Garden State Parkway, where they would be subject part of the time to ocean breezes as well as to continental winds. Each set of two towers placed at half-mile intervals would straddle the roadway and be connected by suspension cables, which would support 72,000 three-bladed windmills each thirty-two feet in diameter. He estimated the power production at seven billion kilowatts per year, about 60 percent of the state's needs. Even greater amounts could be generated if the windmills were placed on buoys offshore, though the initial cost would be greater and maintenance costs higher.

## Calculating Wind Energy

The theoretical amount of kinetic energy that can be extracted from a wind machine amounts to only 59.26 percent. This is based on a 100 percent efficiency of the wind machine itself, but actually only about 30 to 40 percent of the kinetic energy can be utilized. There are two basic calculations in determining potential wind power: (1) Power increases with the cube of the wind speed. If the wind speed doubles, there will be eight times more power potential. (2) Power increases with the square of the diameter of the windmill. If the diameter is doubled, there will be four times more power potential.

Another consideration in calculating basic potential power lies in the fact that the cubic response to wind speed requires a frequency distribution of speeds, rather than average speed. At sea level under standard conditions, a 10-knot wind would contain 84 watts per square meter ($W/m^2$). If the wind blew at a steady 15 knots, 282 $W/m^2$ would be available. But if it blew at 10 knots half the time and 20 knots half the time, again averaging 15 knots, it would yield 376 $W/m^2$, or 33 percent more.

## Measuring Wind Speeds

Only three first-class weather stations in New Jersey possess wind records going back thirty years or more. These are Atlantic City (1874–present), Trenton (1913–present), and Newark Airport (1931–present). There are no official wind-reporting stations in the northern highlands, where one might expect relatively high wind speeds.

March is the windiest month at all three stations and August the least windy. Thermal contrasts, which power the winds, are the greatest in March and the least in August.

Atlantic City Airport at Pomona, with an anemometer exposure at 20 feet (6.1 m) above ground, has the highest monthly wind average with 12.5 miles per hour (20 km/h) in March; Newark Airport, with an exposure 11 feet (3.4 m) above the runways, has 12.0 miles per hour (19 km/h); Trenton has 10.7 miles per hour (18 km/h), with an exposure of 107 feet (32.6 m) atop the Post Office building.

During the past forty years the highest sustained mile of wind passing a station occurred at Newark Airport during the November 1950 storm, when a speed of 82 miles per hour (132 km/h) was measured; in the same storm Trenton attained a peak fastest mile of 64 miles per hour (103 km/h). Atlantic City Airport's highest wind came in Hurricane Donna in September 1960, with a speed of 60 miles per hour (97 km/h). A momentary gust of 108 miles per hour (173 km/h) was reported at Newark during the November 1950 storm.

Old Weather Bureau wind records prior to 1928 must be treated with caution. The former 4-cup anemometer tended to overregister by about 20 percent at high wind speeds. Three-cup anemometers are now standard at most major stations.

# Solar Energy

The sun is a source of safe, clean, abundant energy. It serves as a giant nuclear reactor whose surface temperature of about 10,400°F (5,700°C) radiates at the rate of 43,000 kilowatts per hour per square meter (kWh/m$^2$). The total amount of solar energy reaching the top of the earth's atmosphere is about $7 \times 10^7$ kWh, or about 30,000 times as much energy as employed in all man-made devices. This prodigious flow of energy warms the earth and through the process of photosynthesis produces all the food, fuel, and oxygen upon which life depends.

Solar radiation falling on a surface normal to the sun's rays at the outer limit of the earth's atmosphere has an average intensity of 1.37 kW/m$^2$* or 445 Btu/ft$^2$/h. This quantity, known as the solar constant, varies to a slight degree periodically but has remained essentially the same, it is believed, for several billion years.

On its path to earth solar radiation is absorbed and weakened by various constituents of the atmosphere. It is also scattered by air molecules in the shorter wavelengths, causing the apparent light-blue color of the sky. In the stratosphere, with fewer air molecules above the observer, the sky appears dark.

In the upper atmosphere ozone is an effective absorber of solar radiation, which forms by a photochemical process at heights of about twenty miles (32 km) and filters out much of the shortwave radiation such as ultraviolet rays. Equally important as an absorber in the infrared range is carbon dioxide.

In the lower layers of the atmosphere, water vapor, dust, and other particulate material scatter and absorb much radiation effectively. In early morning and evening when the rays of the sun cut through a long path of turbid air, the radiation is attenuated and short wavelengths scattered. This causes the red color of the sunrise and sunset and permits one to look directly into the sun. The scattering of radiation by air molecules and atmospheric impurities is called *diffuse radiation* and makes up a considerable part of total radiation.

There is no easy way to estimate the intensity of diffuse radiation, since it depends on the amount of dust, moisture, and degree of cloudiness of the sky. On a completely cloudy day, the only radiation that we receive is the diffuse component; on a clear day it depends upon just how clear the sky is and how much invisible water vapor the atmosphere contains.

Water vapor in the lower atmosphere is a primary factor in determining how much direct radiation reaches the earth's surface, since there is a marked variation in water vapor content throughout the year. Only about 46 percent of the incoming solar energy actually reaches the earth's surface; on the average 32 percent is reflected back into space by clouds and the remaining 22 percent is absorbed by the atmosphere. The amount of insolation received through various types of clouds of average thickness (in percent of clear sky radiation) is estimated at: cirrus 83, cirro-stratus 78, alto-cumulus 49, strato-cumulus 32, stratus 25, nimbo-stratus 20, and fog 18 percent.

Since the earth's axis is tilted from the vertical at an angle of 23°26′ and its orbit around the sun is elliptical, solar radiation reaches different portions of the earth in varying amounts according to the season. The apparent path of the sun across the sky changes every day, both in altitude and duration above the horizon. At the winter solstice at New Jersey's latitude the sun travels through an arc of 120° from dawn to dusk, but at the summer solstice it travels through an arc of 240°. The difference in the zenith altitude from winter to summer amounts to 47°—at the summer solstice it climbs at noon to 73°30′, but at the winter solstice it rises to only 26°30′.

The duration of sunlight at 40°N varies from about nine hours and thirty minutes to about fifteen hours, a difference of two hours and forty-five minutes at each end of the day. These figures, of course, do not take into consideration the variable cloud cover that restricts direct sunlight at the earth's surface. Meteorologists calculate the hours of sunshine as a percentage of the possible if the sky had been completely clear of clouds all day. This varies throughout the state each month: Atlantic City in December drops as low as 43 percent and

Trenton rises as high as 65 percent in July. For the state as a whole, the annual average of possible sunshine is about 57.5 percent.

The total hemispheric radiation received also varies considerably throughout the season. At 40°N, the average monthly input is 367 $W/m^2$. It drops as low as 41 percent of this figure in December and rises as high as 153 percent in July.

## Solar Index

The *solar index* is a number between 0 and 100 that gives the percentage of heat that could be supplied on a given day by a typical solar domestic water-heating system. For example, if the solar index were 84, then roughly 84 percent of the water-heating load for a household* could have been provided by a solar system. Collector areas are chosen to give an annual load fraction of 70–75 percent. The solar index is only a relative indicator of system performance. Its main purpose is to create a broader public awareness of the sun's ability to meet a portion of our energy needs.

The solar index is calculated from data describing weather conditions and a representative solar domestic water-heating system for a given locale. The formula involves the percentage of possible sunshine as determined by a radiation indicator and the mean temperature for the day. For example, if the percentage of possible sunshine for Philadelphia is 70 and the average temperature is 30°F, the prepared chart would indicate a solar index of 64. Charts for major cities can be obtained from the United States Department of Energy in Washington, D.C. 20585.

*This windmill stood at Paulus Hook, Jersey City, from 1815 to 1839. New York City is in the background. (Courtesy of Princeton University Library)*

APPENDIX B

# Climate Data

## Monthly Mean Temperature, Based on 1951–1980 Data (in degrees Fahrenheit)

| Station | January | February | March | April | May | June | July | August | September | October | November | December | Annual |
|---|---|---|---|---|---|---|---|---|---|---|---|---|---|
| Atlantic City | 34.2 | 35.3 | 41.7 | 53.3 | 59.4 | 68.3 | 74.0 | 73.8 | 68.1 | 57.8 | 47.8 | 38.5 | 54.1 |
| Belleplain | 32.9 | 34.5 | 42.5 | 52.4 | 62.2 | 70.2 | 75.1 | 73.9 | 67.5 | 56.5 | 46.6 | 36.9 | 54.3 |
| Belvidere | 27.3 | 29.3 | 38.5 | 49.7 | 59.5 | 67.9 | 72.3 | 70.8 | 63.9 | 53.1 | 42.3 | 31.2 | 50.5 |
| Boonton | 27.4 | 28.7 | 37.8 | 49.3 | 58.7 | 67.6 | 72.4 | 70.9 | 63.6 | 52.7 | 42.8 | 31.7 | 50.3 |
| Canoe Brook | 27.3 | 28.9 | 38.0 | 49.1 | 58.8 | 68.1 | 73.2 | 71.6 | 64.5 | 53.2 | 42.9 | 31.7 | 50.6 |
| Cape May | 34.5 | 35.2 | 42.2 | 51.8 | 60.8 | 69.8 | 75.2 | 75.0 | 69.5 | 59.3 | 49.1 | 39.1 | 55.1 |
| Charlotteburg | 25.6 | 26.5 | 35.3 | 47.0 | 56.5 | 65.2 | 70.0 | 68.4 | 61.4 | 50.9 | 41.1 | 29.8 | 48.1 |
| Essex Fells | 27.4 | 29.3 | 38.1 | 49.5 | 59.4 | 68.4 | 73.2 | 71.5 | 64.2 | 53.6 | 43.3 | 31.7 | 50.8 |
| Flemington | 27.9 | 29.6 | 38.6 | 49.5 | 59.2 | 68.6 | 73.7 | 72.2 | 64.7 | 53.4 | 42.9 | 32.1 | 51.0 |
| Freehold | 30.5 | 32.0 | 40.1 | 50.8 | 60.6 | 69.5 | 74.2 | 72.7 | 66.2 | 55.4 | 45.4 | 34.6 | 52.7 |
| Glassboro | 31.6 | 33.1 | 41.7 | 52.4 | 61.9 | 70.8 | 75.6 | 74.4 | 67.7 | 56.1 | 46.0 | 35.6 | 53.9 |
| Hammonton | 31.5 | 33.0 | 41.6 | 52.2 | 61.8 | 70.9 | 75.8 | 74.5 | 67.5 | 56.0 | 46.2 | 35.6 | 53.9 |
| Hightstown | 30.4 | 32.2 | 40.5 | 51.2 | 60.8 | 69.8 | 74.4 | 73.1 | 66.1 | 55.2 | 45.1 | 34.6 | 52.8 |
| Indian Mills | 30.9 | 32.7 | 40.8 | 51.2 | 60.9 | 69.6 | 74.2 | 72.9 | 66.0 | 54.9 | 44.8 | 34.7 | 52.8 |
| Jersey City | 30.6 | 32.1 | 39.9 | 50.5 | 60.4 | 69.4 | 74.6 | 73.3 | 66.3 | 55.8 | 45.5 | 34.5 | 52.7 |
| Lambertville | 30.3 | 32.3 | 40.8 | 51.6 | 61.7 | 70.7 | 75.2 | 73.9 | 67.0 | 55.6 | 44.8 | 34.2 | 53.2 |
| Little Falls | 29.5 | 31.1 | 39.8 | 50.9 | 60.6 | 69.8 | 74.8 | 73.2 | 65.9 | 54.8 | 44.8 | 33.7 | 52.4 |
| Long Branch | 31.6 | 32.9 | 40.1 | 50.1 | 59.4 | 68.7 | 74.0 | 73.0 | 66.6 | 56.0 | 46.1 | 35.9 | 52.9 |
| Long Valley | 26.6 | 28.2 | 36.7 | 48.0 | 57.4 | 66.0 | 70.7 | 69.2 | 62.1 | 51.4 | 41.3 | 30.5 | 49.0 |
| Millville | 31.8 | 33.5 | 41.7 | 52.1 | 61.9 | 70.8 | 75.8 | 74.6 | 67.9 | 56.2 | 46.0 | 36.0 | 54.0 |
| Moorestown | 30.9 | 32.9 | 41.4 | 51.9 | 61.5 | 70.2 | 74.9 | 73.6 | 66.6 | 55.3 | 44.8 | 34.8 | 53.2 |
| Morris Plains | 27.4 | 29.0 | 37.8 | 49.1 | 58.6 | 67.5 | 72.4 | 70.9 | 63.7 | 52.9 | 42.6 | 31.6 | 50.3 |
| New Brunswick | 30.2 | 32.0 | 40.4 | 51.3 | 60.9 | 69.7 | 74.7 | 73.3 | 66.4 | 55.4 | 45.2 | 34.3 | 52.8 |
| Newton | 24.5 | 26.2 | 36.0 | 47.8 | 57.5 | 66.5 | 71.1 | 69.3 | 61.7 | 50.5 | 40.4 | 29.1 | 48.4 |
| Pemberton | 31.4 | 33.2 | 41.4 | 51.5 | 61.1 | 69.8 | 74.3 | 73.3 | 66.7 | 55.8 | 45.8 | 35.4 | 53.3 |
| Plainfield | 30.1 | 32.2 | 40.6 | 51.4 | 61.1 | 69.9 | 74.8 | 73.5 | 66.5 | 55.4 | 44.7 | 34.1 | 52.9 |
| Shiloh | 32.6 | 34.3 | 42.5 | 52.8 | 62.4 | 70.9 | 75.7 | 74.5 | 68.3 | 57.3 | 46.8 | 36.8 | 54.6 |
| Somerville | 28.6 | 30.3 | 39.1 | 50.2 | 60.1 | 69.2 | 74.1 | 72.6 | 65.4 | 54.0 | 43.5 | 32.7 | 51.7 |
| Sussex | 24.1 | 25.9 | 35.3 | 47.3 | 57.2 | 66.1 | 70.7 | 69.1 | 61.6 | 50.8 | 40.6 | 28.7 | 48.1 |

SOURCE: National Climatic Center, Asheville, N.C.

## Monthly Mean Total Precipitation, Based on 1951–1980 Data (in inches)

| Station | January | February | March | April | May | June | July | August | September | October | November | December | Annual |
|---|---|---|---|---|---|---|---|---|---|---|---|---|---|
| Atlantic City | 3.25 | 3.22 | 3.71 | 3.12 | 2.91 | 2.88 | 3.89 | 4.54 | 2.73 | 2.76 | 3.54 | 3.51 | 40.06 |
| Audubon | 3.31 | 2.99 | 4.07 | 3.74 | 3.69 | 4.20 | 4.10 | 4.90 | 3.68 | 3.21 | 3.75 | 3.71 | 45.35 |
| Belleplain State Forest | 3.34 | 3.33 | 4.21 | 3.44 | 3.47 | 3.45 | 4.45 | 4.99 | 3.30 | 3.64 | 3.62 | 3.96 | 45.20 |
| Belvidere | 3.33 | 2.94 | 3.81 | 3.99 | 3.58 | 3.87 | 4.32 | 4.83 | 4.06 | 3.44 | 3.77 | 3.69 | 45.63 |

## Monthly Mean Total Precipitation, (continued)

| Station | January | February | March | April | May | June | July | August | September | October | November | December | Annual |
|---|---|---|---|---|---|---|---|---|---|---|---|---|---|
| Boonton | 3.39 | 3.08 | 4.22 | 4.15 | 4.12 | 3.98 | 4.09 | 4.54 | 4.53 | 3.74 | 4.08 | 3.93 | 47.85 |
| Branchville | 3.25 | 2.75 | 3.68 | 4.07 | 3.52 | 3.80 | 3.96 | 4.62 | 3.75 | 3.41 | 3.70 | 3.58 | 44.09 |
| Canoe Brook | 3.54 | 3.26 | 4.50 | 4.07 | 4.01 | 3.79 | 4.28 | 4.91 | 4.36 | 3.69 | 4.13 | 4.08 | 48.62 |
| Cape May | 3.28 | 3.19 | 3.92 | 3.24 | 3.25 | 3.14 | 3.58 | 4.37 | 3.38 | 3.14 | 3.49 | 3.82 | 41.80 |
| Charlotteburg | 3.75 | 3.37 | 4.70 | 4.34 | 3.95 | 4.19 | 4.23 | 5.01 | 4.39 | 4.15 | 4.66 | 4.23 | 50.97 |
| Essex Fells | 3.61 | 3.20 | 4.37 | 4.07 | 3.93 | 3.82 | 4.51 | 4.46 | 4.34 | 3.74 | 4.16 | 4.14 | 48.35 |
| Flemington | 3.66 | 3.22 | 4.18 | 4.04 | 3.68 | 3.75 | 4.36 | 4.60 | 3.93 | 3.45 | 3.84 | 3.95 | 46.66 |
| Freehold | 3.55 | 3.28 | 4.44 | 3.69 | 3.75 | 3.47 | 4.04 | 4.63 | 3.67 | 3.50 | 3.96 | 3.91 | 45.89 |
| Glassboro | 3.48 | 3.18 | 4.18 | 3.60 | 3.59 | 3.60 | 4.11 | 4.62 | 3.75 | 3.42 | 3.59 | 3.72 | 44.84 |
| Greenwood Lake | 3.93 | 3.55 | 4.78 | 4.61 | 4.01 | 4.27 | 4.13 | 4.86 | 4.59 | 4.17 | 4.74 | 4.46 | 52.10 |
| Hammonton | 3.31 | 3.23 | 3.99 | 3.57 | 3.51 | 3.50 | 4.58 | 4.55 | 3.71 | 3.29 | 3.73 | 3.90 | 44.87 |
| Hightstown | 3.31 | 2.96 | 3.96 | 3.65 | 3.60 | 3.25 | 4.33 | 4.72 | 3.99 | 3.42 | 3.52 | 3.68 | 44.39 |
| Indian Mills | 3.55 | 3.28 | 4.17 | 3.60 | 3.36 | 3.33 | 4.19 | 4.98 | 3.50 | 3.32 | 3.66 | 4.07 | 45.01 |
| Jersey City | 3.28 | 2.86 | 4.24 | 3.81 | 3.68 | 3.26 | 3.81 | 4.30 | 3.82 | 3.36 | 3.67 | 3.69 | 43.78 |
| Lambertville | 3.40 | 2.87 | 4.10 | 3.73 | 3.71 | 3.34 | 4.16 | 4.70 | 3.73 | 3.11 | 3.66 | 3.62 | 44.13 |
| Little Falls | 3.53 | 3.25 | 4.52 | 4.11 | 3.99 | 3.91 | 4.24 | 4.77 | 4.70 | 3.92 | 4.31 | 4.15 | 49.40 |
| Long Branch | 3.60 | 3.59 | 4.63 | 3.78 | 3.85 | 3.12 | 3.88 | 5.11 | 3.65 | 3.59 | 3.88 | 4.24 | 46.92 |
| Long Valley | 3.86 | 3.30 | 4.43 | 4.33 | 4.07 | 3.91 | 4.68 | 5.22 | 4.22 | 3.92 | 4.38 | 4.26 | 50.58 |
| Mays Landing | 3.62 | 3.40 | 4.27 | 3.72 | 3.35 | 3.11 | 4.63 | 4.78 | 3.42 | 3.55 | 3.68 | 3.99 | 45.52 |
| Midland Park | 3.41 | 3.20 | 4.51 | 4.14 | 4.11 | 4.20 | 4.59 | 5.25 | 4.51 | 4.02 | 4.44 | 4.17 | 50.55 |
| Millville | 3.22 | 3.24 | 3.99 | 3.40 | 3.20 | 3.49 | 4.00 | 4.58 | 3.21 | 3.31 | 3.59 | 3.72 | 42.95 |
| Moorestown | 3.24 | 2.99 | 3.90 | 3.63 | 3.63 | 3.55 | 4.33 | 4.91 | 3.61 | 3.38 | 3.50 | 3.69 | 44.36 |
| Morris Plains | 3.65 | 3.12 | 4.46 | 4.40 | 4.20 | 4.02 | 4.32 | 5.05 | 4.47 | 3.79 | 4.34 | 4.10 | 49.92 |
| New Brunswick | 3.45 | 2.96 | 4.04 | 3.77 | 3.90 | 3.26 | 4.39 | 4.90 | 3.93 | 3.33 | 3.82 | 3.75 | 45.50 |
| New Milford | 3.10 | 2.92 | 4.04 | 3.60 | 3.58 | 3.40 | 3.74 | 4.29 | 3.77 | 3.23 | 4.05 | 3.62 | 43.34 |
| Newton | 3.12 | 2.63 | 3.51 | 4.01 | 3.50 | 3.93 | 4.14 | 4.78 | 3.92 | 3.39 | 3.64 | 3.46 | 44.03 |
| Oak Ridge | 3.85 | 3.44 | 4.43 | 4.21 | 3.80 | 4.48 | 4.24 | 5.44 | 4.58 | 4.01 | 4.53 | 4.27 | 51.28 |
| Pemberton | 3.46 | 3.05 | 4.22 | 3.62 | 3.45 | 3.57 | 4.56 | 5.28 | 3.67 | 3.29 | 3.61 | 4.02 | 45.80 |
| Plainfield | 3.55 | 3.30 | 4.56 | 4.02 | 4.11 | 3.42 | 4.76 | 5.37 | 4.09 | 3.66 | 3.91 | 4.05 | 48.80 |
| Princeton | 3.35 | 3.11 | 4.11 | 3.57 | 3.50 | 3.36 | 4.78 | 4.89 | 3.97 | 3.32 | 3.59 | 3.75 | 45.30 |
| Rahway | 2.93 | 2.84 | 3.86 | 3.67 | 3.43 | 3.28 | 4.56 | 4.52 | 3.70 | 3.16 | 3.56 | 3.41 | 42.92 |
| Ringwood | 3.51 | 3.14 | 4.27 | 4.14 | 3.66 | 3.77 | 3.82 | 4.50 | 4.07 | 3.77 | 4.15 | 4.00 | 46.80 |
| Shiloh | 3.07 | 2.64 | 3.47 | 3.11 | 3.23 | 3.48 | 4.23 | 4.21 | 3.41 | 3.28 | 3.51 | 3.36 | 41.00 |
| Somerville | 3.33 | 2.93 | 4.04 | 3.78 | 3.66 | 3.49 | 4.54 | 4.92 | 3.88 | 3.42 | 3.63 | 3.74 | 45.36 |
| Split Rock Pond | 3.52 | 3.06 | 4.23 | 4.21 | 4.11 | 4.41 | 4.38 | 4.84 | 4.57 | 4.14 | 4.57 | 4.10 | 50.14 |
| Sussex | 3.33 | 2.68 | 3.55 | 4.07 | 3.58 | 4.14 | 4.26 | 4.97 | 3.83 | 3.55 | 3.85 | 3.58 | 45.39 |
| Toms River | 3.55 | 3.42 | 4.28 | 3.95 | 3.61 | 3.41 | 4.65 | 4.98 | 3.78 | 3.91 | 3.92 | 4.22 | 47.68 |
| Wanaque Dam | 3.55 | 3.18 | 4.37 | 4.03 | 3.66 | 3.92 | 3.93 | 4.41 | 4.24 | 3.71 | 4.07 | 4.07 | 47.14 |
| Woodcliff Lake | 3.47 | 3.22 | 4.49 | 4.06 | 3.68 | 3.53 | 4.26 | 4.77 | 4.29 | 3.55 | 4.34 | 3.92 | 47.58 |
| Woodstown | 3.31 | 2.99 | 3.77 | 3.60 | 3.18 | 3.37 | 4.03 | 4.18 | 3.63 | 3.27 | 3.74 | 3.74 | 42.81 |

SOURCE: National Climatic Center, Asheville, N.C.

## Monthly New Jersey Average Temperature, Based on 1931–1980 Data (in degrees Fahrenheit)

| Year | January | February | March | April | May | June | July | August | September | October | November | December | Annual |
|---|---|---|---|---|---|---|---|---|---|---|---|---|---|
| 1931 | 31.9 | 33.7 | 39.3 | 49.9 | 60.7 | 69.7 | 76.8 | 73.7 | 70.8 | 58.3 | 50.0 | 40.0 | 54.6 |
| 1932 | 42.9 | 36.1 | 36.9 | 48.5 | 60.7 | 69.6 | 74.0 | 73.6 | 66.5 | 56.4 | 42.4 | 36.4 | 53.7 |
| 1933 | 39.0 | 33.9 | 38.6 | 50.6 | 63.4 | 71.2 | 73.6 | 73.1 | 68.3 | 53.8 | 41.0 | 32.3 | 53.2 |
| 1934 | 34.1 | 18.8 | 36.8 | 49.6 | 62.5 | 72.8 | 76.1 | 70.3 | 67.5 | 52.9 | 47.6 | 33.2 | 51.8 |
| 1935 | 28.7 | 30.4 | 43.3 | 48.9 | 58.0 | 69.1 | 76.2 | 72.7 | 63.4 | 55.0 | 48.1 | 29.2 | 51.9 |
| 1936 | 27.5 | 24.8 | 45.6 | 48.3 | 63.4 | 69.3 | 74.8 | 74.4 | 67.1 | 56.0 | 41.5 | 37.9 | 52.5 |
| 1937 | 39.9 | 34.4 | 36.3 | 49.7 | 62.9 | 70.9 | 75.0 | 75.6 | 63.8 | 53.6 | 44.0 | 33.5 | 53.3 |
| 1938 | 31.5 | 35.9 | 43.6 | 53.3 | 59.5 | 68.9 | 74.9 | 75.5 | 63.9 | 56.4 | 45.9 | 35.2 | 53.7 |
| 1939 | 31.1 | 36.8 | 39.9 | 48.4 | 63.3 | 70.8 | 73.5 | 75.4 | 66.5 | 55.1 | 41.8 | 35.4 | 53.2 |
| 1940 | 22.5 | 32.2 | 34.9 | 45.8 | 60.0 | 68.9 | 74.1 | 69.6 | 63.5 | 50.2 | 43.7 | 37.3 | 50.2 |
| 1941 | 29.7 | 29.7 | 34.7 | 55.6 | 62.7 | 69.6 | 73.9 | 71.3 | 67.7 | 59.3 | 46.9 | 37.4 | 53.2 |
| 1942 | 29.1 | 30.0 | 42.5 | 51.7 | 64.6 | 70.1 | 74.8 | 71.7 | 66.5 | 56.2 | 45.1 | 30.3 | 52.7 |
| 1943 | 30.6 | 33.3 | 40.0 | 45.9 | 62.1 | 74.6 | 74.4 | 73.7 | 65.2 | 53.7 | 42.6 | 31.2 | 52.3 |
| 1944 | 32.8 | 32.6 | 37.4 | 48.2 | 65.6 | 70.6 | 75.9 | 74.4 | 67.1 | 53.8 | 44.0 | 30.9 | 52.8 |
| 1945 | 24.7 | 32.5 | 50.0 | 54.8 | 58.7 | 69.9 | 73.5 | 71.3 | 69.2 | 54.2 | 46.4 | 29.2 | 52.9 |
| 1946 | 32.9 | 32.8 | 48.1 | 50.4 | 61.1 | 68.2 | 73.4 | 69.4 | 67.8 | 59.0 | 48.5 | 36.9 | 54.0 |
| 1947 | 37.2 | 28.4 | 36.6 | 50.7 | 60.4 | 67.9 | 73.9 | 74.8 | 67.3 | 60.6 | 42.2 | 32.2 | 52.7 |
| 1948 | 24.5 | 30.0 | 42.4 | 50.6 | 60.1 | 69.0 | 74.8 | 73.3 | 66.4 | 53.8 | 49.9 | 36.7 | 52.6 |
| 1949 | 38.3 | 38.4 | 42.5 | 51.8 | 61.5 | 72.2 | 78.1 | 74.7 | 64.0 | 60.1 | 44.0 | 37.4 | 55.2 |
| 1950 | 41.2 | 31.9 | 36.8 | 47.9 | 58.9 | 68.7 | 73.4 | 71.4 | 62.9 | 57.6 | 46.6 | 32.3 | 52.5 |
| 1951 | 34.9 | 35.0 | 41.3 | 51.4 | 61.6 | 68.8 | 74.5 | 72.6 | 66.0 | 57.6 | 41.4 | 36.8 | 53.5 |
| 1952 | 35.4 | 35.4 | 39.5 | 53.4 | 59.4 | 72.1 | 77.2 | 72.8 | 66.5 | 52.2 | 45.3 | 36.7 | 53.8 |
| 1953 | 36.4 | 37.5 | 42.6 | 51.2 | 63.0 | 70.5 | 74.8 | 72.5 | 67.2 | 56.7 | 45.4 | 38.4 | 54.7 |
| 1954 | 30.0 | 38.0 | 41.2 | 53.4 | 58.5 | 70.1 | 74.2 | 71.6 | 66.3 | 59.1 | 43.3 | 34.5 | 53.3 |
| 1955 | 29.8 | 33.0 | 41.8 | 53.4 | 63.5 | 67.6 | 79.3 | 76.6 | 65.8 | 57.6 | 43.3 | 28.8 | 53.4 |
| 1956 | 31.1 | 35.9 | 37.2 | 47.7 | 58.5 | 70.4 | 72.2 | 72.3 | 63.8 | 56.1 | 45.6 | 40.5 | 52.6 |
| 1957 | 27.7 | 36.4 | 40.6 | 53.1 | 61.9 | 72.9 | 74.7 | 70.8 | 67.9 | 53.4 | 46.8 | 38.4 | 53.7 |
| 1958 | 30.3 | 26.9 | 38.9 | 52.0 | 58.7 | 66.1 | 75.9 | 72.6 | 65.4 | 54.2 | 46.2 | 27.9 | 51.3 |
| 1959 | 30.5 | 31.8 | 40.0 | 52.8 | 64.4 | 70.8 | 74.8 | 75.3 | 69.3 | 58.8 | 44.6 | 36.9 | 54.2 |
| 1960 | 33.4 | 35.8 | 32.1 | 54.8 | 60.5 | 69.8 | 72.6 | 73.6 | 66.3 | 54.7 | 46.5 | 27.7 | 52.3 |
| 1961 | 24.6 | 34.0 | 41.2 | 47.7 | 58.4 | 69.6 | 74.8 | 73.4 | 72.0 | 57.2 | 46.6 | 33.2 | 52.7 |
| 1962 | 30.8 | 30.3 | 39.9 | 51.6 | 62.6 | 70.5 | 71.7 | 71.4 | 62.8 | 55.6 | 41.6 | 30.0 | 51.6 |
| 1963 | 28.1 | 26.4 | 42.3 | 51.2 | 59.3 | 69.5 | 74.5 | 70.9 | 62.2 | 58.4 | 48.6 | 28.3 | 51.6 |
| 1964 | 32.2 | 30.8 | 42.1 | 48.7 | 63.1 | 69.5 | 74.8 | 70.7 | 66.5 | 52.6 | 47.1 | 35.5 | 52.8 |
| 1965 | 27.7 | 32.1 | 37.9 | 47.9 | 65.0 | 68.9 | 72.9 | 72.4 | 67.5 | 53.0 | 44.1 | 36.6 | 52.2 |
| 1966 | 29.1 | 31.5 | 41.4 | 46.9 | 58.1 | 70.7 | 76.1 | 73.8 | 64.2 | 53.3 | 46.4 | 34.6 | 52.2 |
| 1967 | 35.5 | 28.6 | 37.1 | 50.1 | 54.2 | 70.5 | 73.5 | 71.8 | 63.7 | 54.2 | 40.7 | 36.0 | 51.3 |
| 1968 | 26.2 | 28.5 | 42.6 | 52.6 | 58.2 | 69.0 | 75.1 | 74.2 | 67.5 | 57.4 | 45.2 | 31.9 | 52.4 |
| 1969 | 29.2 | 31.3 | 37.9 | 53.1 | 61.7 | 70.8 | 73.0 | 73.8 | 66.3 | 54.3 | 43.8 | 32.0 | 52.3 |
| 1970 | 23.7 | 32.1 | 36.9 | 49.6 | 62.0 | 68.9 | 74.4 | 74.3 | 68.9 | 57.1 | 46.6 | 34.3 | 52.4 |
| 1971 | 26.6 | 33.1 | 38.9 | 48.7 | 58.1 | 70.7 | 73.5 | 72.1 | 68.7 | 60.6 | 43.9 | 39.9 | 52.9 |
| 1972 | 33.5 | 30.1 | 38.7 | 47.6 | 60.4 | 66.3 | 74.9 | 72.4 | 66.9 | 50.8 | 42.4 | 38.5 | 51.9 |
| 1973 | 33.7 | 31.7 | 45.6 | 51.9 | 58.1 | 72.2 | 75.2 | 75.2 | 67.3 | 57.0 | 46.6 | 37.6 | 54.3 |
| 1974 | 34.6 | 30.8 | 42.0 | 53.3 | 60.1 | 67.4 | 74.5 | 73.6 | 65.5 | 51.5 | 45.6 | 37.7 | 53.0 |
| 1975 | 35.6 | 34.5 | 39.1 | 46.1 | 63.7 | 69.7 | 74.1 | 73.7 | 63.0 | 58.4 | 49.8 | 35.4 | 53.6 |
| 1976 | 27.1 | 38.5 | 44.0 | 53.7 | 59.7 | 72.0 | 72.4 | 72.0 | 64.5 | 50.9 | 39.3 | 29.0 | 51.9 |
| 1977 | 20.3 | 32.5 | 45.7 | 53.2 | 63.2 | 67.7 | 75.2 | 73.4 | 67.5 | 53.4 | 46.9 | 33.1 | 52.7 |
| 1978 | 27.5 | 23.3 | 37.3 | 49.6 | 58.3 | 68.9 | 72.0 | 74.6 | 64.2 | 53.6 | 46.2 | 36.3 | 51.0 |
| 1979 | 31.5 | 22.0 | 44.0 | 49.9 | 62.1 | 66.7 | 73.2 | 72.8 | 65.9 | 53.8 | 48.8 | 37.2 | 52.3 |
| 1980 | 31.4 | 28.8 | 38.5 | 52.1 | 63.0 | 67.5 | 75.7 | 75.8 | 68.7 | 53.0 | 41.8 | 30.8 | 52.3 |

## Monthly New Jersey Average Temperature, (continued)

| Year | January | February | March | April | May | June | July | August | September | October | November | December | Annual |
|---|---|---|---|---|---|---|---|---|---|---|---|---|---|
| Mean | 31.2 | 31.9 | 40.3 | 50.6 | 61.0 | 69.8 | 74.5 | 73.1 | 66.3 | 55.4 | 45.1 | 34.4 | 52.8 |
| Number of years | 50 | 50 | 50 | 50 | 50 | 50 | 50 | 50 | 50 | 50 | 50 | 50 | 50 |

SOURCE: National Climatic Center, Asheville, N.C.
NOTE: Divisions weighted by area.

## Monthly New Jersey Average Precipitation, Based on 1931–1980 Data (in inches)

| Year | January | February | March | April | May | June | July | August | September | October | November | December | Annual |
|---|---|---|---|---|---|---|---|---|---|---|---|---|---|
| 1931 | 2.14 | 2.01 | 4.22 | 2.69 | 3.55 | 4.67 | 4.15 | 5.56 | 1.84 | 2.84 | .83 | 2.18 | 36.68 |
| 1932 | 4.52 | 2.00 | 5.78 | 2.74 | 3.04 | 3.77 | 2.90 | 2.70 | 2.39 | 5.70 | 7.45 | 2.94 | 45.93 |
| 1933 | 2.46 | 3.27 | 4.90 | 4.68 | 4.99 | 2.84 | 3.77 | 10.71 | 5.59 | 1.81 | 1.08 | 3.23 | 49.33 |
| 1934 | 2.79 | 2.87 | 3.29 | 3.72 | 4.49 | 3.69 | 3.46 | 3.83 | 8.61 | 2.44 | 2.86 | 2.85 | 44.90 |
| 1935 | 4.05 | 2.86 | 2.49 | 2.44 | 1.91 | 4.67 | 4.52 | 2.74 | 6.60 | 4.69 | 5.14 | 1.80 | 43.91 |
| 1936 | 6.38 | 3.13 | 5.05 | 3.05 | 2.59 | 4.79 | 2.66 | 4.04 | 4.67 | 3.24 | 1.10 | 6.26 | 46.96 |
| 1937 | 6.29 | 2.28 | 2.78 | 4.69 | 3.08 | 4.60 | 2.55 | 6.80 | 2.51 | 5.49 | 4.48 | 1.61 | 47.16 |
| 1938 | 3.47 | 2.40 | 2.09 | 2.69 | 3.48 | 7.73 | 8.86 | 3.05 | 9.78 | 2.55 | 3.55 | 2.66 | 52.31 |
| 1939 | 4.02 | 5.60 | 4.96 | 5.14 | 1.37 | 3.69 | 2.41 | 7.26 | 1.45 | 4.24 | 1.87 | 1.44 | 43.45 |
| 1940 | 1.87 | 3.09 | 4.95 | 5.57 | 6.24 | 3.07 | 2.61 | 6.15 | 4.63 | 2.36 | 4.73 | 2.97 | 48.24 |
| 1941 | 3.53 | 2.47 | 2.73 | 2.31 | 1.87 | 5.12 | 6.76 | 3.73 | .27 | 1.87 | 2.88 | 3.59 | 37.13 |
| 1942 | 2.96 | 2.63 | 5.71 | 1.39 | 2.37 | 3.12 | 6.94 | 7.76 | 4.40 | 3.51 | 4.08 | 4.50 | 49.37 |
| 1943 | 2.96 | 1.98 | 3.02 | 2.82 | 4.84 | 3.38 | 4.13 | 2.02 | 1.65 | 7.48 | 2.88 | 1.44 | 38.60 |
| 1944 | 3.50 | 2.29 | 5.72 | 5.42 | 1.62 | 4.05 | 1.44 | 2.83 | 8.14 | 2.54 | 6.41 | 3.00 | 46.96 |
| 1945 | 2.97 | 3.21 | 2.32 | 3.28 | 4.64 | 4.11 | 9.56 | 4.31 | 4.54 | 2.57 | 5.49 | 5.12 | 52.12 |
| 1946 | 1.83 | 2.16 | 3.33 | 1.51 | 6.48 | 5.34 | 5.73 | 4.27 | 3.12 | 1.53 | 1.47 | 2.40 | 39.17 |
| 1947 | 3.75 | 1.97 | 2.62 | 4.18 | 7.20 | 3.60 | 4.32 | 4.13 | 2.59 | 2.07 | 6.17 | 2.76 | 45.36 |
| 1948 | 5.06 | 2.57 | 3.61 | 3.65 | 8.02 | 5.24 | 4.11 | 6.04 | 1.19 | 2.30 | 4.77 | 6.39 | 52.95 |
| 1949 | 5.96 | 3.78 | 2.72 | 3.60 | 4.78 | .24 | 3.76 | 3.65 | 4.19 | 2.52 | 1.64 | 2.89 | 39.73 |
| 1950 | 2.37 | 3.82 | 4.36 | 2.14 | 3.67 | 2.69 | 5.14 | 4.97 | 3.52 | 1.92 | 5.50 | 3.77 | 43.87 |
| 1951 | 3.20 | 4.23 | 5.19 | 2.98 | 4.16 | 3.70 | 3.99 | 2.91 | 1.77 | 4.38 | 6.74 | 5.49 | 48.74 |
| 1952 | 5.17 | 2.24 | 5.46 | 6.58 | 5.72 | 3.66 | 4.75 | 7.33 | 3.71 | .84 | 4.85 | 4.19 | 54.50 |
| 1953 | 5.19 | 2.64 | 6.91 | 5.41 | 5.79 | 2.90 | 3.89 | 3.39 | 1.44 | 3.73 | 2.92 | 4.34 | 48.55 |
| 1954 | 2.12 | 1.79 | 3.72 | 3.52 | 3.86 | 1.12 | 1.71 | 6.76 | 5.64 | 2.26 | 5.16 | 3.68 | 41.34 |
| 1955 | .68 | 3.03 | 4.58 | 2.59 | 1.43 | 4.10 | 1.14 | 11.44 | 2.45 | 6.96 | 2.20 | .39 | 40.99 |
| 1956 | 2.46 | 4.98 | 4.92 | 3.21 | 2.71 | 4.49 | 5.72 | 3.49 | 3.43 | 4.27 | 3.82 | 4.28 | 47.78 |
| 1957 | 1.93 | 2.73 | 3.22 | 4.68 | 1.63 | 2.22 | 1.34 | 2.17 | 2.88 | 2.73 | 4.08 | 6.33 | 35.94 |
| 1958 | 4.86 | 4.78 | 5.33 | 5.72 | 4.42 | 3.14 | 6.02 | 6.21 | 3.78 | 5.41 | 2.74 | 1.57 | 53.98 |
| 1959 | 2.26 | 2.02 | 3.98 | 2.90 | 1.86 | 3.97 | 7.35 | 5.05 | 1.89 | 4.55 | 4.32 | 4.10 | 44.25 |
| 1960 | 3.19 | 4.42 | 2.40 | 2.99 | 3.72 | 1.98 | 7.40 | 4.67 | 7.73 | 2.34 | 2.22 | 3.05 | 46.11 |
| 1961 | 3.14 | 3.68 | 5.44 | 4.97 | 3.58 | 3.10 | 6.11 | 4.08 | 2.64 | 2.78 | 2.54 | 3.47 | 45.53 |
| 1962 | 2.91 | 3.98 | 3.67 | 3.94 | 1.66 | 4.36 | 2.95 | 5.87 | 3.64 | 2.60 | 4.87 | 2.76 | 43.21 |
| 1963 | 2.50 | 2.37 | 4.31 | .90 | 2.64 | 2.67 | 2.73 | 2.88 | 4.76 | .32 | 6.94 | 2.13 | 35.15 |
| 1964 | 4.67 | 3.44 | 2.11 | 5.99 | .94 | 2.16 | 4.83 | .90 | 3.22 | 1.91 | 1.97 | 4.49 | 36.63 |
| 1965 | 3.10 | 2.59 | 3.31 | 2.49 | 1.62 | 1.77 | 3.27 | 3.44 | 2.43 | 2.11 | 1.42 | 1.80 | 29.35 |
| 1966 | 3.20 | 4.11 | 1.70 | 2.92 | 3.97 | 1.15 | 2.08 | 2.44 | 7.82 | 4.72 | 2.72 | 3.93 | 40.76 |

## Monthly New Jersey Average Precipitation, (continued)

| Year | January | February | March | April | May | June | July | August | September | October | November | December | Annual |
|---|---|---|---|---|---|---|---|---|---|---|---|---|---|
| 1967 | 1.35 | 2.42 | 5.14 | 2.81 | 3.93 | 2.79 | 6.04 | 9.11 | 2.15 | 2.40 | 1.98 | 5.76 | 45.88 |
| 1968 | 2.56 | 1.07 | 5.08 | 2.05 | 6.15 | 5.33 | 2.07 | 2.99 | 1.55 | 2.70 | 4.92 | 3.31 | 39.78 |
| 1969 | 2.12 | 2.61 | 3.02 | 3.04 | 2.49 | 3.80 | 9.60 | 3.67 | 4.40 | 1.77 | 3.19 | 7.21 | 46.92 |
| 1970 | .97 | 3.03 | 3.83 | 5.21 | 2.68 | 3.83 | 3.28 | 3.37 | 1.60 | 3.74 | 5.40 | 2.84 | 39.78 |
| 1971 | 2.56 | 5.36 | 3.02 | 2.59 | 4.19 | 1.34 | 4.34 | 10.36 | 5.68 | 4.69 | 5.33 | 1.98 | 51.44 |
| 1972 | 2.74 | 4.79 | 3.40 | 3.77 | 5.50 | 8.41 | 3.96 | 2.00 | 2.37 | 5.45 | 9.06 | 6.11 | 57.56 |
| 1973 | 4.25 | 3.71 | 3.65 | 6.64 | 4.87 | 5.92 | 3.26 | 3.00 | 3.54 | 3.94 | 1.43 | 7.38 | 51.59 |
| 1974 | 3.58 | 2.14 | 5.19 | 3.19 | 3.67 | 3.59 | 2.14 | 6.34 | 5.54 | 2.11 | 1.49 | 5.15 | 44.13 |
| 1975 | 5.33 | 3.29 | 4.26 | 3.42 | 4.68 | 6.38 | 9.06 | 3.85 | 8.16 | 3.88 | 3.75 | 2.79 | 58.85 |
| 1976 | 5.35 | 2.50 | 2.06 | 2.09 | 3.68 | 2.87 | 3.79 | 4.59 | 2.60 | 6.29 | .59 | 2.43 | 38.84 |
| 1977 | 2.29 | 2.13 | 4.85 | 3.73 | 1.37 | 3.96 | 2.57 | 5.46 | 4.26 | 4.24 | 7.59 | 6.01 | 48.46 |
| 1978 | 7.50 | 1.45 | 4.19 | 1.99 | 7.06 | 2.66 | 4.58 | 7.06 | 2.53 | 1.71 | 2.52 | 4.93 | 48.18 |
| 1979 | 9.09 | 5.30 | 3.71 | 3.75 | 5.78 | 3.77 | 3.92 | 5.71 | 6.13 | 3.90 | 3.45 | 2.09 | 56.60 |
| 1980 | 2.39 | 1.01 | 6.92 | 6.28 | 2.51 | 3.49 | 3.47 | 2.09 | 1.97 | 4.10 | 3.21 | .86 | 38.30 |
| Mean | 3.51 | 3.00 | 4.02 | 3.60 | 3.77 | 3.70 | 4.34 | 4.78 | 3.87 | 3.33 | 3.76 | 3.57 | 45.26 |

SOURCE: National Climatic Center, Asheville, N.C.

# Bibliography

*A series of specialized studies on various aspects of New Jersey's meteorology and climatology have been published by two institutions in New Brunswick. The authors are either faculty members or students in the Departments of Meteorology and Physical Oceanography, Rutgers, the State University.*

*Bulletin*. New Jersey Academy of Science. New Brunswick, N.J.: Rutgers, the State University, 1955–.

*The Journal Series* of the New Jersey Agricultural Experiment Station, New Brunswick, N.J.: Cook College, Rutgers, the State University.

## New Jersey's Climate

Biel, Erwin. "New Jersey's Climate." In *The Economy of New Jersey*, edited by Salmon J. Fink, pp. 53–98. New Brunswick, N.J.: Rutgers University Press, 1958.

Blodget, Lorin. *Climatology of The United States*. Philadelphia: Lippincott, 1857.

Smock, John C. *Climate of New Jersey. Final Report of the State Geologist.* Vol. 1, pp. 325–439. Trenton: Geological Survey of New Jersey, 1888.

U.S. Department of Agriculture, Weather Bureau. *Climatic Summary of the United States. Section 90—New Jersey*. Washington, D.C.: Government Printing Office, 1934.

U.S. Department of Commerce, National Oceanic and Atmospheric Administration, Environmental Data Service. *Climatography of the United States No. 81—New Jersey. Monthly Normals of Temperature, Precipitation, Heating and Cooling Degree Days 1941–70*. Asheville, N.C.: National Climatic Center, 1973.

———. *Climatology of the United States No. 85—New Jersey. Monthly Averages of Temperature and Precipitation for State Climatic Divisions 1941–70*. Asheville, N.C.: National Climatic Center, 1973.

U.S. Department of Commerce, Weather Bureau. *Climate of the States: New Jersey*. Agricultural Yearbook Separate No. 1848. Washington, D.C.: Government Printing Office, 1941.

———. *Climatography of the United States No. 60–28. Climates of the States: New Jersey*. Washington, D.C.: Government Printing Office, 1959. Revised edition, 1973.

# For General Readers


Anthes, R. A., H. A. Panofsky, J. J. Cahir, and A. Rango. *The Atmosphere*. 2d ed. Columbus: Charles E. Merrill, 1977.

Barry, R. G., and R. J. Chorley. *Atmosphere, Weather and Climate*. New York: Methuen, 1977.

Battan, Louis J. *Fundamentals of Meteorology*. Englewood Cliffs, N.J.: Prentice-Hall, 1979.

———. *Weather*. Englewood Cliffs, N.J.: Prentice-Hall, 1974.

Bentley, W. A., and W. J. Humphreys. *Snow Crystals*. New York: Dover, 1962.

Bernard, Howard W., Jr. *Weather Watch*. New York: Walker, 1979.

Biswas, M. R., and A. K. Biswas, eds. *Food, Climate, and Man*. New York: Wiley, 1979.

Bryson, R., and T. J. Murray. *Climates of Hunger*. Madison: University of Wisconsin Press, 1977.

Calder, Nigel A. *The Weather Machine*. New York: Viking Press, 1975.

Dunn, G. E., and B. I. Miller. *Atlantic Hurricanes*. Baton Rouge: Louisiana State University Press, 1960.

Flora, Snowden D. *Hailstorms of the United States*. Norman, Okla.: University of Oklahoma Press, 1960.

———. *Tornadoes of the United States*. Norman, Okla.: University of Oklahoma Press, 1956.

Heuer, Kenneth. *Rainbows, Halos, and Other Wonders—Light and Color in the Atmosphere*. New York: Dodd, Mead, 1978.

Holford, Ingrid. *The Guinness Book of Weather Facts and Feats*. London. Guinness Superlatives Limited, 1977.

Hughes, Patrick. *American Weather Stories*. Environmental Data Service, National Oceanic and Atmospheric Administration, Washington, D.C.: U.S. Department of Commerce, 1976.

Imbrie, J., and K. P. Imbrie. *Ice Ages: Solving the Mystery*. Short Hills, N.J.: Enslow, 1979.

Kotsch, William J. *Weather for the Mariner*. 2d ed. Annapolis: U.S. Naval Institute Press, 1977.

Landsberg, Helmut E. *Weather and Health*. New York: Doubleday, 1969.

Lave, L. B., and E. P. Seskin. *Air Pollution and Human Health*. Baltimore: Johns Hopkins University Press, 1978.

Lowry, William P. *Weather and Life: An Introduction to Biometeorology*. Corvallis, Oreg.: Oregon State University Press, 1967.

Ludlum, David M. *The American Weather Book*. Boston: Houghton Mifflin, 1982.

———. *Early American Hurricanes, 1492–1870*. Boston: American Meteorological Society, 1963.

———. *Early American Tornadoes, 1586–1870*. Boston: American Meteorological Society, 1970.

———. *Early American Winters, 1604–1820*. Boston: American Meteorological Society, 1966.

———. *Early American Winters II, 1821–1870*. Boston: American Meteorological Society, 1968.

———. *New England Weather Book*. Boston: Houghton Mifflin, 1976.

———. *New Jersey Historical Weather Data: Temperature and Precipitation, 1885–1980*. Princeton: American Weather History Center.

———. *Weather Record Book: United States and Canada*. Princeton: Weatherwise, 1971.

Miller, Albert. *Meteorology*. 3d ed. Columbus: Charles E. Merrill, 1976.

Riehl, Herbert. *Introduction to the Atmosphere*. 3d ed. New York: McGraw-Hill, 1978.

Ruffner, James A. *Climates of the States*. Detroit: Gale, 1978.

Scorer, Richard. *Clouds of the World*. North Pomfret, Vt.: David and Charles, 1972.

Simpson, Robert, and Herbert Riehl. *The Hurricane and Its Impact*. Baton Rouge: Louisiana State University Press, 1981.

Sloane, Eric. *For Spacious Skies*. New York: Funk & Wagnalls, 1979.

Thompson, P. D., and R. O'Brien. *Weather*. 3d ed. Alexandria, Va.: Time-Life Books, 1973.

Tufty, Barbara. *1001 Questions Answered about Storms and Other Natural Disasters*. New York: Dodd, Mead, 1970.

Ward, R. *Floods, A Geographical Perspective*. New York: Halsted Press, 1978.

Wilson, C. L. *Inadvertent Climate Modification*. Cambridge: Massachusetts Institute of Technology Press, 1972.

World Meteorological Society. *International Cloud Atlas* (Abridged Atlas). Geneva, Switzerland, 1956.